WHAT YOU NEED TO KNOW BEFORE YOU INVEST

Third Edition

An Introduction to the Stock Market and Other Investments

by Rod Davis

BARRON'S

To Nancy.

Illustrations by Tom Kerr.

© Copyright 2003, 1999, 1996 by Rodney G. Davis.

All inquiries should be addressed to:
Barron's Educational Series, Inc.
250 Wireless Boulevard
Hauppauge, New York 11788
www.barronseduc.com

ISBN-13: 978-0-7641-2493-8
ISBN-10: 0-7641-2493-5

Library of Congress Catalog Card No.: 2003044413

Library of Congress Cataloging-in-Publication Data
Davis, Rod.
    What you need to know before you invest :
an introduction to the stock market and other
investments / by Rod Davis. — 3rd ed.
        p.   cm.
    Includes bibliographical references and index.
    ISBN 0-7641-2493-5
    1. Stock exchanges. 2. Investments. I. Title.
    HG4551.D33   2003
    332.6—dc21   2003044413

PRINTED IN THE UNITED STATES OF AMERICA
9 8 7 6 5

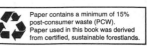

Paper contains a minimum of 15% post-consumer waste (PCW). Paper used in this book was derived from certified, sustainable forestlands.

Table of Contents

Preface to the Third Edition

The more things change, the more they stay the same. I have been working in the financial services industry as a broker, teacher, and writer for nearly 30 years. In this business, that makes me a dinosaur. When I first started out, the ticker tape had only been out of commission a few years. Stock transactions were consummated with lots of pieces of paper.

My clients would bring stock certificates for shares that they wanted to sell into my office. There we would converse across a massive wooden desk while I self-confidently reclined in my high-backed red-leather chair and put on professional airs. I tried to look older and wiser, as befitted my desk and chair. I would carefully examine the signature when my clients endorsed the back of the certificate, and I would nod authoritatively. Then I would have my efficient, no-nonsense secretary, whom I shared with five other brokers, run it up to the cashier, who worked behind a metal-barred teller's cage. She would return a few minutes later with a neatly printed receipt. Then I would write a ticket with triplicate carbon copies so those shares could be sold and another ticket (with carbon copies) so new shares could be purchased. My clients would go home and probably worry about whether or not they had made the right decision. "He looked so young, but he must know what he's doing. Did you see that massive wooden desk, red-leather chair, and official-looking secretary?" Then they would eagerly await the delivery of their new certificate.

The popular companies of the day had names like E. I. duPont de Nemours, Standard Oil of New Jersey, and Pan American Airways. Some still trade by the same name, though you may not recognize it. Some have changed their name and/or merged with another company. Some no longer exist, except as memories and entries in the *Obsolete Securities Directory*.

The new stock certificate for the shares my clients had purchased would arrive in their mailbox about a month later. They would carefully slit open the large, official-looking envelope and admire the craftsmanship of the certificate. It would usually feature an engraving of a scantily clad woman printed on banknote paper, your great-grandparents' version of eye candy. They would then hustle on down to the First Bank of Wherever to the hide it away in a safe-deposit box. Then they would hope it went up.

Today if you use the word "ticker tape," many people think you are referring to an EKG. If they associate the term with the stock market, they will probably picture a desktop antique ticker under a glass dome, associated with Monopoly—the original version. Today there are only massive wooden desks and red-leather chairs in firms that are so stodgy they haven't got a clue about what century they're in. Your trades are executed electronically, and even your signature is verified on-line. There is no paper in cyberspace. If you want a paper trail of a securities transaction, you print a hard copy of your execution report. Instead of a banknote certificate featuring a scantily clad woman, you have banner ads, pop-ups, and e-mail alerts for porn sites. You make your investment decision, and then you hope it goes up. Well, some things never change.

Everyone still wants to get rich. We have all heard stories about how many "millionaires next door" amassed their wealth through savvy stock picking. We all want to be one of those. Of course, we have also heard the horror stories about how much money some guy at work lost by gambling on the market. Obviously he was a fool who didn't know what he was doing. You wouldn't make the same mistakes he made. Before you put any money into the stock market you're going to make sure it's in something that checks out. Something like that new company that has found the guaranteed cure for cancer, or AIDS, or obesity, or that company that has invented the new smart pill. You know what you're doing; this one's a real money-maker. You can beat the system. Some things never change.

Inherent in our very nature is a propensity for greed. Now, before you think I'm about to knock greed, let me tell you that it's not necessarily all bad. If we had enough money that we didn't have to worry about maintaining our financial security, we could afford to be more philanthropic. We'd be glad to help others, if only we didn't have to spend all of our time helping ourselves. Being financially secure would afford us the luxury of focusing our attention on perhaps more worthwhile, life-fulfilling dreams and goals.

Greed does serve a more noble purpose. It represents that part of our nature that motivates us to achieve financial goals so that we can get on with the really important things in life. The problem with greed is that too often it ceases being the means to an end and becomes the end itself. This too is human nature. We no longer hunt just for food; we hunt for the thrill of the hunt, completely forgetting what the original purpose of hunting was. In other words, money gathering becomes our life-consuming passion, and we forget why we were doing it in the first place.

The stereotype of a corporate executive is someone who is so wrapped up in work and business that he or she completely neglects his or her family. Although the original intent may have been to provide financial security for loved ones, with that goal achieved, he or she now abandons loved ones for the love of the corporation. Does the executive love work and business more than his or her family? The answer is yes.

There seems to be something inherently askew with our very nature. We long for love, but when we have it, we long for something else. It's as if longing, not achieving, is what life is all about. Life is a game played with illusions and dreams that don't fit the physical model in which we live.

I'll bet you didn't expect a discourse on life in the preface to a book on stock market investing. Well, this book is not about human nature; it is just about investing. However, I went through this elaborate ruse to simply highlight that the biggest problem you will ever have at being a good investor is your very nature. That's not something that is easily changed, nor is it something that a book like this will likely influence. However, it remains the number one lesson. Do not get so caught up in the business of investing that you forget why you started doing it in the first place. This book will give you the information you need to become an astute, well-informed investor.

This is a book of tools. What you build with these tools is your decision, whether it is a monument to yourself or a legacy for others. Just keep in perspective what you are trying to achieve, and make sure it's really a worthwhile goal. Don't let greed become an end in itself. Keep your goals in proper perspective, constantly examining why you do what you do. Be aware that your nature is a great distraction. Some things never change.

There have been many changes in the securities industry since the second edition of *What You Need to Know Before You Invest* went into print. Many of these changes pertained to tax-advantaged investments and plans for retirement and college education expenses—the same things that necessitated revisions to the first edition. Keeping up with the rapidly evolving field of tax-advantaged investments can be a full-time job in itself. Much of that information becomes obsolete every year.

New types of tax-advantaged investments for college education and retirement planning is necessitated because most people do not take the steps necessary to plan for these costly events and lifestyle changes. This lack of planning is having an adverse affect on society, and the government is stepping in to fill the void.

However, although the government can provide the means of encouraging you to save for your future or the future of your children or loved ones, it cannot provide the impetus that motivates you to follow through with those financial plans. To help with that, this book provides the information you need to make sound financial and investment decisions. So take the information from this book and share it with those who need to know.

Introduction

Many people feel intimidated by the stock market. Since they don't understand how it works, they don't feel comfortable investing. They think that only professionals can understand the strange language of investing. This book should help change that perception. There are innumerable books that give investment advice, such as when to buy stocks or what to buy, but there are few books that explain in nontechnical language just what the stock market is. *What You Need to Know Before You Invest* will help you understand how the market works and explain various securities that are popular with individual investors. It is written for the nonprofessional. You will find it much easier to understand than most other books on the subject, and it will help you to feel more comfortable with the investment process.

I have been teaching about the stock market for twenty-five years and have examined hundreds of books on the subject. In spite of the voluminous amount of material on investing, I have still to find one book that adequately introduces all aspects of investing to an individual who does not already have some background information. Most college texts are written for students who are in an economics or a business or finance program, and those who are not specializing in these areas generally find the material difficult to comprehend. Most books for the general population are written by professionals who cannot (or will not) bring the material down to the level of the "common man." This is truly unfortunate. Basic information on the stock market is not difficult to understand. There is, however, a scarcity of nontechnical information on the stock market for individual investors.

In any free enterprise economic system, an individual's ability to participate in stock market investing is a *right*. Indeed, the stock market exists because of this economic state. It is not the *symbol* of a free market system, it *is* the free market system. The word *free* implies that *everyone* is free to participate, not just business professionals. So, everyone should avail themselves of some fundamental information about investing. Your ability to capitalize on money-making opportunities should be limited only by the amount of your finances, not by your lack of knowledge. Fundamental information about stock market investing should be presented so that everyone can understand it. Everyone should have access to the education they need to capitalize on investment opportunities, without having to get a college degree in business or economics.

As an instructor, I have heard the same questions asked year after year: What exactly is a stock? Why do stock prices go up and down? Is the stock market risky? How are my rights as an investor protected?, and so on. Even for individuals who have invested in the stock market for years, some fundamental questions have *never* been adequately answered. So, here is a book that answers them. This book was written so that it could be understood by those who use the business section of the newspaper for lining the garbage can or the bottom of the birdcage. However, it will also provide seasoned investors with a foundation they may have never established. It will explain fundamental terms and present a thorough overview of the most popular areas of investing. When you finish this book, you will not only be able to read the business section but also be able to use the information as well. Then, if you are interested in learning more, you will have no problem comprehending other books that pick up where this one leaves off.

About the Author

Rod Davis is an independent financial executive in Fountain Valley, California affiliated with Investacorp, Inc. He won an L.A. Area Emmy award for his work on *Dollar$ and Sense: Personal Finance for the 21st Century*, a telecourse offered through Coastline Community College District. He teaches stock market investing at Cerritos College and has worked in the securities industries for more than twenty-five years.

Chapter 1

What Is the Stock Market?

In many ways the economy is like a living person, probably most like a hyperactive teenager. The economy is a dynamic organism, ever growing, changing, and evolving. Like an adolescent, it can go through dramatic growth spurts that are usually followed by extended periods of lethargy. It is hardly ever static, and it seems impossible to get it to just stand still. Economists, like parents, never come to a point where they can say, "Stop everything now. You are just perfect as you are. Don't change a thing." Whether they want it to or not, the economy is going to change. There is no way to stop it, and there is no way to predict exactly how it is going to grow.

Also, the nature of the economy is such that there always seems to be a problem looming around the corner. Everything is dramatic to the economy. It is continually confronted with one earthshaking crisis after another. Regardless of the actual size of the problem, it always looks ominous. "This time it's really different. Nobody understands me. I must be the most miserable economy alive." Thus, economists—who, as the economy's parents, are responsible for monitoring its growth—never seem to know whether their charge is really exhibiting a relatively minor problem, which is easily taken care of, or if they are dealing with a potential catastrophe. It is difficult to tell whether that blemish is a simple pimple, problematic acne, or a cancerous lesion. Accelerated diagnosis of economic problems is usually difficult. Does this problem deserve a Band-Aid, prescription medicine, or radical surgery? Such uncertainty heightens the tension around the search for a solution to the problem. One can never be completely certain the proposed solution will solve the problem, or even whether the proposed solution will address the problem.

In addition, the nature of the economy is such that the solution to every problem will always create another problem. If the symptom is lethargy, an economist parent may recommend a strong dose of caffeine; however, the caffeine may create a whole new set of problems, perhaps super-hyperactivity, requiring a prescription sedative. Also, there is the possibility that your mother was right—caffeine really does stunt your growth; however, the real problem may not be simple lethargy. It may be manic depression, in which case a stimulant may only worsen the problem and create an even deeper depression. Economists are continually trying to figure out what is wrong with their child, and blame each other for their lack of parenting skills. Their ward suddenly seems so foreign to them. "That child I thought I knew has turned on me. When did it go so wrong? What's the matter with kids these days?"

The stock market is a convex mirror to the economy. It reflects and magnifies every economic imperfection. When the economy looks good, the stock market looks glamorous. When the economy looks bad, the stock market can get downright ugly. The fact that you can own stock in any one of the over 10,000 different domestic or foreign publicly traded companies means that you can directly participate in the fortunes or misfortunes of the economy. You can experience both its good and bad times. The stock market reacts with the same juvenile level of imitation that the economy does. "When it's good, it's very, very good; but when it's bad, it's horrid." So, what is the stock market, really?

It is a place where shares of stock can be *exchanged* from one owner to another. (Note that an exchange does not create new stock.) It is simply a physical location where buyers of *securities* can find sellers and where sellers can find buyers. **"Securities" is a broad term for investment instruments issued by businesses, usually corporations. Securities are available through broker/dealers and include stocks, bonds, and several other types of investments.**

You may have heard someone say, "The market was up today because there were more buyers than sellers" or it was down because "there were more sellers than buyers." These statements are misleading. There are never any more shares bought than were sold, or sold than were bought. Every time you buy a security, another investor in that security has sold it to you. Every time you sell a security, another investor buys it from you. This is true of all securities except those that are sold on the primary, or new issue, market, which will be discussed in Chapter 2. So, you should realize from this description of stock market transactions that an exchange does not create a security. It simply provides a service for buyers and sellers.

Illustration 1.1 shows the classic relationship between supply and demand curves. If supply is high and demand is low, the price per unit of a commodity will remain relatively low. As demand increases, supply decreases, and the price per unit goes higher. Only at the point where the supply is equal to the demand, where the two lines cross, will the price of the unit remain stable. Relating supply and demand to the stock market, every company has a *relatively* fixed number of shares available for investment. This number is said to be *relatively* fixed, because within certain limits a company can sometimes issue more shares, such as by giving perks or bonuses to employees through profit-sharing plans or stock options. Under no circumstances can a company issue more shares than it is *authorized* to issue. So, since there is a limited supply of shares available, the more motivated investors are to buy these shares, the higher the price they are willing to pay for them. This demand will drive the price higher. As demand increases, the price will increase because supply is limited. The more motivated investors are to sell a stock, the lower the price they will ask for their shares. So, stock prices tend to follow this same pattern illustrated by the supply and demand curves.

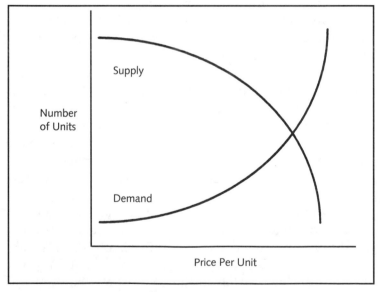

Illustration 1.1

All shares of stock on U.S. exchanges trade on a decimalized system—in U.S. dollars and cents. Usually the smallest incremental change in price for a share of stock is one cent. The incremental change for some high-priced shares may be changed to a higher minimum, such as 5 cents or 10 cents. Also, some low-priced shares, usually below $1, can trade at 1/10 (or even 1/100) of a cent minimum. However, when you see a company's stock quoted at 25.89, that means that ownership of shares of stock were exchanged for $25.89. If stock is quoted at 0.075, that represents a share price of seven and one-half cents.

The term used to describe each incremental change in a stock's price is called a "tick." So, if you hear someone say, "The stock is on an up tick," that simply means that the last price at which the stock traded was higher than the previous price. Also, business reporters will frequently comment on the *closing tick*. **The "closing tick" is computed by subtracting the number of companies whose last trade of the day was on a down-tick from those companies whose closing trades were on an up-tick.** The purpose of reporting on the closing tick is to indicate the sentiment of buyers and sellers just before the close of the market. This measure of investor activity at the close of that day's market could be an indicator of how the market might open on the next trading session. A high closing tick number would indicate that there was a surge of buying activity at the end of the trading day, which could carry over into the activity when the market opens the next day.

Contrary to what many people think, a stock does not have to open the next trading day at the same price it had closed at on the previous day. Investors may put in orders to buy and sell securities after the market is closed. These *overnight* orders will be entered before the market opens the next day and will determine at what price the stock will open for trading. **Most major stock exchanges in the United States are open every business day from 9:30**

A.M. to 4:00 P.M. local time in New York City, which would be 6:30 A.M. to 1:00 P.M. on the West Coast.

Additionally, there is an increasingly active market for trading securities after the NYSE has ended its regular day and before it opens the next. Several companies and exchanges offer extended-hours trading, available an hour and a half before the market opens and up to four hours after the close. This means that you can trade securities from 8:00 A.M. to 8:00 P.M. Eastern time.

This extended-hours market activity is managed by Electronic Communication Networks, or ECNs. The largest and most active company in this area is Instinet Group. Instinet ECN and its subsidiaries handle most of the volume of extended-hours trading. Much of this trading volume comes from institutional investors, such as mutual funds. However, individual investors also have access to the system, and an increasing number of small investors use extended-hours trading services. Instinet is a subsidiary of the British conglomerate Reuters Company. Two other exchanges offering extended-hours trading are Island ECN and Archipelago ECN. Most brokers use one of these three services, but others are available.

The stock market is a pure expression of a free market economy in action. It is more than a symbol for a free market—it is the free market. Without government or outside intervention, individuals can decide for themselves whether the price that someone is charging to sell their share of ownership in a company is a fair price or not. If they decide that it is a fair price, they can choose to purchase an ownership interest in the company.

What Is the Dow Jones Industrial Average?

When you hear someone say, "The market was up

today," they are *not* generally referring to the total market value for all securities, or even the total of the securities listed on the New York Stock Exchange, the largest stock exchange in the world. They are generally referring to the average change in price of the 30 companies that make up the *Dow Jones Industrial Average*. This average may also be abbreviated DJIA, DJ, Dow Industrials, or just the Dow. **The 30 companies that make up the Dow Jones Industrial Average are considered to be leaders in their industries, have a large capitalization, are actively traded, and usually pay a *dividend*. A "dividend" is a quarterly payment to stockholders that represents a portion of the company's earnings for that quarter.** The Wall Street jargon for the type of companies that are included in the Dow is "Blue Chip"—the color of the gaming chip with the highest value.

The fact that the term "the market" seems ambiguous is another example of how slowly traditions change on Wall Street. The Dow Jones Industrial Average started in 1884, when Charles H. Dow and Edward D. Jones began computing it by hand. The average covered 11 stocks and grew to 30 by 1928. Originally, the closing prices of the stocks were added up, and the total was divided by the number of companies to get a simple mathematical average. However, because of *stock splits* (explained shortly) and changes of the companies that made up the average, the divisor has evolved to about 0.15. You can find the current divisor, accurate to 8 decimal places, in the *Markets Lineup* section of *The Wall Street Journal*.

The divisor is useful because it gives you a reference point for figuring out how much the price movement of individual stocks affects the total market average. Consider how much the market would be changed if all 30 stocks in the Dow were up just one point. Dividing the total (30) by the divisor (0.15) reveals that the market would be up an astonishing 200 points! Also, the divisor may be used to determine how much a particular stock is a factor in the total market change. For example, assume that the market is up about 35 points, and one of the 30 stocks is up 5. If you divide 5 by the divisor, the result will reveal how much that stock contributed to the market's rise. In this case, those 5 points alone would account for nearly the whole 35-point rise in the average (5 ÷ 0.15 = 33). Thus, you may also deduce that the changes in the other 29 stocks would average out approximately to zero.

You should also note that this method of averaging favors higher-priced stocks, because of the diminishing percentage change as numbers increase. For example, a $1 increase in the price of a $100 stock is only 1 percent. A $1 increase in a $10 stock, however, is 10 percent—ten times as much. So, it is much more likely for a stock at 100 to move to 101 than it is for a stock at 10 to move to 11. Thus, the Dow is said to be *price-weighted*, because higher-*priced* stocks add more to the total than do lower-priced ones.

Now let us consider how the divisor has changed due to stock splits. **When a stock "splits," the number of shares an investor owns will increase and the price per share decrease, so that the total *market value* of the shares owned will be the same as it was before the split.** In other words, the percentage of the price reduction after the split will be the same as the percentage of increased shares resulting from the split. When a stock splits 2-for-1, for example, the total number of shares an investor owns will be doubled, and the price per share will be cut in half. The number of shares that will be added as a result of the split will be 50 percent of the new total. So, the total market value of the investment will remain the same. A shareholder who owns 100 shares of a stock selling for $50 (worth $5,000) will receive an additional 100 shares as a result of the split. That will make the total number of shares owned 200. The new shares represent 50 percent of the total shares owned after the increase. The price of the stock, however, will be cut to $25. So, the total market value of the shares will remain the same, $5,000. One hundred shares of a $50 stock has the same total market value as 200 shares of a $25 stock ($5,000). Also, stock splits may be made at ratios other than 2-for-1. A 3-for-2 stock split would result in a 33 percent price reduction; a 4-for-3 split, a 25 percent reduction.

A stock split is generally viewed very favorably by investors. It is a sign that the price of the stock has appreciated substantially. The board of directors of the company has decided that they would like to keep the price of the stock in a range that would attract more investors. However, you should be aware that there is no direct material benefit to the shareholders when a company declares a stock split.

To illustrate how the divisor for the DJIA has been reduced, imagine what would have happened if the original 30 stocks had all split 2-for-1. (This, of course, has never happened and never will.) However, if it did, to compute the average you could either multiply the split share prices by 2 and continue to divide by 30, or you could reduce the divisor by one-half—from 30 to 15. For example, if the prices of the 30 stocks totaled $3,000 before the split, the DJIA would be at 100 ($3,000 divided by 30 is 100). After the stocks split 2-for-1, however, the total market value would be reduced to $1,500. So the divisor would have to be reduced to 15 to maintain the average at 100. Fifteen hundred divided by 15 would still be equal to 100. It is less complicated to compute the Dow by changing one divisor than by changing the multiplier for each company every time there is a change in one of those 30 components.

There have been many deletions from and additions to the 30 companies that make up the Dow Jones Industrial Average. Usually companies whose Blue Chip status has faded are replaced by other companies that have emerged as leaders in their industries. A common criticism of using averages (or indexes) to measure the stock market is that they are constantly being artificially improved when under-performing companies are replaced with better performing ones. If companies that have done poorly were left in the average, the market would not appear to be doing as well as the historical record would indicate. In the case of the DJIA, this is not a major factor, since changes of the component companies only occur every few years. In other broader indexes, however, many component companies can change every year. Formulating a completely accurate method of measuring the market is very difficult.

Even though computers have made using the Dow Jones Industrial Average as an *overall* market indicator quite obsolete, everyone has always followed it—it's tradition. Other broader market indexes, however, are becoming very popular. Most institutional money managers, such as those who manage *mutual funds*, use the *Standard & Poor's 500 Index*. **"Mutual funds" are professionally managed portfolios in which each share of the fund represents ownership of many different individual securities** (mutual funds will be discussed in detail in Chapter 8). Whereas 30 companies make up the Dow Jones Industrial Average, the Standard & Poor's 500 Index (S&P 500) is made up of 500 companies. The difference between an *index* and an *average* is that an index is usually adjusted or weighted by other criteria. Also, an index will begin its measure with a base being assigned an arbitrary number, such as 0 or 100. For the S&P 500 the base period was established in the years 1941–1943. **The "S&P 500" is**

called *value*-weighted because the closing price of each
company in the index is multiplied by its number of
shares outstanding. Thus, the index is used to compute
the average of the total "market value" for each of the
500 companies.

Whether you are watching an average or an index, the
importance of the resulting computation of that market
indicator is not the number itself, but its relative change
over a period of time. If the DJIA was at 10,000, for example, and it went up 1,000 points, then you know that the
market was up 10 percent over that period of time. One
thousand is 10 percent of 10,000. The number that is
reported for the Dow Jones Industrial Average or for the
S&P 500 Index is not as important to an investor as the relative change in that number over any particular period of
time.

Other representative stock indexes include the popular
New York Stock Exchange Index. The NYSE Index represents the average closing price of all the approximately 2,800
companies on the "Big Board." The Value Line Index represents about 1,700 companies from all the major markets. All
of the companies on which Value Line publishes research
reports will be included in that index. The Russell 2000
Index measures the market capitalization changes of 2,000
small-cap U.S. corporations. It does not include any foreign
companies. "Small-cap" companies are mainly corporations
whose capitalization is less than $2 billion. Mid-cap indexes
measure companies whose capitalization generally ranges
between $2 billion and $10 billion. Different financial publications use different criteria for labeling companies small-
cap or mid-cap, however. So, these ranges are meant to be
guidelines, not rules. By far the *broadest* of the most frequently quoted market index is the Wilshire 5000 Equity
Index. It is composed of *more* than 5,000 companies (cur-

rently over 7,000). All of the actively traded companies that are *not* included in the S&P 500 make up the Wilshire 5000. Although these other market indexes are more representative of the overall market than the Dow Jones Industrial Average, you are not likely to see any change from this most quoted indicator in your lifetime.

In addition to the Industrials Average, Dow Jones & Company also publishes the Dow Jones Transportation Average of 20 stocks and the Dow Jones Utilities Average of 15. These averages represent companies in those specific industry groups. The total of all three indexes is combined into the 65-stock Dow Jones Composite Average.

How Do You Read Market Quotes in the Newspaper?

The biggest problem that most people have when they first try to look up stock quotes in the newspaper is figuring out how the names of the companies are abbreviated. The abbreviated names in the newspaper are *not* standardized. They are shortened by the wire service that supplies the quotes to that particular newspaper. However, the names of the companies are organized in alphabetical order *as if their names were spelled out completely*.

The abbreviated names used by the wire service have no relationship to **the "ticker symbols," which are the computer symbols assigned by the exchange where the stocks are traded.** If you wanted to find the quote for General Electric Company, for example, it would be listed alphabetically as if its name were spelled out. It would not be listed alphabetically under "GE," which is what the company is usually called, or under its ticker symbol, which is also "GE." If a company changes its name, its position in an alphabetical list will, of course, also change.

When Philip Morris Companies, Inc. changed its name to Altria Group, Inc. in 2003, many investors were concerned that they could no longer find the stock quote in the newspaper. In fact, it had simply changed its order in the alphabetically arranged list.

If you have ever seen the ticker tape in a brokerage office or on television, you have seen the *ticker symbols* scrolling across. The ticker symbol is always a one-, two-, or three-letter symbol for *listed* stocks. **"Listed" is a term used to describe stocks that trade on an exchange,** such as the New York, American, or Pacific. Securities that are not listed trade *over-the-counter* and will always have a four- or five-letter symbol. **The over-the-counter market, which is usually abbreviated OTC, differs from an exchange in that it has no central location. It is a computer network for trading securities.** The largest such network is called the National Association of Securities Dealers Automated Quotation System (NASDAQ). More information on how the over-the-counter market differs from the exchanges will be presented in Chapter 2.

New York Stock Exchange Composite Transactions										
YTD % CHG	52 WEEK Hi	Lo	STOCK	SYM	DIV	YLD %	PE	VOL 100s	CLOSE	NET CHG
6.2	41¹/₂	17³/₄	UniqueIn	INC	1.40	3.8	17	135000	37	+0.25

Illustration 1.2

Different newspapers may organize the stock quote information differently, but *The Wall Street Journal* has the most complete listing. Illustration 1.2 shows how a market quote would look in the *Journal*. It presents information on a stock you'll be hearing more about in the future, Unique Inc., ticker symbol "INC." The information to the left of the name of the company gives the year-to-date percentage change—that is, the percentage of the closing price from last December 31 the stock is currently up or down. You can see that the closing price of Unique Inc. at 37 was up 6.2 percent from the previous year's closing price. In other words, last December 31 Unique Inc. shares closed at about 34.84. This is followed by last year's high and low prices—that is, the high and low for the previous 52 weeks. This information gives you some idea of the recent trading range for that company. You can tell whether it is currently trading near the high end or low end of that range.

Next you see the name of the company as the wire service abbreviates it and the ticker symbol. This is followed by the annual dividend and yield. The "dividend," which will be explained in greater detail in Chapter 3, **represents the current rate of payments that the company is making to its shareholders.** The payments are made quarterly, but the amount reported in the paper represents the annualized rate, or four times the quarterly payment. So, Unique Inc. is currently paying a $.35 quarterly dividend, or $1.40 per share annually. **The dividend "yield" is the percentage return that the dividend would represent if you bought the stock at the closing price quoted in the paper.** In this case, the $1.40 dividend represents a 3.8 percent yield, based on a price of $37 per share, the closing price. This would be approximately the same amount of interest you would earn if you put $37 in a savings account at 3.8 percent interest for one year. If a company does not have a policy of paying the same quarterly dividend, the rate noted in the paper will be followed by a footnote, usually "e," indicating that the company does not have a policy of paying a regular quarterly dividend.

PE stands for price earnings ratio and is sometimes written "P/E." This number represents the closing price of the stock divided by its earnings per share. The earnings per share, abbreviated EPS, is the company's net earnings for the last year divided by the number of shares outstanding. This may not mean much to you right now, but you will learn about the significance of the price earnings ratio in Chapter 5, "How Do You Read Financial Statements?"

"Vol 100s" means the total number of shares traded on that day, divided by 100. **Stocks usually trade in a block of 100 shares, which is called a "round lot."** So, that volume record represents the number of round lot trades. The total number of shares of Unique Inc. that traded on that day was 13,500,000, that is 135,000 times 100.

The next column reflects that the closing price, or the last trade of the day, was executed at $37 per share. The net change is the difference between the previous day's closing price and the current day's closing price—"+" means higher and "–" means lower. Since Unique Inc. closed "+0.25," you know that the previous day's closing price was $36.75.

Should You Invest in the Stock Market?

Even if you don't think you have any investments in the stock market directly, you probably do have some indirectly. Over half of all Americans participate either directly or indirectly in the stock market. Part of the investments that you have in insurance policies or retirement accounts or even in banks or credit unions is probably in securities. This is not by coincidence. Professional *fiduciaries* realize that the stock market on average has given a better inflation-adjusted rate of return on their investments than any other alternative. **A "fiduciary" is someone who acts on behalf of another in making financial decisions.**

Unfortunately, too many people approach the stock market with a get-rich-quick attitude. This hinders their objective point of view on the stock market, and usually contributes to their making very poor and ill-timed investment decisions. Millions have been made by investing in stocks, but you should note that these millions were made at the expense of those who have lost. When it comes to investing, slow and steady wins the race.

We live in a risk-oriented economy. **"Inflation," the measure of the loss of purchasing power of money due to an expanding economy or rising prices,** is a constant reality. The greatest risk you can take with your investment capital is to do nothing. If you keep your money in your mattress or in any other way "sleep on it" and do nothing to keep ahead of inflation, you virtually guarantee that your net worth will steadily decline. Do you remember what it cost you to go to a movie when you were a child? Do you know what your parents paid for their car or for their house? You don't have to have a very long memory to realize that a dollar does not go as far as it used to. Only if you make investments that at least maintain pace with inflation will the dollar you have in your pocket now be able to buy an equivalent amount of goods next year.

For the last century, the best-performing inflation-adjusted investment, of all investment possibilities, has been common stocks. Other investments may have outperformed stocks for short periods of time, but compared to bonds, gold, real estate, oil, collectibles such as stamps, rare coins, art, and baseball cards, or any other investment to which comparisons are usually made, the stock market has consistently given better long-term returns. There is a place for stock market investments in almost everyone's financial plan. Regardless of your current economic status, you could benefit in some way from security investments.

An individual financial plan will usually begin with an itemization of your assets. These can be separated into financial assets and real assets. Financial assets would include your bank accounts, brokerage accounts, insurance, and retirement plan investments. Real assets would include your house, car, jewelry, collectibles, and so on. Next itemize your debt, or liabilities. You should list your home mortgage balance, car loan, credit card balances, and any other debt you currently have. The difference between your assets and your liabilities will be your net worth, or equity. You'll see how corporations compute their net worth in Chapter 5.

Most financial planners will organize your personal spending or investing priorities something like this: (1) insurance or risk management, (2) home ownership, (3) tax and estate planning, (4) capital accumulation. Quite honestly this list looks as if it were organized by (1) insurance salespeople, (2) real estate brokers, (3) attorneys, and (4) bankers. Some financial planners imply that the stock market is for risk capital only, and that there is no place for those types of investments until after you have met all your other financial goals. This assessment assumes that all securities are high-risk investments, which is false. Certainly, risk capital should be on the bottom of your financial priorities, but the stock market should *not* always be approached as a risk capital area of investing. Many security investments are *not* high risk.

Perhaps a more logical approach to financial planning is to consider your own basic personal needs. They are the same for you now as they were in your childhood. Most of us were taught as children that our needs, in order of priority, are: food, shelter, safety, and love. Sound financial planning should be prioritized on this same basis. First and foremost, you need to provide for adequate personal income to meet all your current and anticipated future needs. In other words, you need to keep food on the table. If you don't have any finances, you won't need a financial plan.

Second, your goal should be to achieve home owner-ship—shelter. This is becoming increasingly more difficult in today's complex real estate market, but you should have a workable plan to achieve the goal of saving enough money to purchase and to finance your own home.

Third, financial safety should be taken care of through proper insurance coverage for protection from catastrophic events. Also, you need an adequate plan for retirement. Your goal here should be to have enough income at retire-ment to maintain the same lifestyle you had as a wage earner.

The fourth personal need is love, and, as every country-and-western songwriter knows, all the money in world can't buy that. In fact, some would say that money is a major hindrance to love—but that's another book. Your fourth goal in financial planning, however, is to anticipate the future financial needs of your loved ones. Make provi-sions for your children's college education or other major expenses. Also, every financial plan should include charita-ble giving, or tithing.

Anyone who has capital to invest has a very good rea-son to take advantage of the opportunities in the securities industry, no matter what his or her financial position is. At all levels of financial planning there are some securities investments that could help you achieve your goals. If you approach investing with a desire to study and be involved in your investment decisions, you will avoid the common pitfalls of novice investors and increase your chances of reaching your goals. Do not approach the market as a means to get rich quick, and do not take unnecessary risks. A little psychological study of how your investments affect your emotions can be invaluable to your success.

How Do You Know When to Buy or Sell?

Perhaps the most difficult question for anyone to answer about the stock market is, "When should I buy, and when should I sell?" There have been innumerable books written on these subjects, but none of them has found the perfect answer yet. The best advice on this subject has come from studies on the psychology of investing, which have resulted in a theoretical cycle known as the "Greed-Hope-Fear Cycle." This cycle illustrates the fact that your emotions tend to be your worst enemy when it comes to investment timing. If you are able to separate your emotions from your logic, you will greatly improve your timing of when to buy and when to sell. The Greed-Hope-Fear Cycle is also known as the Individual Investor Cycle or the Small Investor Syndrome, implying that this cycle is representative of individuals rather than of institutions. It should be noted, however, that institutions are made up of individuals, and the most dramatic illustrations of this cycle in action have come primarily from poor institutional timing.

On October 19, 1987 (Black Monday), the stock market dropped over 500 points, and for a four-day period it fell about 770 points, approximately 30 percent. This was the largest *numerical* drop in stock market history, although the actual loss in market value was small compared to the loss following the Crash of 1929. From peak to trough the market crash from October 1929 to June 1932 was approximately 89 percent. The so-called "crash of '87" was perpetuated in a large part by *institutional*, not individual, investors. Insurance companies, pension and retirement funds, brokerage firms, and mutual funds were primarily responsible for the huge increase in trading volume during that time. In fact, several insurance companies announced that they would increase their insurance premiums as a result of investment losses they incurred following the "crash." Many astute individual investors, however, took advantage of the price drop, buying after the crash. The value of their investments, on average, rose to new highs within the next 12 months.

To illustrate the Greed-Hope-Fear Cycle, here is a typical example of how some investors choose what stock to buy and when to buy it. *Usually, curiosity about a particular company is initially aroused by an animated conversation with your hairstylist, neighbor, relative, or friend—but seldom with your stockbroker—about a company that has invented a new widget that is going to revolutionize life as we know it. Though you may listen with a justifiably skeptical ear to this conversation, your curiosity has been sufficiently aroused that you start to follow how this company is doing. You look it up in the business section of the newspaper.*

To your surprise the company is doing quite well. It started out at 20 (dollars per share), and over the next few days has run up to 24½. Doing a little simple arithmetic you realize that an investment of $2,000 for 100 shares would now be worth $2,450, and that $450 profit represents a 22.5 percent return on your investment—in less than a week's time. Hey, that beats that CD you've got all to heck. If that stock comes back down a little bit, maybe you'll pick up 100 shares.

So, you continue watching it more intently, and it does come back. It moves down to 23. "Should I buy it now?" you think to yourself. "No, it was 20 a little over a week ago, and it's coming down, I'll wait." Over the next few days, however, you watch the stock go back up—now it's 27! "What a fool," you say to yourself. "If I had just bought that stock when I heard about it, I'd be rich now. If I had bought 1,000 shares at 20, that stock would now be worth $27,000! Why don't I ever take advantage of what I think I should do?"

The stock continues to go up and down for a few more weeks. Down to 26, up to 28, down to 27, up to 30. Then something happens. The company puts out a press release explaining how this widget really will change life as we know it, and the stock immediately shoots up to 35. Well, you can't just sit there any longer. It's too depressing to compute how much money you lost by not investing in that stock just a few months ago. You know the widget works—there it is in black and white—and in a fit of desperation, you call up your broker and tell him to get you 100 shares at the market. Your broker calls you back in 20 minutes, "Your order was filled at 38¼."

Over the past few months, you've watched this stock run from 20 to 38¼. Now, where does your logic tell you that this stock is going to go from here? How much higher do you think this stock can go? Look at the motivation for your decision. It is purely and simply GREED. You became so obsessed with how much money you could have made from an investment in this company that you failed to analyze the overall picture. Greed caused you to buy at the top of the market. *So, of course, the day that you bought this stock at 38¼, it closed at 37. The next day it closed at 35½, and within a week it dropped to 33.*

Your attitude toward this company has rapidly soured. The greed that motivated you when you bought it is now a faint memory. As you open the newspaper each day and hastily turn to the business section to look up your stock quote, it's not with eager anticipation to see how much money you've made on your investment; it's with the firm resolve that if that turkey ever gets close to what you paid for it, you're going to sell it in a flash. Your emotional attachment to your investment has subtly changed from greed to HOPE. You hope that if you can just get out of this situation without it costing you too much, you will have learned your lesson never to invest in the stock market again.

After that initial drop, your widget company does begin to come back. *From the low of 30, it moves slowly up to around 35. In a few more days, it hits 36¼. You begin thinking, maybe this isn't the catastrophe you thought it would be. It's moved up over three points in a few days. In a few more days, you'll be able to get your money back. The next day, however, you find your finger running down the column of stock quotes in the paper and stopping at...34½. You double check to make sure that you're on the right company. You are. You begin anew beating yourself up in your mind, "That was it. That was my chance to get out, and I didn't take it. Why don't I do what I say I'm going to do? Why don't I take action when I know I should?"*

For the next several months only the HOPE that you may someday be able to get your money back sustains you. The stock goes up and down, but mostly down. In fact, over this period of time it has gone from 34 to 30 to 28 to 25—not straight down, up and down—but every upward move seems to be followed by a greater downward move. The farther away from 38¾ it gets, the dimmer the glimmer of hope that you will ever get your money back.

Then one day you look at your morning paper, and there on page three is an article about your widget company. That widget, in fact, may not do what it is supposed to do. It may not change life as everyone knows it; it may only change life as some people know it. But it certainly has changed life as you know it. You flip to the business section to look up your quote. You have a little trouble finding it this time because you haven't looked at it in several weeks, and the longer your finger runs up and down that quote column the harder it is to focus on the name of your company. There it is—21½! You've lost almost half of your investment. In a panic you call your stockbroker. He tells you that the company is currently trading at 18⅜. You yell, "Sell!"

Your attitude toward your investment had long ago changed from one of GREED, anticipating high profits.

And now your HOPE of recouping your money has eroded to a FEAR that you may lose it all. *Your broker calls you back in about 10 minutes and says, "We got 17¾ for the stock." You hang up the phone in a fit of despair and try to sort out what you have learned from this experience. "I'll never do this again. Never. Never. Never."*

Now stop for just a minute. You've watched this company go from 38¾ to 17¾ in a relatively short period of time. Logically, not emotionally, where do you think this stock is going to go from here? The next day the stock closes at 20½. The day after that at 21¼, then 23. It begins moving slowly and steadily back up.

This narrative is meant to be a somewhat exaggerated look at the Greed-Hope-Fear Cycle. Unfortunately, it may be too close to a real-life experience to be humorous for some investors. The point, however, is this: Your emotions are always going to be working against you when it comes to making good decisions concerning market timing. The best time to buy is when the majority of people is selling, and the best time to sell is when the majority is buying.

You may have heard market commentators advising investors to be *contrarians*, and this is an illustration of what that means. If you had been a buyer of securities after the "crash of '87," you could have doubled your investment over the next year. There weren't, however, many investors scrambling to buy on that day. It goes against the grain to buy when everyone else is selling, or to sell when everyone else is buying. This is true whether you are an individual investor or an institutional investor—we are all individuals. So, what is called the Small Investor Syndrome or Individual Investor Cycle is really true of institutions as well.

If you want to avoid falling victim to this cycle, you will need to make investment decisions based on logic and research, not on emotions. This investor's mistake was not that he did not quickly buy the stock when he first heard about it; it was that he did no research or analysis on the company. He did not look at the company's financial statements or analyze the company's market potential for selling widgets. Some investment advice you will often hear quoted is, "Buy low and sell high." This advice is so simplistic that most people take it as a joke, but no one will deny that it is true. Take it seriously, and you'll always have the last laugh.

Do You Know What You Need to Know?

To check up on what you learned from this chapter, answer the following questions in your own words, then compare your answers with the answer key.

1. Why is the economy described as dynamic, and why does it always seem to be in trouble? How do economists try to predict how the economy should be regulated— expansion or contraction?

2. Why is it incorrect to say that the market went up today because there were more buyers than sellers?

3. How do supply and demand factors affect security prices? What causes increased demand or limited supply?

4. How does the Greed-Hope-Fear Cycle illustrate that one's emotions will often cause investors to buy or to sell securities at the wrong time? What is the right time to buy and the right time to sell?

5. What is a stock split and in what way, if any, does it benefit shareholders? Does a 2-for-1 stock split mean that the value of shareholders' stock will double?

6. Why is the Dow Jones Industrial Average most commonly referred to as "the market?" What index do most professional investors use to measure the market? Why?

7. What is the difference between a price-weighted average, such as the DJIA, and a value-weighted index, such as the S&P 500?
8. What is a *contrarian* investor? Should you be one? Why, or why not?

Answer Key

1. The economy is dynamic because it is always on the move and always changing. Economists who try to monitor its growth are always dealing with a problem that keeps changing. The solution to one problem will eventually lead to another problem. Lowering interest rates stimulates growth to avoid recession; however, that will eventually cause inflation. Raising interest rates will slow inflationary growth, but may lead to a recession.
2. There are never any more shares bought than sold, or sold than bought. The function of the stock market is to match buyers with sellers and vice versa. One could say that at times buyers are more desperate than sellers, thus willing to pay higher prices for securities, or more desperate to sell and willing to accept lower prices. However, every time a share is bought, it is sold by someone else, and vice versa.
3. Companies have a limited number of shares issued and outstanding. The greater the demand, the higher the price investors may be willing to pay for securities.
4. Greed may cause you to want to buy at or near the top of a normal market cycle. If you think that everyone is making money in the stock market except you, watch out—that's most likely a market top. The ideal time to buy is probably when the market is going through an irrational fear (down) cycle.

5. Companies usually have a stock split to make shares more affordable to average investors. A 2-for-1 split means shareholders will own twice as many shares as they did previously, but the price will be half as much. Thus, the total value of an investment after a split remains approximately the same.

6. The DJIA is the oldest of the market indicators, and it is usually referred to as "the market" simply because it is traditional. Most professional investors, such as mutual fund managers, use a broader index called the S&P 500 for their comparative measure of the market.

7. The DJIA was originally computed by adding up the prices of the stocks in the average and dividing by the number of companies. The divisor has changed over the years due to stock splits and the different prices of new companies added. The S&P 500 measures the total market capitalization of each security in the index. Market capitalization is equal to the price of the security multiplied by the number of shares outstanding.

8. A contrarian is an investor who buys when the prevailing wisdom says to sell and who sells when the prevailing wisdom says to buy. Yes, you probably should be a contrarian. See the Greed-Hope-Fear Cycle.

This book will help you avoid common pitfalls of securities investing.

— Chapter 2 —

What Is a Stock?

Businesses in the United States are organized either as sole proprietorships, partnerships, or corporations. A "sole proprietorship" is a business owned by an individual, who is solely responsible for its success or failure. Most often a proprietorship will be a retail business serving a local market, a professional in private practice, or a small business operating out of a home. It will generally remain a proprietorship as long as the owner does not need to raise more money for expansion than what he or she has available.

If the proprietorship business grows and the individual does need to raise more capital for expansion, the next step may be to get a partner. The addition of a partner would change the sole proprietorship to a partnership. **The expenses, or liabilities, and the profits of the "partnership" business would be divided between the partners in whatever arrangements they have agreed upon.** Usually this sharing arrangement is in the same proportion as the amount of capital they have invested in the business.

More businesses than most people realize in the United States are organized as partnerships. Some family-owned operations have remained in the family for generations, and they have never opted to expand out of their partnership status. Also, in the last few years there has been a wave of partnership-financed buyouts of public corporations. In these cases, multimillion-dollar financiers have raised enough personal capital or have borrowed enough capital to buy out large public corporations, thus turning them into partnerships. Many states also allow the formation of a limited liability partnership (LLP). However, such a partnership structure is usually restricted to the businesses of attorneys or accountants.

If a partnership business needs additional capital beyond the resources it has available under this structure, the next step is usually to incorporate. There are two popular corporate structures for small businesses: S corporations and limited liability corporations (LLCs). In many ways these types of companies are more like partnerships than they are like public corporations. They are both non-public corporate structures, which means that the general public cannot invest in them. S corporations, so called because they make a special tax election under subchapter S of the Internal Revenue Code, are limited to no more than 75 shareholders. These types of small business structures shelter the owners' personal assets from corporate liability. They act as "pass through" businesses, meaning that all corporate profits are passed through to the individual owners, who then pay taxes on those profits. Taxes are not paid by the corporate entity itself, which is why these structures are so popular. Also, LLCs usually require less paperwork by easing required document filing and record keeping.

The corporations just mentioned are usually referred to as "private companies." In fact that term may also be applied to almost any company owned by only a small number of shareholders, regardless of their corporate structure. Such companies are private because they have few owners and seldom sell shares to anyone else. Consequently, they are not required to disclose financial information to the general public about their business operations. The shareholders keep all profits from the business, and they are solely responsible for making financial decisions. Larger corporations that allow anyone to invest in them are legally called C corporations. In this book, whenever the word "corporation" is used, it almost always refers to a public company.

Corporations have two basic methods of raising capital. They can borrow money, or they can sell some of their equity. If they borrow, they can get a loan from a bank or other financial institution, or they can borrow money from other investors by issuing bonds. If the company borrows money, it will have to pay a fixed rate of interest on the amount borrowed, and it will have to pay back the principal when the loan comes due or the bond matures. If, however, the company decides to sell some of its equity, it won't have to pay interest or pay back principal. The company will, however, lose some of the control over its business. If it needs to raise a large amount of capital and must sell a large number of shares to investors not currently associated with it, the company would then *go public*.

By "going public," the company makes available shares of stock, representing ownership in that business, to anyone who wants to invest. How this process works is explained in the next section. When it goes public, the new company will raise additional capital, but now it must disclose to its new owners, the shareholders, and usually to the general public as well, all of its financial information. It must also update the shareholders quarterly, every three months, of all changes in the finances of the company. These quarterly statements will correspond to the four quarters of its fiscal calendar.

At the time the corporation is formed it will begin a fiscal year, thus establishing the quarterly cycle for reporting its finances. Some corporations still use the fiscal year that began in the month in which the corporation was formed. Many corporations, however, have adjusted their fiscal year to correspond to the calendar year, that is, a year ending December 31. Thus, their quarterly statements are sent to shareholders following the months of March, June, September, and December. The large number of companies reporting their earnings on this quarterly cycle can cause some volatility in the stock market around the time of their reporting period. A large number of companies reporting higher than expected earnings, for example, can cause the stock market to rally.

Probably the most important difference between a proprietorship or a partnership and a corporation, at least from the viewpoint of the investor, is the financial liability assumed by the owners. **If a business is organized as a proprietorship or a partnership, the owners have unlimited liability.** If the business fails, those who loaned money to the business, the creditors, have the legal right to seize not only assets of the business, but personal assets of the owners as well. In other words, under this type of structure, the owner's capital risk can be greater than the amount of the investment. When a proprietorship or partnership business fails, that is, declares bankruptcy, the owners are often forced to declare *personal* bankruptcy as well. The liability of investors in a public corporation, however, is limited to the amount of their investment.

How Do Companies Sell Shares of Stock?

The process of initially bringing shares to market is called "underwriting," and it is the job of investment bankers. The market for an initial public offering of stock is called the "primary market." When a company has completed its initial public offering, its shares may start trading on other exchanges or on the over-the-counter market. **The New York Stock Exchange, the American Stock**

Exchange, the regional exchanges (Midwest, Pacific, Boston, and so on), and the over-the-counter market are all "secondary markets." There is also a "third market." This term refers to the trading of *listed* securities off the floor of the exchange. Member firms of the NYSE, for example, might match buy and sell orders for clients from the firm's own inventory. This type of trading is referred to as 19c3, the rule in the NYSE charter that allows it. Also, institutions will sometimes negotiate large block trades between themselves without going to the exchange where that security is normally traded. The execution of that type of trade is referred to as the "fourth market."

Most major brokerage firms and money center banks have large investment banking departments. These departments can be very profitable for these financial institutions. The investment banker will advise the officers of a company on their various options for *going public*. The officers may decide to issue bonds or preferred stock, instead of issuing common stock. If they decide to issue common stock however, the investment banker will compute the number of shares that it feels the company can sell and fix the price per share. The price will be determined on the basis of various financial ratios of other comparable companies.

The only information that can be distributed to the public before the initial offering is the preliminary prospectus, known as a "red herring." It is so called because it has a red disclaimer statement on the cover page. The disclaimer simply states that the Securities and Exchange Commission (SEC), the governing Federal agency with which the red herring is filed, cannot guarantee the authenticity of the information. This is to protect the SEC so you can't sue them for any misinformation that the company may have put in the document. **The prospectus represents "full disclosure" of the company's business.** Any other information, while it may not be inaccurate, will not fulfill the Securities and Exchange Commission requirement of full disclosure.

After the company goes public, the only information that may be publicly disseminated is the *final prospectus*. It is a copy of the red herring that includes the final offering price, the total number of shares sold, the proceeds to the issuing company, and so on, but does not include the red ledger. The investment banker may not issue any other information about the company, except in what is called a "tombstone ad," so called because of its stark appearance.

The tombstone ad is the only way the investment banker can advertise its success in bringing this company to the market. The only way the investment banker can distinguish itself in the ad is by the border it puts around the announcement. So, you may notice that some of the borders around the tombstone ads are a little flashier than most tombstones. From the investment banker's point of view, you have to do the best with what little the regulators give you. The first name in the list of firms that participated in the offering is the lead underwriter. That firm gets to pick the border.

Once the company has gone public, it has changed from a proprietorship, partnership, or closely held company. It is now owned by its shareholders.

What Are Your Rights as a Shareholder?

Under the corporate structure the liability of shareholders is limited to the amount of their investment. Investors cannot lose any more than what they paid for their stock. As a corporate shareholder, your personal assets are not at risk, as they could be in a proprietorship or a partnership. Obviously, the shareholders do not have nearly as much control over the business's operations as the proprietor or partners do over their businesses. The shareholders may own the company, but they don't manage it. **Most common stock shareholders have the right to vote for who will represent their interests on the board of directors for that corporation. They may also vote on any proposals that would materially change the structure of their corporation**, such as increasing the number of shares outstanding. However, the shareholders have no say over the day-to-day operations of the company's business.

Usually one vote is granted for each share owned of a company's common stock. Since the number of outstanding shares is relatively constant, your percentage ownership of the company will remain relatively constant. Admittedly, if you own 100 shares of a company with 100 million shares outstanding, your voting influence is not very significant. You own 0.0001 percent of the company. As a result of the large number of minority interest shareholders, corporations frequently propose issuing nonvoting stock. The New York Stock Exchange, however, has always had a policy of guaranteeing the right of "one share, one vote" for every share of common stock listed on the exchange. To the NYSE board of governors, this is such an inalienable right that every share of common stock listed on the "Big Board" must have it, and proposals to list nonvoting shares have always been rejected.

Voting is accomplished by issuing a *proxy card* to all registered shareholders. **A "proxy" is someone who is given the authority to carry out the instructions from someone else. When you sign and return your "proxy card," your votes will be cast by a proxy at the annual shareholders' meeting.** If you do not vote by proxy, you may vote your shares directly at the meeting itself. Although quite often a majority of shares may have already been voted by proxy on all the issues that will be brought up at the meeting, shareholders should not underestimate the power of their right to vote. Many large shareholders, such as pension funds or institutions, have been increasing their clout in recent years by using their votes to change the board of directors at a company or to influence management to follow a course that would be more beneficial to their interests. Although minority shareholders may feel somewhat powerless, their votes as a whole can greatly influence management. If they feel their company is being mismanaged, shareholders do have the power to do something about it.

If a company issues shares of stock that have some restriction on voting rights, or have some other unusual restriction, such shares will be labeled as "classified." Instead of being common stock, these shares will be identified as Class A or Class B, or some other class designation. You will not usually find classified shares on the New York Stock Exchange (NYSE) because of the "one share one vote" rule. However, there are some exceptions. Class B shares of the *Washington Post* trade on the NYSE. Those shares do hold to the one-share-one-vote rule; however, the Class A shares, which are not publicly traded and are owned mainly by insiders, maintain a voting majority for the company.

Another noteworthy situation is Berkshire Hathaway Co. Class A and Class B. These are actually two different companies. However, they are both run by the same CEO, legendary billionaire Warren Buffet, and they both are in the same business of buying other companies. Class A shares of Berkshire Hathaway have long been the most expensive shares on the NYSE (around $75,000 per share at the time of this writing). The "poor man's version" is Class B, which are just a few thousand dollars per share. Both of these companies guarantee full voting rights for shareholders. In fact, many investors purchase one share of the company so they can attend the annual shareholders' meeting and glean insight on the market from Mr. Buffet's keynote address.

If shares of a company's stock are classified due to a limitation of voting privileges, those shares will not be listed on the New York Stock Exchange. They would have to be listed on the American Stock Exchange or one of the regional exchanges, or trade on the over-the-counter market. **The "over-the-counter market,"** you should recall from Chapter 1, **is a system for trading shares of stock without having one central location. A computer network will match individuals who want to buy or to sell shares of stock with "market makers," professional traders for that security.** The OTC market will be discussed in greater detail in Chapter 4.

The other basic right of a shareholder is the right to participate in the profitability of the company. In many companies, the board of directors has a policy of declaring a dividend when they report their quarterly earnings. **A "dividend" is a payment made to all shareholders, which would represent a percentage of income the company made from its revenues for that quarter.** Once the board of directors has declared a dividend payment to shareholders, there is an unwritten law that they must continue to pay that same dividend, or a higher one, thereafter. Indeed, this is analogous to granting a child a certain privilege. As all parents know, once a privilege is granted to a child, it becomes a God-given right thereafter.

Obviously, a company's earnings are not always the same every quarter, so the board of directors doesn't usually declare a regular dividend until they have sufficient equity to continue paying the same dividend even if they have a bad quarter. Investors should take note, however, that if a company's earnings per share (EPS) are below their regular dividend payments, that dividend is probably in imminent jeopardy of being reduced or eliminated. Sometimes the board of directors of a company will vote to continue to pay a dividend even if the earnings are insufficient to cover it. This is done to save face. The officers of the company realize that cutting a dividend is usually the kiss of death, causing the company's stock price to drop precipitously.

The dividend "yield" on equity investments is analogous to the interest rate paid on debt investments, such as bonds or bank CDs. Interest, however, is a term associated with a fixed, or guaranteed, rate of return, and, as previously pointed out, the dividend is *not* guaranteed—except by the social pressures exerted on the board of directors by the shareholders. The dividend yield would be computed by dividing the *annualized* dividend—the sum of the four quarterly dividends—by the price per share. If you pay $25.00 per share for a company that is paying a $1.00 (that is, $.25 per quarter) dividend per year, the dividend yield would be 1 divided by 25, or 4.00 percent. Note that if you pay more for the stock, the dividend yield will go down. If the share price should rise from $25 to $30, the $1.00 dividend represents a 3.33 percent yield (1 divided by 30). So, the dividend yield on a stock will change daily, as the stock's price changes.

Many companies choose not to pay a dividend. This type of policy is usually associated with a *growth stock*. If the company does not pay out part of its earnings to its shareholders, then it retains the use of that money for its own expansion purposes. The company should be able to grow faster if it has the use of that capital. If the management of that company is competent, they should be able to increase the company's earnings at a much faster rate than what the individual investor could receive as a return on that dividend from a savings account or another investment. If, however, a company has a policy of not paying dividends, and its earnings are not growing at a faster rate than other alternative investments with less risk, then the investor may be wise to seek a company with better management or at least a better dividend-paying policy. The mechanics of how a dividend is paid will be discussed in Chapter 4, when the terms "trade date" and "settlement date" are explained.

The dividends that a company pays will be issued by the transfer agent for that company. **A "transfer agent" is a financial institution contracted by a corporation. Its functions, among many others, include keeping records of the company's stockholders, issuing certificates for the company's stock, and sending out dividend checks.** Most transfer agents are departments of major banks, and they will usually act as an agent for many, perhaps even hundreds, of companies. The transfer agent will send the dividend checks to the holders of record of the company's stock. If the shareholder has a stock certificate issued in his or her name, the dividend will be mailed directly to him or her. If the shareholder leaves the stock certificate on deposit in his or her account at a brokerage firm, the dividend will be paid directly to that account.

The discussion of securities up to this point has assumed that these were shares of an American company. Foreign companies, however, can also trade shares in the United States. You should be aware that foreign companies do not fall under the jurisdiction of the Securities and Exchange Commission. Also, foreign companies may employ different accounting principles and standards than are applicable to U.S. corporations. However, this lack of U.S. regulation has not slowed down the trading of these securities.

The volume of trading of foreign securities on U.S. markets has risen sharply in recent years. This is mainly due to U.S. companies being bought out by foreign ones. AXA, BASF, BP (British Petroleum), China Telecom, DaimlerChrysler, GlaxoSmithkline, Honda, Matsushita,

Nestlé, Nokia, Phillips Electronics, Royal Dutch, Sony, Unilever, and Vodafone are just a few of the many thousands of foreign-owned companies that actively trade in the United States. Some foreign companies may trade in the U.S. as a class of shares that are identical to the shares that trade on exchanges in that company's country of origin. These are called "ordinary shares." However, most trading of foreign companies is accomplished through the issuance of American Depositary Receipts (ADRs). **An ADR is a certificate issued by a U.S. bank representing shares of the foreign stock that have been put on deposit at the bank.** The bank, for a small fee, issues certificates printed in English and converts any dividends paid by the company into U.S. currency. American Depositary Receipts are either classified as "sponsored" or "unsponsored." A sponsored ADR, represented by the companies mentioned on the above list, means that the foreign corporation provides financial information to the bank. An unsponsored ADR company does not.

Is the Stock Market Risky?

"Risk" can be defined as the potential for an unpredictable result, in particular, a potential for loss. The rates of return on investments assume that the investor has an aversion to risk. So, the lower the risk associated with an investment, the lower the expected rate of return. **The willingness to assume greater risks with investments is what differentiates "investing" from "speculating."** A speculator is obviously willing to assume greater risks in hopes of realizing a greater return, or he or she may be trying to achieve high returns in a short period of time.

Investing and speculating both involve a good deal of research before any money is put into an investment. The stock market is sometimes compared to gambling, and though it is possible to gamble on the market, investing or speculating in the stock market involves much more research and study than gambling. In later chapters we will discuss how to analyze financial statements to select good investments. Proper investment analysis is what distinguishes investing or speculating from gambling.

One may still assume high risk when making an investment decision, but at least that risk is based on certain assumptions regarding the company's future business. This is a completely different process than making a decision with no research or analysis whatsoever. A good investment decision is not made on the basis of someone's interpretation of that stock's past price performance, as can be presented in various charts, or on the basis of a rumor overheard by someone about a new product or business development at the company. Making decisions without thorough research is gambling.

Risk, however, is a very difficult quantity to measure. It can be broadly categorized as either macroeconomic risk or microeconomic risk. **"Macro," meaning large, would be that risk that would affect all investments of like kind.** Inflation, recession, interest rates, changing government policies, economic cycles, and business trends would all be components of macroeconomic risk.

"Micro," meaning small, on the other hand, would be those risk factors that are peculiar to that particular company. Microeconomic risk factors would include: quality of management, the structure of the company's finances, the company's competitive position in the marketplace, the quality of the company's product or service, and the company's ability to control its overhead costs. Obviously, most of these risk factors require a judgment call on the part of the investor. They are very difficult to quantify, but one should attempt to research and draw an informed conclusion on all of these factors.

The statistical measure of risk most often used is a number identified as *beta*. **"Beta" is a measure of the movement of a stock's price relative to the movement of the overall market.** For statistical purposes, the "market" is not the Dow Jones Industrial Average, which, as you already know, includes only 30 Blue Chip stocks. As mentioned in Chapter 1, a more widely used measure of the broad market is the Standard & Poor's 500 Index. Standard & Poor's is a financial service publishing firm that is well known for its stock reports, *Stock Guide*, newsletters, and statistical services. The S&P 500 Index includes some companies from industries that are not included in the Dow, such as utilities.

The "beta" of a company is the measure of that company's price movement relative to the S&P 500 Index. A beta of 1.0 would mean that company's price change was the same as the overall market change as measured by the S&P 500. In other words, if the market was up 10 percent over the last year, and this particular company's stock price was also up 10 percent, it would have a beta of 1.0. If, however, the stock happened to be up 15 percent while the market was up 10 percent, it would have a beta of 1.5. If the stock was only up 7 percent over the same period of time, it would have a beta of 0.7. It is obviously very easy to compute beta if the market is up 10 percent— the numbers will be the same as their relative change over that time. However, the same principle applies no matter what the change in the market. If the market is up 18 percent, and a particular stock is up 27 percent, it will have a beta of 1.5; or if a stock is up 9 percent over the same period of time, the beta will be 0.5.

Beta is a measure of the volatility of a stock relative to the volatility of the market. The same principle would apply when the market is down as when it is up. So, a stock with a low beta would be considered less risky, because when the market drops, such a stock would probably be down less than those with higher betas. If a stock has a beta of 0.5 and the market is down 20 percent, you would expect this stock to be down only 10 percent. The major drawback of beta as a measurement of risk is that it only measures past performance. Because a particular company had a beta of 0.86 last year does not necessarily mean that it will have the same beta this year. In fact, every company's beta will vary from year to year, but it is as close as we can come to having a statistical measure of risk.

The relationship between risk and expected rate of return (reward) is usually expressed graphically in a chart such as Illustration 2.1. The higher the risk, the higher the expected rate of return. The lower the risk, the lower the expected rate of return.

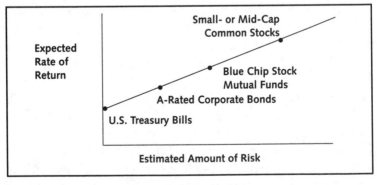

Illustration 2.1

What is most odd about this chart is the investment used to define the "riskless" rate of return. The "riskless" rate is the rate of return on U.S. Treasury bills. The reason why this is so odd is that what is backing these bills is a political entity that has issued over $6 trillion of unsecured debt—a deficit unparalleled in history, and an amount that grows at a rate so fast publishers are unable to update books to report on it.

The term "riskless" is still applied to debt of the U.S. government because of the powers given to its elected public servants. Unlike other entities, which must back their credit borrowings with either specified assets or future revenues, the U.S. government backs its indebtedness by its ability to print more money or to raise taxes. Obviously, printing more money not only does not solve the problem, but compounds it, and raising taxes has the effect of reducing the personal income of the electorate.

Nevertheless, proponents of deficit spending are quick to point out that if the government goes bankrupt, all other less creditworthy borrowers are likely to follow suit. So, we are likely to continue to use the U.S. Treasury bill rate as the measure of the "riskless" rate of return for all investments. When selecting an investment, you should choose those that would be placed above the average. Your goal should be to get the highest rate of return with the least amount of risk.

Do You Know What You Need to Know?

To check up on what you learned from this chapter, answer the following questions in your own words, then compare your answers with the answer key.

1. How does a corporate structure differ from that of a sole proprietorship or a partnership?
2. Explain some of the key differences between a stock and a bond.
3. Since shareholders are technically the owners of a corporation, can they influence the management of their company? If so, how?

4. Why do shareholders usually assume that a company will continue to pay future dividends at the same rate as the last one it declared? Is a company under any legal obligation to continue paying future dividends at its current rate?

5. What is an American Depositary Receipt (ADR), and how does it differ from common stock?

6. What are the key differences between investing, speculating, and gambling? Does speculating involve as much research as investing? Explain.

7. What is the difference between *macro*economic risk and *micro*economic risk? How might macroeconomic factors affect micro factors?

8. How is *beta* used to measure the risk of a particular investment? What market indicator is used as a standard for the beta of a particular company to be measured against?

Answer Key

1. The liability of the shareholder-owners of a corporation is limited to the amount of their investment. Proprietorships or partnerships usually have unlimited liability to the investor.

2. A stock represents equity ownership in a company. A bond represents a loan to a company, for which the investor usually receives a fixed rate of interest.

3. Shareholders have the right to vote for the Board of Directors of a company, but their participation in management decisions is passive.

4. Although the Board of Directors must meet each quarter to declare each dividend payment, most investors assume the rate will remain unchanged. Thus, reporting agencies, such as the newspapers, show dividend yields

at the annualized rate of the last quarterly payment unless noted differently by a footnote comment.

5. An American Depositary Receipt is a certificate for shares of a foreign company issued by a U.S. financial institution. Some foreign companies—such as Canadian companies—trade ordinary shares, not ADRs. In order for foreign companies to trade in the United States, they must meet SEC (and in some cases NYSE) requirements to have their financial statements reconciled to the auditing standards of U.S. "generally accepted accounting principles."

6. Investing and speculating involve thorough research of an investment before putting money into it. Speculators, however, expect a higher rate of return in a shorter period of time than investors do. Gambling is the correct description for putting money into something that you know nothing about.

7. Macroeconomic risk is that which affects all like investments. Such risk factors are usually related to the overall economy. Inflation is an example of macro risk. Microeconomic risk is associated with an individual investment only, such as the management of a particular company.

8. Beta is the measurement of a company's return versus the S&P 500 Index. A beta of 1.0 would mean that the company performed as well as the market did for the same period of time. A high beta indicates more volatility and thus more risk. A low beta indicates a historically less risky investment.

Stockholders own their company, but they do not manage it.

— Chapter 3 —

How Do You Open a Brokerage Account?

The process of opening a brokerage account is similar to that of opening a bank account. You will need to provide such information as your address, social security number, employment, date of birth, and whether or not you have any other brokerage accounts. The broker will probably also request information such as your marginal tax bracket, annual income, and net worth. A full-service broker will likely also ask what goals you want to achieve from your investments and what level of risk is acceptable to you to achieve those goals. This will help the broker make appropriate investment recommendations designed to meet your objectives.

The brokerage industry today is sharply divided between full-service and discount firms. Full-service brokers usually offer professional research and analysis and make specific investment recommendations to meet predetermined financial goals. Discount brokers offer significant savings on transaction costs because they do not have the overhead of full-service firms. However, the lines between these two groups is cloudy because many full-service firms offer discounted on-line trading, and some discount brokers now offer financial advice. Regardless of the firm's designation, most provide many nontraditional brokerage services that are usually associated with banks, such as checking accounts and credit cards.

Probably the most significant response of full-service brokers to the threat of losing clients to discount brokers is "wrap fee" accounts. A wrap fee allows the client to execute all transactions free of charge, while the broker charges the account an annual flat fee for transaction services. Usually this fee amounts to about 1.5 percent of the account value (it can be less). Such a wrap fee designation might pay off for an actively traded account. However, if the client is a "buy and hold" type, he or she may be paying a large amount of money for little or no service. A $100,000 account, for example, would be charged $1,500 per year. If the client only makes three trades per year, that wrap fee amounts to a charge of $500 per trade. So, the lesson here is tailor your account to your particular trading style.

The commissions that a full-service broker charges to execute a transaction will generally fall in a range from 1 percent to 5 percent of the amount of money being invested, depending on the number of shares and the price per share. The average commission will generally be about 2 percent. Discount brokers often advertise that they can save investors up to 90 percent of full-service brokerage fees. As dramatic as that sounds, the investor's actual savings are usually only about 0.5 percent to 2 percent of the amount of the investment. For example, a 50 percent discount on a 2 percent commission would be 1 percent.

Another way of looking at this is that an investor can buy professional securities analysis for about 0.5 percent to 2 percent of the total investment. That sounds like a good bargain, especially if the analysis is insightful. Certainly, professional analysis should be able to direct investors into securities that would make more than 1 percent, the average commission savings they would realize from a discount broker.

In a free enterprise economy, *competition* is the key to the system's success. The ability to compete effectively in a world market is what has made the United States an economic leader today. The United States became a great world power because it fostered an environment where anyone who had an imaginative and marketable idea could capitalize on it. If you had the brains and the brawn to build a better mousetrap, you had the opportunity to make money on your idea. This is not true of many other economic systems. What was unique about "the land of opportunity" was that you did not have to come from a wealthy family to get rich. Competition will inevitably lead to the best product at the best price.

Competition in the brokerage industry has also benefited consumers. Since discount brokers have become popular in recent years, this competition has forced full-service brokerage firms to deliver extra service for the extra commissions they charge. What is true of other industries is true of the brokerage industry as well: a competitive environment fosters better service and fairer pricing. If full-service brokers charge higher prices, then they must provide better service to justify the additional cost. As a direct result of competition from discount brokers, the professional analysis available from most full-service brokers today is about the best it has ever been. In addition, the price differential between discount brokers and full-service brokers is about as low as it has ever been.

A final consideration when you establish a brokerage account is what legal designation you would like on the account. If you wish to have more than one name on the account, such as a husband and wife, there are several choices that will clarify how you would like the investments distributed in the event of your death. **The most commonly used designation is "joint tenants with rights of survivorship," which is sometimes abbreviated "JTWROS" or "Jt Ten." This designation simply means that the property is**

jointly owned by both individuals named on the account, and if one tenant dies, the account will become the sole property of the surviving tenant. Other options for account designations are "community property" or "tenants in common." These designations both denote that if one tenant dies, half of the property goes to that tenant's estate and the other half goes to the survivor. A community property designation means not only that half of the property goes to the estate, but also that it will take a court order to transfer it out of the estate. This type of designation is usually used by individuals who arrange prenuptial agreements for keeping their personal property separate or who do not want their property to go to their spouse after their death. The laws governing the legal disposition of an individual's wealth after his or her death are set by state law. Not all states have community property laws.

There is no "and/or" designation for security account titles as there can be for bank accounts, because *securities* are legally defined as *property,* whereas bank accounts are not. Because securities are defined as such, these types of investments must be owned either by one party or by both parties jointly. Property cannot be legally owned *both* by two parties jointly *and also* by either one party or the other, as an "and/or" designation would indicate. However, all the standard joint account designations allow for one party or the other to make investment decisions. So, your broker will not require both parties to tell him to buy or to sell a security. Either party can make a decision. In that sense it is similar to an "and/or" designation. However, *both signatures* would be required on written transactions. If a stock certificate is registered in joint name, it must be properly endorsed by both parties before it can be negotiated.

Stock certificates, however, do not have to be held in the investor's name. If the broker holds the certificate for the client, he will usually hold it in *street name*. **A stock certificate that is held in "street name" is held in the name of the brokerage firm, or the nominee name of the brokerage firm.** This means that the security can be sold without the beneficial owners having to sign the certificate. The owner can simply tell his broker to sell the stock, and the transfer to the new owner can be accomplished without the seller's signature. Your legal proof of ownership of the stock is represented by your brokerage account statements—in the same way that the proof of your bank account balance is represented by your bank statements. However, you will probably have a much closer and more personal relationship with your stockbroker than you have with your banker.

How Do You Select a Broker?

Most people will spend a lot of time selecting an investment, but they will not spend any time selecting an investment advisor. This can be a big mistake. A good investment advisor can be worth much more to you than a good investment. The usual way of selecting a broker, once you have chosen an investment, is to call up your local brokerage office and let the receptionist direct you to whomever is free at the time. Usually this is someone who has been designated as the "floor broker," the person who has been asked to answer all call-ins who do not already have a broker.

Contrary to popular perception, most brokers are honest and professional. There are dishonest brokers, but they usually do not stay in the business very long. The regulators in the securities industry, particularly the Securities and Exchange Commission, have become increasingly diligent in recent years at prosecuting broker fraud, mismanagement, or client abuse cases. More information on what resources are available if you feel your broker is mismanaging your account will be discussed in Chapter 10, *How Are Your Rights as an Investor Protected?* In any business where financial services are involved, there is a potential for dishonesty. Money can make people do strange things.

Most brokers, however, realize that maintaining their clients' best interests is in their own best interest. Critics are quick to point out that brokers generally are paid by the commissions they generate from the investments clients make, and that there is a conflict of interest inherent in the brokerage business. In other words, brokers may be inclined to recommend trades simply to generate a commission, rather than to truly benefit the investor. However, most brokers realize that if they do not make money for their clients, they are probably going to lose them. Brokers are very aware that unless they give you sound investment advice, they are not going to retain your business.

Common investor complaints about their brokers, however, include making inappropriate investments, such as making highly risky investments for a client who is a conservative investor. Another common complaint is **"churning," a term used to describe a broker's making frequent buy and sell trades in an account without benefiting the investor**. If you feel you have been victimized by your broker in any way, you should first talk to the manager of the broker's office. If you are unable to resolve the grievance to your satisfaction, you can contact the SEC, the **"Securities and Exchange Commission," the main government agency for regulating the securities industry.** The phone number at the SEC for investor complaints against brokers is **(212) 748-8055**, or you could write to them at Mail Stop G-9 U.S. SEC, 450 5th Street NW, Washington, D.C. 20277-2820. The web site address for the SEC is *www.sec.gov.*

You may also contact the NASD, **the "National Association of Securities Dealers." It is a self-governing**

body of securities professionals, responsible for establishing standards of ethics, fair trading practices, and educational testing for members. The NASD has an arbitration board established to hear investor complaints about brokers. The arbitration process is usually considered the least costly and most efficient manner for settling broker disputes. The main phone number for the NASD is (212) 858-4400 (more about this organization will be discussed in Chapter 10). The web site address for the NASD is *www.nasd.com*. Serious legal matters can also be decided in a court of law with an attorney. Investors should be cautioned, however, to seek the counsel of attorneys who specialize in the securities industry.

Hopefully, you will be able to avoid any of these problems by first taking time to select a good broker. It is a frequent practice in the medical profession to get a second opinion before making a major medical decision, and the same practice would be advisable before making a major financial decision. Make appointments with several brokers and interview them. Evaluate how well they communicate with you.

Brokers will always have investments that they are recommending at the time. That's their job. If they don't have a good investment recommendation, you should probably be a little worried. However, determine if brokers are just trying to sell you something that they have available or if they are really listening to your needs and recommending something that meets your objectives.

Ask the broker for three or four referrals. This is a frequent practice in many other professions. People will often ask for referrals from the plumber, but never bother to check out the person to whom they are about to hand over their life savings. When you have been given the referrals, follow up on them. It takes only a few minutes to talk to some other people who will have something in common with you.

If you have any questions, call your broker. Do not be intimidated by anything you do not understand. No question is trivial or unimportant. The brokerage business is a service business, and your broker's job is to service your account. Develop a good working relationship with your broker from the beginning, and you may not have to lose any sleep later on.

How Do You Make an Investment?

Once your account is established and you have been assigned an account number, you are ready to make an investment. **When you make any investment**, such as purchasing a stock, bond, or mutual fund, **there are two dates involved—trade date and settlement date. The "trade date" is the date on which the purchase is made, and the "settlement date" is the date by which the trade must be paid for.** By the same token, if you are selling, the trade date is the date of the sale, and the settlement date is the date on which you will receive the proceeds of the sale.

For regular way trades, there is currently a three-*business-day* time period (abbreviated T+3) between the trade date and settlement date. A *business day* is any day that banks are normally open, that is, every day except weekends or bank holidays. To illustrate how this works, a trade made on Monday would settle on the following Thursday—three business days later. However, if one of the days in that period happens to be a holiday, the trade would settle on Friday. Because of the weekend, a trade made on Wednesday would normally settle on the next Monday. The settlement date will always be three business days after the trade date. It is important that you understand the relationship between the trade date and the settlement date when you read "How Do Companies Pay Dividends?" at the end of this chapter.

Most securities transactions settle *regular way*, that is, T+3. However, you do have an option to request a special settlement date on some trades. If you request a **"cash settlement," the trade will settle on the same date as the trade date.** If you are purchasing stock on this basis, the cash to pay for the purchase must be in the account before the trade is made. If you are selling on a cash basis, the proceeds of the sale could be released to you on the same date as the trade date. In order for such a trade to be executed, however, the specialist or executing broker must find another party who is willing to settle the trade on a cash basis. Because of the special handling this type of trade requires, it may cost 10¢ to 25¢ or more per share to be executed. The trade may not even be executed at all if the specialist cannot find a cash basis investor for the opposite side of your trade. It is also possible to request a special "next day," or ND, settlement.

The investor must also be aware that there are three different types of orders that can be entered: *a market order, a limit order, and a stop order.* The market order is the most common. **A "market order" will be executed at the best available price at the time the order is received by the specialist or market maker.** If you are a seller, this would normally be at the *bid* price, and if you are a buyer, it would be at the *ask* price. **The "bid price" is the highest price at which anyone is offering to purchase shares at that time, and the "ask price" is the lowest price at which anyone is offering to sell their shares.** Bid and ask prices are easier to understand when you know what a *limit order* is.

A "limit order" is an order that the seller of a stock
will enter at a price equal to or above the current market price of the stock and the buyer of a stock will
enter at a price equal to or below the current market
price. A limit order may be filled only at the limit price
or better. For example, if Unique Inc. is currently selling at
18½, you could enter a limit order to sell it at 19. Then if
the stock went up to 19, your order would be executed at
that price, or a higher price. If you wanted to purchase the
stock, you could enter a limit order to buy it at 18. Your
order, however, would be executed only if the stock
dropped to that price. If Unique Inc. did not come down to
18, your order would never be executed. Frequently, limit
orders are entered on a **"good-till-canceled" basis, or
GTC. This means that your order will remain in effect
until you cancel it. GTC orders are also referred to as
"open orders."** Any order that is not designated GTC,
however, will be in effect for one day only. It will be considered to be canceled at the close of the market on that day.

These good-till-canceled limit orders will remain on the
specialist's books until they are either executed or canceled.
They will frequently represent "bid" or "ask" orders on the
specialist's books. The stock market is described as an auction market. Like an auction, investors continually *bid* for a
stock they want to buy from a seller, while sellers ask for a
slightly higher price at which they will sell their shares.
**The difference between the highest current bid price
and the lowest current ask price is called the "spread."**
If you are a buyer, you will be buying at the ask side of the
market, and if you are a seller, you will be selling to the
highest bidder.

**The "specialist" is the title of the individual who is
responsible for matching buy and sell orders on the
floor of an exchange.** The specialist may also buy or sell

stock in his or her own account, but only for the purpose of maintaining a fair and orderly market. **On the over-the-counter market, the function of the specialist is performed by "market makers," who execute buy and sell orders from the inventory of shares they personally own.** This is one of the fundamental differences between the listed markets, such as the NYSE and AMEX, and the over-the-counter market.

The third type of order is the *stop order*. **A "stop order" to sell a stock is entered at a price below the current market price, and a stop order to buy a stock is entered at a price above the current market price.** Notice that this is the opposite of a limit order. A stop order is usually used to preserve a profit or to limit a loss. This type of order will not be executed unless the stock drops to the stop price. **When the stop price is reached, the order becomes a market order; that is, it will be executed at the best available price at that time.** In other words, a stop order guarantees an execution once the stop price is reached. However, it does *not* guarantee a minimum price at which the order will be executed, as the limit order does.

Another way to enter a stop order is to enter a stop-limit order. This is the same as a regular stop order, except that once the stop price is reached, instead of becoming a market order, it becomes a limit order. If Unique Inc. is now trading at 22.90 and you think that the stock is probably going higher, but you want to make sure you sell it at 21 or better in order to preserve a certain profit, you could enter a stop-limit order at "21 Stop 21 Limit GTC." This would mean that if the stock did drop to 21, your order would then become a limit order to sell your stock at 21. If, however, the stock continued to go up, never dropping to 21, the stop order would never be activated.

Stop orders to *buy* securities are rather rare. There are not too many instances where an investor wants to spend more than the current market price for a stock. A buy stop order would almost exclusively be used by someone who had sold the stock *short* and wanted to cover the short at a certain profit or to limit a loss. *Short sale* is a term that will be explained in the next section, "How Can You Make Money When Stocks Go Down?" Stop orders are not used very often, and they probably shouldn't be. If you watch a stock closely you can make a better decision about when to sell or when to buy than you can by using a stop order. In most cases, about all the stop order does is to guarantee that you'll get less money for the sale of your stock than you would have gotten if you had just sold at the market.

When you establish your brokerage account, you will also be asked if you want to establish a cash account or a margin account. **A "cash account" is one in which all of your investments must be paid for in full by the settlement date. If you establish a "margin account," you may borrow a certain percentage of the total cost of your investment from the brokerage firm.** Currently, you can borrow up to 50 percent of your total equity investment and pay interest to the brokerage firm on the amount you borrow. **This so-called margin requirement is set by the Federal Reserve Board, the Fed, and is called "Regulation T"** (Reg. T), or Reg. U for institutions. This is the Federal Reserve Board's only regulatory involvement in the securities industry. The Fed is much more involved in regulating the banking industry. Reg. T may be changed by the Fed at anytime. However, it has not changed from 50 percent for equity investments in over two decades. The current Reg. T requirement for most corporate bonds is 30 percent and for U. S. government bonds, 10 percent.

The margin rate of interest that the brokerage will charge on your debit balance is determined by the *broker loan rate*. This is the rate at which major banks will lend money to securities brokers to loan for margin accounts. The brokerage firm will usually charge some *marginally* higher percentage over the broker loan rate. That fact may have been the reason why the word margin came to be used in this context. Whenever that rate changes, the brokers will change the rate they charge their margin accounts.

In addition to the Reg. T requirement set by the Federal Reserve Board, **brokerage firms will set a "minimum maintenance requirement." This means that if the market value of your securities drops below this level, which is usually set at 30 percent, you will be required to deposit additional funds to keep your equity above 30 percent.** In other words, you can borrow no more than 70 percent of the market value of your investment from the brokerage firm. The reason why most brokers set the minimum maintenance requirement at 30 percent is that the New York Stock Exchange requires the brokers to have a 25 percent minimum maintenance requirement. The brokers, therefore, will set their minimum above that so they will not be in violation of the NYSE rules.

Let's look at an example to understand this (see Illustration 3.1). If you purchase 200 shares of Unique Inc. at $30 per share (it has gone up in the last few pages), your total investment will be $6,000. On margin, you would deposit $3,000 and borrow the remaining $3,000. So, you have $6,000 in market value, minus $3,000 debit, leaving $3,000 in equity. If the price of Unique Inc. drops to $20 per share, the total market value on your 200 shares is going to drop to $4,000. Your debit balance, the amount you borrowed from the brokerage firm, is still the same—$3,000. So your equity is now just $1,000, that is, $4,000 market

value minus $3,000 debit balance equals $1,000 equity. And
that $1,000 equity is only 25 percent of the total market
value of the investment, $4,000. You will consequently have
a maintenance call that will require you to deposit additional money into the account to bring up the equity to 30
percent. This will be about $200. Thirty percent of $4,000 is
$1,200. So, in addition to the $1,000 you have in equity, you
will have to deposit $200 more, assuming you haven't had
any interest charges added to the total debit.

Computing Margin Accounts				
200 shares	Bought at $30	Drops to $20	Rises to $40	
Market Value	$6,000	$4,000	$8,000	total amount of proceeds if security was sold
Debit Balance	–3,000	–3,000	–3,000	amount of money borrowed from broker
Equity	$3,000	$1,000	$5,000	net amount received after selling the stock and paying off the loan
Margin Maintenance	50.0%	25.0%	62.5%	equity divided by market value

Illustration 3.1

The use of margin will magnify your profit or loss by
the same percentage as the equity of the market value. In
our example the stock dropped $10 per share—from $30 to
$20. The total market value of the investment dropped 33
percent, from $6,000 to $4,000. However, the equity
dropped twice as much, 67 percent—from $3,000 to
$1,000. You should also realize, however, that if the stock
had gone up $10 per share, from $30 to $40, instead of
making only 33 percent on your equity, you would have

made 67 percent. Your total market value would have gone from $6,000 to $8,000, but your equity would have gone from $3,000 to $5,000. That $2,000 profit on your original investment of $3,000 is a 67 percent total return. If you margin your account at 50 percent, you will double the profit or double the loss that you would have made if you had a cash account. This is called leverage.

"Leverage" is a general term for describing the process of using a smaller amount of money to control the total amount of an investment. In other words, although a margin investor hasn't paid for an investment with his own money, he still will realize the profit or loss from the total amount of the investment. Simply put, leverage involves borrowing money to make an investment. Most people use leverage when they buy a house. By putting $25,000 down on a $250,000 house, just 10 percent, you would still make all of the appreciated value on the house above that purchase price. So, if the house appreciated 10 percent in value, you would receive 100 percent return on your investment. However, if the house depreciated just 10 percent in value, you would lose 100 percent of your investment. This example is overly simplified. It does not include any costs associated with the real estate transaction or any interest paid. The point is that using leverage obviously requires a strong likelihood of price appreciation to be effective. Excessively leveraging yourself in risky investments would be considered gambling in most cases.

How Can You Make Money When Stocks Go Down?

Another example of a leveraged investment is short selling. **"Short selling" is the process of selling shares borrowed from a lender, such as a brokerage firm, with**

the promise to buy them back in the future, hopefully at a lower price. Selling something you don't own is often an irresistible attraction to speculators. Short selling is a strategy used when investors think a stock is going to drop. When you sell short, you may *not* withdraw the proceeds from the sale of the stock. Those funds are kept in a separate short account and must be applied to repurchasing the stock, or "covering" the short sale.

In order to sell a stock short, you must first borrow the shares from the brokerage firm. The source of those shares is usually other clients' margined stock. When clients set up margin accounts, they are required to sign a margin agreement (sometimes called a loan agreement or client agreement), which gives the brokerage firm the right to sell securities if the account is in violation of margin requirements, and it also gives the brokerage the right to use some of those shares for other purposes. The brokerage firm obviously must maintain the right to sell the shares in case they must be liquidated to meet minimum margin maintenance requirements. Investors, however, may not realize that their shares may also be lent out to someone else for the purpose of short selling. The loaning of your stock to a short seller, however, does not change your status of ownership. You still own the stock, and the brokerage firm guarantees availability of the stock for delivery if you should decide to sell. Remember the brokerage can borrow the stock from other margined accounts.

The brokerage will also require an equity deposit when shares are sold short. This is usually 30 percent. This equity must be on deposit in a margin account separate from the proceeds of the short sale in the short account. You cannot withdraw money from the short account. That money is earmarked for the future repurchase of the shares of stock that had been shorted. If you sold short $20,000 worth of stock, you would have to deposit $6,000 (30 percent), or have that much equity in a margin account. Say that Unique Inc. has gone up to $40 per share, and now you think it is likely to drop. This is a good possibility, since it was under $20 only a few pages back. You could sell 500 shares *short* at $40 for total proceeds of $20,000. Now, if the stock drops to $30 per share, you could buy the 500 shares back for $15,000, and you would have made $5,000 on that stock's price drop. Keep in mind that since this is a leveraged investment, your original capital requirement was only $6,000. So, that $5,000 profit represents an 83 percent return on the amount of equity you were required to maintain for that trade.

Also, the execution of an order for a short sale is subject to the **"up-tick rule." This means that when a stock is dropping, it must up-tick, or sell at a higher price than the previous trade, before a short sale can be executed.** The intent of the up-tick rule is to prevent additional selling that would compound the problem when a stock is dropping dramatically. The price at which the short sale is executed must be the same price or a higher price once the up-tick has occurred. This rule is analogous to the piling on rule in football after the ball carrier has been tackled.

Once the short position is established, **the short account must be "marked to the market"** by the margin department of the brokerage firm. **This means that the short account must always maintain a credit balance equal to the market value of the stock that has been shorted.** After each day's close, the brokerage firm will "journal," or move, funds from the short account to the general margin account if the stock has gone down. It will also journal funds to the short account from the margin account if the stock has gone up. This is why the short account must always be kept separate from the general margin account.

Although there are no specified time limits as to how long a short seller can maintain that position, short selling is usually a short-term strategy. Historically, stocks go up more than they go down. So, the odds are usually with the purchaser, not the short seller. If the stock goes up, the short seller is going to lose money. For example, if you sold Unique Inc. short at $40 per share and it goes up to $45, it is going to cost you $22,500 to buy back the 500 shares. You will lose $2,500 on that position, or approximately 42 percent of your original equity. If you remember the discussion of buy stop orders, you should now understand why these types of orders are usually placed in a short account. A buy stop order would preserve a profit or limit a loss on a short position, as a sell stop order would if you had purchased the stock.

Another reason why short selling is usually a short-term strategy is that if the company pays a dividend, you will have a dividend *claim* every time it is paid. In other words, whenever the stock pays a dividend, the short seller will have to remit that amount in cash. So, you usually don't want to hold that position through the payments of too many dividends. That will either reduce your profit or increase your loss.

How Do Companies Pay Dividends?

There are three important dates that a stockholder must be aware of when a company declares a dividend. They are the ex-dividend date, the record date, and the payable date (or just pay date). The "pay date" is the date on which that dividend will be paid. The "record date," usually about two weeks to a month before the pay date, it is the date on which you must own the stock if you are to receive that dividend when it is paid.

If you are a purchaser of a stock about to pay a dividend, the *settlement date* for that purchase must be on or before the record date, or you *will not* receive that dividend.

The "ex-dividend date" is the date on which, if you bought that stock, it would settle the day *after* the record date. "Ex-" means without, so the purchaser of the stock on the *ex*-dividend date would *not* receive the dividend when it was paid. These same dates are also applicable to the seller. If you sold the stock on the ex-dividend date, you would still be the registered owner on the record date, and you *would be* entitled to receive the next dividend on the pay date. Since there can be a long lag time between the record date and the pay date, individuals who sell stock after the ex-date are sometimes surprised to receive the payment.

Remember that there are always three business days between the trade date and settlement date when you buy or sell stock. If you understood the preceding paragraph, you should also deduce that **there will always be exactly two business days between the ex-dividend date and the record date.** So, the record date is the date on which you must own the stock to receive the dividend, and the ex-dividend date is the date on which, if you trade the stock, it will settle the day after the record date. The number of days between the ex-dividend date and the record date will always be one day less than the number of days between the trade date and the settlement date.

Another reason why the ex-dividend date is important is that the market price of the stock will be reduced by the approximate dollar amount of the dividend on that date. The price for all open orders (good-till-canceled orders) for a stock will be reduced by the amount of the dividend on the ex-date, unless they are specified "DNR"—do not reduce. In other words, the investment will still represent the same net amount of actual cash value on the ex-dividend date as it did the day before. For example, if Unique Inc. is currently trading at 38¾, and is going to pay a $.25 dividend, then the stock will have the same net market value at 38½ without the dividend that it had at 38¾ with it. If you bought the stock at 38¾ with the dividend, you could consider the dividend a $.25 refund on the price of the stock. In other words, the stock really only cost you 38½ out of pocket.

In fact, stock quotes will appear in the newspaper reflecting this change on the ex-dividend date. If Unique Inc., for example, closed at 38¾ the day before the ex-dividend date, and closed the next day, the ex-date, also at 38¾ the newspaper would show the net change as "+¼," instead of unchanged. If it closed on the ex-date at 38½, the newspaper would show the stock unchanged, even though the actual market price of the stock was ¼ lower than the previous day's close. The effect of the dividend on a stock's market price is sometimes misunderstood by individual investors.

Another important factor regarding dividends is the dividend payout ratio. Keep in mind that dividend payments represent the portion of quarterly earnings that the company pays out to shareholders. **The dividend payout ratio is the percentage of earnings that are paid out.** Most companies will have a policy of keeping the dividend payments within certain ratios. This will vary widely from industry to industry. The dividend payout ratio will be highest in those industries where companies do not have high cash needs to maintain their business. As an industry group, electric utility companies generally have the highest dividend payout ratio, because the profit margins on their core business are regulated by government agencies. In most cases, electric utility companies pay dividends ranging from 50 percent to 80 percent of their earnings.

Also, many companies offer dividend reinvestment programs (DRIPs). These programs allow investors to purchase additional shares of the company with their dividends, instead of receiving them in cash. So, if you participate in this type of program, on the pay date you will receive a statement from the transfer agent showing the number of shares purchased, rather than a dividend check. Usually, there are no fees for purchasing shares through these programs. Plus, they allow investors to receive dividends on the shares they purchased with their dividends. After a few years, the additional shares received from participation in these programs dramatically increase the total return to investors. This is called compounding and will be discussed next, after you learn about bonds.

DRIPs must be set up directly with the transfer agent for the company involved. You can get information about this by searching the web for the name of the company in which you are interested. A helpful web site for DRIPs with many links to other web resources is *www.dripcentral.com*. Some DRIPs, well over one hundred at the time of this writing, also offer a 5 percent bonus on reinvested dividends. That's like buying the stock with a built-in capital gain. If you are a long-term investor, check this out.

Do You Know What You Need to Know?

To check up on what you learned from this chapter, answer the following questions in your own words, then compare your answers with the answer key.

1. Why can't brokerage accounts in joint name be identified with an "and/or" designation as bank accounts are? What designations are normally used for brokerage accounts?

2. What are the SEC and the NASD, and why are they important to you as an investor? How do their functions compliment one another? How do they overlap?

3. Explain the significance of *trade date* and *settlement date* regarding both the purchase and the sale of securities. Why are these dates significant as they relate to companies' dividend payments?

4. A *business day* is defined as any day when banks are normally open for business. If there is a holiday when most of the major stock exchanges are open, but the banks are generally not, would this be considered a business day for settlement date purposes of security transactions?

5. What is Regulation T, and who sets it? How does the use of margin increase an investor's expected rate of return on his or her investment? Is the anticipated amount of increased return equivalent to the increased amount of risk? Explain.

6. Compare and contrast the roles and functions of the specialist, who trades listed securities, with that of the market maker, who trades over-the-counter securities. What are some of the limitations to fair trading practices of each?

7. Who sets the *minimum maintenance requirement* and how does it differ from the initial margin requirement?

8. Why is short selling a strategy used by speculators when they expect the price of a security to decline? Who owns the share that short sellers sell?

Answer Key

1. Securities are defined as property, and property cannot be owned by either one party or another and by both. The standard designation is Joint Tenants with Rights of Survivorship.

2. The Securities and Exchange Commission (SEC) is the primary government agency with legislative authority over the securities industry. The National Association of

Securities Dealers (NASD) is a self-governing professional organization that sets standards for ethics and qualification for brokers.

3. An investor who purchases a security on a trade date must pay for that trade by the third business day after that date, the settlement date. In order to receive a dividend, an investor's trade must settle on or before the record date for the dividend payment.

4. No. If a day is a bank holiday, it is not considered a business day, even though the stock market is open for business.

5. Regulation T, set by the Federal Reserve Board, is the minimum percentage equity requirement for investors to purchase stock on margin. It is currently 50 percent and increases the amount of risk because of the use of leverage.

6. Specialists on the NYSE match buy and sell orders for other members. They may also trade a limited number of shares of stock for their own accounts in order to stabilize a volatile market. On the other hand, market makers for over-the-counter stocks buy securities from sellers for their own accounts and sell securities from their accounts to investors.

7. The minimum maintenance requirement for margin accounts is set by the New York Stock Exchange at 25 percent; that is, the equity must equal 25 percent of the total market value of the account. Most brokerage firms, however, set the minimum maintenance requirement at 30 percent.

8. A short seller sells shares of stock that are borrowed from the brokerage firm. The short seller is committed to buying back those shares to pay back the loan from the broker. The short seller hopes that the price of the security will drop, so that he or she can repurchase them at a lower price than that at which they were originally sold.

Selecting a broker is one of the most important decisions an investor will make.

— Chapter 4 —

What Is a Bond?

Companies can raise capital to finance their operations either by selling shares of stock in the company or by issuing bonds. Each share of stock sold represents to the buyer a share of ownership in the *equity* of the company. Each bond that a company sells, however, represents a *debt*, or a liability. The bond investor is lending his or her money to the company. A bond is a loan. When a company issues a bond, it is borrowing money from the bond investor. **A "bond" is a loan agreement made by the issuer to pay a fixed rate of interest to the lender (the bond investor) for a predetermined period of time and to repay the principal at the end of that period.** To the bond issuer this is a liability, or debt. **"Equity" and "debt" are broad terms for securities that would most frequently refer to the former as stocks and the latter as bonds.** There are other equity securities than stocks, and other debt securities than bonds, but those are the most common types of equity and debt issues.

Another set of contrasting terms to identify stocks and bonds in financial jargon is "variable-return" investments and "fixed-return" investments. Variable return obviously draws attention to the unpredictability of the stock market, and fixed return explains quite plainly the nature of bonds. A bond is a fixed-return investment because it will pay a fixed rate of interest for the life of the bond, and when the bond comes due, or matures, the "principal," or amount of money the bond investor loaned to the corporation, must be repaid.

Bond issues may be either collateralized or uncollateralized. **A "collateralized" bond will have a specific asset assigned to replace the bond's principal in the event of default.** Most often these are mortgage bonds, which have real estate holdings pledged as collateral, but a company could also pledge other assets, such as equipment. Airline companies, for example, might pledge their airplanes as collateral for bond issues. **An uncollateralized bond is called a "debenture," and a large majority of bonds are debentures. If a company already has some debentures outstanding, it may also issue *subordinated* debentures, which would rank below the other uncollateralized bonds.** In other words, if the company declares bankruptcy, the debentures will be paid off before the subordinated debentures.

The formal agreement specifying the terms of the bond and the rights and obligations of the bond issuer and the purchaser is called the "indenture." The indenture appears on the face of the bond certificate. From the indenture, the bond investor knows exactly how much interest that investment will pay every year, and the investor will get no more and no less than that amount. With only a few exceptions all bonds pay interest semiannually, twice a year. The full description of a bond must include: (1) the name of issuer, (2) the coupon rate of interest, and (3) the due date, or maturity date, when the bond's principal will be repaid. Bonds are generally sold in denominations of $1,000 principal amount, or face value. A bond of less than $1,000 face amount is called a *baby bond*. Such bonds are rather uncommon.

Illustration 4.1 is an example of typical municipal bond certificate. A municipal, or *muni*, bond is one of the types of bonds that will be discussed in the next section.

パス

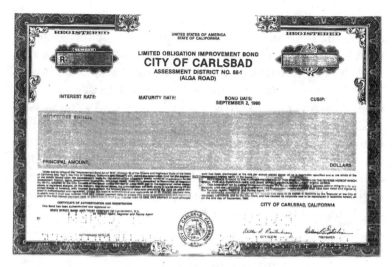

Illustration 4.1

Reprinted with permission, City of Carlsbad.

What Are the Different Types of Bonds?

Bonds can be classified by their issuers. The major bond issuers in the United States are the U.S. government, state and local municipalities, U.S. government agencies, and corporations. Foreign bond issuers, either corporate or government, are becoming increasingly popular for U.S. investors too, especially in the form of mutual funds. Far and away the largest single issuer of bonds is the U.S. government. Debt instruments issued by the U.S. Treasury Department account for about three quarters of the nation's well-publicized federal debt. As was mentioned earlier, at the time of this writing, the debt is well over $5 trillion. However, it may be significantly higher than that when you read this. **"Municipal bonds" are issued by state or local governments or government agencies,**

and their interest is exempt from federal income tax and from state income tax for residents of the state in which the bond is issued. Municipal bonds are usually offered only in five-bond denominations. So, the minimum investment in municipal bonds is $5,000 principal, but that is still referred to as "five bonds." Municipal bonds will usually pay the lowest rate of interest compared to other bond issuers, such as corporations, the federal government, or federal government agencies, because of the tax-exempt status of the interest. When you add the tax savings to the interest you receive from tax-free bonds, the returns are usually quite comparable to those of taxable bonds.

Municipal bonds may be categorized either as *revenue bonds* or *general obligation (G.O.) bonds*. **The payment of interest and repayment of principal for "revenue bonds" is backed by revenues generated from the project for which the bond was issued.** Sewer, solid waste disposal, toll bridge or road, and stadium bonds would all be examples of revenue bonds. **"General obligation bonds" are backed by nonspecified taxes raised by the bond issuer.** Most states issue G.O. bonds backed by the state income taxes they collect. Municipal bond investors used to feel that G.O. bonds represented the highest standard of safety for bonds issued by that state. In light of many states' fiscal crises, however, muni bond investors frequently prefer high-rated revenue bonds.

When you invest in tax-free muni bonds, you can compute the taxable equivalent rate by using a simple formula: The tax-free rate divided by (one minus your tax bracket). If you are investing in tax-free bonds issued by state or local government agencies within your state of residence, you would want to combine your federal and state income tax brackets. Currently, the maximum federal tax rate is 39.6 percent, and if you assume the top state income tax bracket is 11 percent, a high-income taxpayer would be in a total tax bracket over *50 percent*. Most taxpayers, however, will probably be in approximately a 40 percent combined tax bracket. So, if you invested in a 5.00 percent municipal bond, your taxable equivalent rate would be 8.33 percent. This was computed by dividing .05 (the tax-free interest rate) by the quantity one minus .40 (the total tax bracket); that is, $1 - .40 = .60$ and $.05/.6 = .0833$. The formula for equivalent taxable yield is: the tax-free rate divided by (one minus the tax bracket). It is a relatively simple matter for any individual using this formula to figure out if he or she would receive more income by investing in taxable bonds or tax-free bonds. Obviously, the higher the individual's tax bracket, the greater the benefit of tax-free bonds. Regardless of your tax bracket, however, anyone who knows what his or her bracket is can easily compute whether he or she is better off with tax-free or taxable bonds.

All federal government debt obligations offered by the U.S. Treasury Department have minimum denominations of $1,000. The three types of U.S. Treasury issues are T-bonds, T-notes, and T-bills. Treasury bonds and notes are structured almost identically, except for the maturity dates. Bonds have maturities ranging from 10 to 30 years, and notes have 2- to 10-year maturities from the date of their initial offering. Also, bonds may have early call features, whereas notes will not. The interest an investor receives from all federal government debt is *exempt from state income tax*. The interest, however, *is subject to federal income tax*. At the time of this writing, the minimum investment in T-notes with maturities of 2 years and 3 years was $5,000 (or five notes). The 5-year note and all bonds have $1,000 (or one bond) minimums.

U.S. Treasury bills have a somewhat different structure than notes or bonds. The bills will have maturities of three months (91 days, or 13 weeks), six months (182 days, or 26 weeks), or one year (52 weeks), and the bills do not pay semiannual interest. U.S. Treasury bills are sold at a discount to their $10,000 minimum face value, and the interest that the investor receives is the difference between the discounted price and the $10,000 received at maturity. U.S. Treasury bills are offered in $1,000 denominations with a $10,000 minimum.

The next area of fixed-return investing is that of government agency bonds. **"Ginnie Mae"** is an acronym for Government National Mortgage Association, or GNMA. Her close relatives are **"Fannie Mae,"** Federal National Mortgage Association, and **"Freddie Mac,"** Federal Home Loan Mortgage Corporation. **These are all government agencies whose function is to add liquidity and safety to investing in the mortgage market.** FNMA and FHLMC, however, may not even be true government agencies. Both of them have issued publicly traded shares and are legally owned by the shareholders. Mortgage-backed certificates are very different than conventional bonds.

The Government National Mortgage Association is described as a mortgage passthrough agency. It purchases *pools*, or groups, of a large number of home mortgages from conventional lenders and then reissues new certificates of these mortgage pools to **GNMA investors. GNMA is the only government agency whose mortgage pools come with a written U.S. Treasury guarantee as to the timely payment of interest and principal.** Other government agency issues are backed by the agencies themselves and have an implied government guarantee, but not a written government guarantee.

Because of the way GNMAs are formed, there are many differences between these certificates and regular bonds. GNMAs are offered with a minimum $25,000 face amount and $5,000 increments thereafter. They pay interest *and part principal* monthly. As a GNMA investor you are in a position similar to that of a mortgage lender. If you are a homeowner, you know that the monthly check you send to your lender is applied partly to interest and partly to principal. Like the lender, the GNMA investor is the recipient of a monthly check that includes interest and part of the principal. At first, most of your monthly payments are applied to interest payments, and very little is applied to principal. Toward the end of the loan, however, most of the payment is applied to principal and very little to interest.

Most GNMA issues are composed of conventional 30-year mortgages on FHA (Federal Housing Authority) or VA (Veterans' Administration) approved homes. However, some are issued on 15-year loans. In spite of these terms, GNMA interest rates are usually compared with 10- or 12-year Treasury bonds. This is because the average GNMA pool of mortgages only lasts about 12 years. The culture in which we live is very mobile—we move frequently. So, every time a home in a GNMA pool is sold *or refinanced*, which happens at an alarmingly fast rate when mortgage interest rates drop, the portion of principal for that home loan will be included in the next monthly check sent out to the GNMA investor. The unpredictability with which principal can be repaid on GNMA investments is probably the major drawback to this security.

GNMAs have always been very popular because they represent a way for an investor to get a government guarantee on a security that will be paying interest based on the current rate on home mortgage loans, which is usually higher than a 10-year Treasury bond. Also, many investors like the fact that they get paid monthly rather than semiannually, but the fact that the principal can be repaid at any time does add significant interest-rate risk. In the past, when mortgage interest rates came down quickly, some high-yielding GNMAs paid back all the principal in just two or three years. This left the GNMA investor with the task of trying to find another investment during a time when yields were much lower than what he or she had been getting.

There are many mutual funds available that invest primarily, or exclusively, in GNMAs, and these can help considerably with the repayment of principal problem. Since these funds would be composed of a large number of GNMA pools, they offer geographical diversity where some areas of the country may not have as high a turnover rate as other areas. Also, funds are usually structured so that they pay out interest only, and the principal that is repaid each month is reinvested in new GNMAs. This may cause the monthly distributions to be adjusted periodically, because the new GNMAs in the fund would probably not be paying the same interest as the older ones. The underlying principal invested in GNMAs, however, would remain relatively intact.

FNMA, or "Fannie Mae," offers securities somewhat like GNMA, but they are not limited to FHA or VA approved homes. FHLMC, or "Freddie Mac," offers collateralized mortgage obligations, CMOs, and a host of *mortgage derivatives* and residuals. Both FNMA and FHLMC have publicly traded shares on the New York Stock Exchange. **The term "mortgage derivatives" refers to various investments created by these government agencies from one pool of home mortgages or from commercial CMOs.** These derivatives include such investments as IOs (interest-only obligations), POs (principal-only obligations), or various "tranches," a prioritizing of investors as to who gets paid first. Published estimates have set the number of different identifiable mortgage derivatives over 12,000. These can be very sophisticated creations and can be much riskier than the mortgage pools themselves. Millions have been lost in several well-publicized fiascoes involving derivatives. Typically, what can happen is an investor pays a premium for a certain mortgage derivative, expecting to receive a high rate of interest for a certain period of time. If, however, the principal gets repaid quickly, the investor would lose that premium (the amount paid for the security *above* par value) and would not receive the high rate of interest for the period of time expected.

Also, much of the trading in these derivative products is tied to computer programs that create hypothetical scenarios based on interest-rate movements as small as one one-thousandth of a basis point. These programs are much more sophisticated than the actual market. Many of these professional traders learned the hard way that the real world can be very different than the hypothetical one. As they tried to sell their portfolio of securities when their program indicated they should, they found that there were no buyers. As a result, their losses were much higher than forecast. No matter how sophisticated the analysis, an illiquid market is an illiquid market. The lesson to investors is to avoid those products that are overly complex or are made more complex than they already are by the issuing agency.

There are other government agencies that also issue debt instruments such as the Federal Farm Credit Bank, but they are not common investments for most individuals. Additionally there are many agencies of the World Bank that issue marketable debt instruments. These include the International Bank of Reconstruction and Development, the International Development Association, the International Finance Corporation, and so on. In recent years, individual investors have become more interested in securities issued by these global agencies.

The fourth category of bond classification is corporate bonds. Corporate bonds may be listed on the New York Stock Exchange or the American Stock Exchange or may trade over-the-counter. They are sold in denominations of $1,000, with no minimum number of bonds for most corporations. The interest they pay is fully taxable, both federal and state. **A unique variation of corporate bonds is that some of them may be convertible into the common stock of the underlying issuer. A "convertible bond" will include in its indenture the price per share at which the bond may be exchanged for shares of stock.** This conversion price would represent the price you would pay for the stock if you bought the bond at par value, $1,000. So, the important consideration for a convertible bond holder is not necessarily the *price* of each share into which that bond would convert, but the *number* of shares the bond holder would receive upon conversion.

If the bond converts into stock at $20 per share, for example, the investor would receive 50 shares per bond (1,000 divided by 20). So, if the investor purchases the bond at a discount, say at $900, the price per share he or she would pay for the stock upon conversion will not be $20. It will be $900, the price of the bond, divided by 50, the number of shares that will be received. So, the investor will actually pay $18 per share. It also follows that if the investor pays more than $1,000 per bond, he or she will be paying more than $20 for the common stock upon conversion. Most convertible bonds will include in their indenture a clause giving the issuer the right to make conversion mandatory if the stock trades above a certain price.

If you invest in convertible bonds, you need to do double the normal amount of homework. You need to research the stock as well as the bond. In reality, you are investing in both a bond and a stock. Convertible bonds can be a very practical way to achieve both high current income from the bond's interest payments and capital appreciation from the increasing share price of the stock.

Aside from bonds, another common fixed-return investment is *preferred stock*. **"Preferred stock" trades in shares, similar to common stock, but it pays a fixed dividend, similar to bond interest.** In the newspaper stock quotes you will usually see preferred shares identified with a "pf" (often followed by another letter such as A or B, identifying the series) after the name of the company. Preferred shares are usually sold at an initial par value of $25, $50, or $100, which is similar to a bond's principal value of $1,000.

One key difference between a preferred stock and a bond, however, is that the *dividends* paid on a preferred stock are *not interest* payments, as is the case with bonds. To the company issuing the preferred stock, this has an impact on the taxation of its earnings. A company *can deduct interest expenses* before paying income taxes, but it *cannot deduct preferred dividends* in the same way. Thus, corporations are usually more inclined to issue bonds than preferred stock. The board of directors must meet quarterly and declare each preferred dividend, as they do common dividends.

Also, preferred stock does not have a maturity date, as does a bond. Preferred stock may, however, be convertible into common stock or may have some mandatory terms of redemption, or call features. Often this is similar to an early call feature for a bond, which protects the issuer against interest-rate risk. In other words, if interest rates move down, the preferred *issuer* may call the high-yielding series and reissue new shares at a lower-dividend yield.

Another key difference between preferred stock and a bond is that to a *corporate investor 70 percent of the dividend is currently free from federal income tax*. This corporate dividend exclusion was meant to avoid double taxation of corporate earnings. This tax savings greatly increases the net after-tax return to a corporate investor. Thus, the majority of preferred stock investors are corporations. However, even

though individual investors may not get this tax benefit—
individuals must pay taxes on 100 percent of preferred dividends—they may be attracted to preferreds for other reasons.

Preferred dividends are senior to common dividends,
which means that if the issuing company goes into bankruptcy, preferred shareholders have a senior claim to the
company's assets over common shareholders. Almost all
dividends on preferred stock are **"cumulative." This
means that if the company skips a preferred dividend
because of financial problems these dividends accumulate.** All dividends in arrears must be paid before any common stock dividends can be paid.

Preferred stock is somewhat like a cross between a
stock and a bond. It is rated like a bond, but on a company's financial statement it will appear as Shareholder's
Equity, not a liability. You will read more about that in the
next chapter. Preferred stock could be described as fixed-
income equity. From an investor's point of view, it is more
like a bond than it is like a stock.

What Is Compound Interest?

A bond investor should also note that the interest rate
paid on bonds is always quoted at an annualized rate.
Thus, a *three-month* Treasury bill paying 3.00 percent is
actually going to be paying about 0.75 percent for the time
period you hold it. That would be computed as 3 percent
interest divided by four. Three months is one fourth of a
year. The 0.75 percent interest you will receive for the three
months you hold that Treasury bill is a 3 percent *annualized* rate. If the rate remained the same for four successive
quarters (which is very unlikely) and the investor "rolled
over" each bill as it came due, he would receive a full 3 percent return, having held the bill for one full year.

All interest rates are quoted at an annualized rate, regardless of how often that interest is paid, or compounded. "Compounding" **is a term used to describe the effect of having the interest that is paid on an investment reinvested into an interest earning investment,** in other words, earning interest on your interest. Albert Einstein has been credited with stating that compound interest was the greatest invention of man. Whether you are talking about the interest rates on CDs or credit cards or first trust deeds, all interest rates are required to be quoted at an annualized basis. This is done so that investors, or borrowers for that matter, can easily compare that rate with other comparable rates—without being misled by different time frames.

A simple formula to help you understand the effects of compounding is the "Rule of 72." The number of years it will take your investment to double in value at compounded interest rates can be approximated by dividing the interest rate into 72. To illustrate, consider that you had a $1,000 investment that paid 10 percent *simple interest*, that is, not compounded. Your investment would double in value in 10 years. A $1,000 investment would pay $100 interest every year, which in 10 years would total $1,000. However, if you had a $1,000 investment that paid interest that compounded annually, that $100 would begin earning interest when it was paid. So, the extra interest you earn on your interest will mean that your investment will double in approximately 7.2 years. Using the Rule of 72 formula, this would be 10 divided into 72. Obviously, it would take 10 years for your investment to double in value if it paid 7.2 percent interest (7.2 divided into 72). Notice when you use this approximation formula, you don't write the interest rate as it would be correctly written mathematically; that is, 7.2 percent interest is written 7.2, not .072. Also, how often your interest is paid and thus begins compounding will have an effect on how long it takes to double.

A type of bond structure called **"zero coupon bonds"** describes fixed-income investments that do not pay periodic interest. **These bonds, as their name implies, do not pay coupon interest, but rather they may be bought at a discount and the interest is represented by the appreciated value of the bond.** These bonds will have a stated basis, or yield-to-maturity, the total return the investor will realize if he or she owns the bond when the principal is due at maturity. Zero coupon bonds have a structure similar to a Treasury bill, but they generally mature after a much longer period of time.

Since regular coupon bonds pay interest semiannually, the price you pay for a zero coupon bond is computed as if the bond did pay interest twice a year and this interest were reinvested in another bond at the same rate. In other words, the interest is computed as if it were compounding at the same rate. Now this may seem like a small matter—whether the interest, which is usually a rather small amount, is compounded or not—but it has a very dramatic effect on the bond's price, particularly if this is a long-term bond, one that won't mature for 15 years or more.

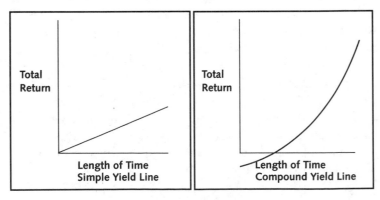

Illustration 4.2

Illustration 4.2 shows two graphs comparing the rate of return on an investment that pays simple interest and one that pays compound interest at the same rate. Simple interest is a straight line, and compound interest is a parabolic curve. For a complete discussion on how simple interest and compound interest is calculated, see the Appendix.

Also, **there are *three* interest rates an investor should be aware of when investing in a bond: the coupon rate, current yield, and the yield-to-maturity. The "coupon rate" is simply the stated rate the bond will pay for every $1,000 invested.** A 6.00 percent coupon, for example, will pay exactly $60.00 per bond—no more, no less. It is called the coupon rate because bonds originally came with actual coupons attached, which the investor had to cut off and redeem at a financial institution. Municipal coupon bonds, however, have not been issued since 1986, and corporations had stopped issuing coupon bonds decades before that. **All bonds issued today are "registered," which means they have the owner's name or a nominee name imprinted on the face of the certificate. Older coupon bonds were usually issued in "bearer" form, which means the bond was considered to be owned by the bearer,** like money. No name was imprinted on the certificate.

The first consideration in bond investing must be the relationship between the coupon rate of interest and the price of the bond. Consider what happens to the yield on a bond if it is selling at **a "discount," an amount less than $1,000**? You'll learn how it's possible for a bond to be selling at a price less than its face amount in the next section, "What Are the Risks of Investing in Bonds?"

If for some reason this 6.00 percent bond is currently selling at $900, then the current yield and yield-to-maturity are going to be different than 6.00 percent. The current yield will be calculated by dividing the dollar amount of interest received each year by the dollar amount paid for the bond. In this case that would be $60 divided by $900, or 6.67 percent. The current yield represents the simple interest you will receive each year on that investment.

"Yield-to-maturity" represents the total return you will receive for the life of a bond, including the coupon interest and the appreciation or loss of principal. The yield-to-maturity calculation in this example would take into account the additional $100 you will receive in principal when the bond matures. Note that the cost of the bond was only $900, but at maturity bonds pay off their full face amount, $1,000. So, the yield-to-maturity will take into account the 6.67 percent current yield and add to it the extra $100 which the investor will receive when the bond comes due. If the bond were to mature in ten years, without adjusting for the effects of compounding, that would amount to $10 per year. An additional $10 each year for ten years will equal $100.

The true yield-to-maturity formula, however, is not computed as if the capital appreciation on the bond follows a simple yield line. It follows a *compound* yield curve, and must be computed using a formula from calculus. Since most people haven't studied calculus, and some of us who have can't remember it anyway, the easiest way to compute yield-to-maturity is to punch it in on a financial calculator. Actually, when you invest in a bond, the price will be quoted on a yield-to-maturity basis, but you can double check it with a financial calculator, if you like. For your information, the yield-to-maturity on the bond in this example would be 7.44 percent.

You should note that when the price of a bond goes down, the yield-to-maturity, which will be the total return on the bond investment, goes up. In other words, there is an *inverse* relationship between bond price and bond yield. So, if you happen to hear a business news reporter say, "The bond market was *down* today," you will know that interest rates were *up*. The opposite of this is also true. As interest rates go down, bond prices will go up.

It is easy to understand this inverse relationship if you look at the interest rate paid on bonds as a fixed dollar amount. In the previous example we were considering a bond that had a 6.00 percent coupon, or paid $60.00 per year. Since that $60.00 was "fixed," that would only represent a 6.00 percent return to the investor if he paid $1,000 for the bond. If you paid less than $1,000, your yield would be greater than 6.00 percent, and if you paid more than $1,000, the yield would be less than 6.00 percent. If you paid $1,100, for example, the current yield would be $60 divided by $1,100, or 5.45 percent. The yield-to-maturity is going to be less than that, because you are going to lose $100 of principal when the bond matures. Actually, the yield-to-maturity for a ten-year bond with a coupon rate of 6.00 percent that costs $1,100 will be 4.73 percent. (This was computed on a bond calculator.) Note that the loss of $100 in principal has a dramatic effect on a bond's yield over a ten-year period.

Now let's look at what can cause bond prices to fluctuate.

What Are the Risks of Investing in Bonds?

As you may have deduced from the previous discussion, **the primary risk of investing in bonds is that interest rates will go higher before the bond matures.** Then you would be locked into a lower than market rate of return, and if you wanted to sell your bond before maturity, you would have to sell it at a discount to face value. This interest-rate risk is inherent in any fixed-return investment: government bonds, municipal bonds, corporate bonds, CDs, second trust deeds, preferred stock, even Treasury bills. You should note, however, that the shorter the term of the investment, the less the interest-rate risk. A Treasury bill that matures in three months will be worth its full face value in a relatively short period of time. So, even if interest rates go up, the bill's price won't drop too much simply because it will be worth the full face amount in a few weeks.

However, a longer-term bond, say a 30-year bond, is by far the most volatile as interest rates move. That's why the 30-year U.S. Treasury bond is the one most frequently quoted by financial reporters—not because it is the bond with the largest number of investors; it isn't. It is the one that will usually have the greatest price volatility corresponding to interest-rate moves.

A popular choice for minimizing the risk of long-term bonds is to invest in money market funds. **"Money market" is the term used to describe very short-term debt instruments.** Most financial institutions today offer a mutual fund that invests in money market investments only. These funds usually have a share price of $1.00 that doesn't change because there is little or no principal price fluctuation. The principal always comes due in a very short time, usually around 30 days.

The most popular investment in these funds is commercial paper. "Commercial paper" is corporate debt, usually with a $100,000 minimum face amount maturing in 5 to 270 days. There are many forms of money market investments other than commercial paper, but since these are not common investments for individual investors, they will not be discussed here.

Another major risk associated with bond investing is *credit risk*, the potential of being downgraded by the bond-rating agencies. Most corporate bonds or municipal bonds are rated by Standard & Poor's Corporation, Fitch IBCA, Duff & Phelps, or by Moody's Investors Service, Inc. Standard & Poor's is a division of McGraw-Hill, Inc. The issuers must pay these agencies a fee to review and to rate their bonds. Bonds are rated from the highest quality to the lowest on a scale as shown in Illustration 4.3.

Standard & Poor's	Fitch IBCA, Duff & Phelps	Moody's
AAA	AAA	Aaa
AA	AA	Aa
A	A	A
DDD	BBB	Baa
BB	BB	Ba
B	B	B
CCC	CCC	Caa
CC	CC	Ca
C	C	C
D	DDD	
	DD	
	D	

Illustration 4.3

To get a triple-A rating (AAA or Aaa) a corporation or municipality must usually have enough revenue generated by the bond project to cover the interest payments on its bonds by over ten times. **Any bond rated in the top four categories, that is, triple-B or higher, is considered an "investment grade" bond.** Fiduciaries such as pension funds, the largest corporate bond investors, must invest only in investment grade bonds. So, if a bond is rated below triple-B, it is not eligible to be bought by the largest number of bond investors. Thus, it will have to pay a much higher rate of interest to attract investors. In fact, interest rates will move up incrementally on bonds as they move down the rating system.

Bonds that are rated D by S&P, DDD by Fitch, or single C by Moody's are in default. This means that the issuer of that bond is not solvent enough to pay the interest. Usually, the issuer of the bond will have filed for Chapter 11. **"Chapter 11"** does not mean that the company, or the municipality, has come to an end. **It is the chapter of the Federal Bankruptcy Code that allows the bond issuer to continue its normal business operations while it attempts to work out a repayment agreement with its creditors.**

The *credit risk* of bond ownership is that if your bond is ever downgraded, say from double-A to single-A, that bond will now have to pay a higher rate of interest. Since you already realize that if interest rates go up, the bond price will go down, guess what is going to happen to that bond's price?

The financial term for bonds in the double-B and lower categories is "junk." However, you will not find too many brokers using that term. Their preferred term for these bonds is "high yield." Most major mutual fund families now offer a high-yield bond fund. They have become very popular funds recently because, as interest rates have come down, investors seeking to replace the yield that they used to receive on their insured CDs or government bonds are now opting for the more attractive yields in these funds. Investors should realize, however, that there is greater risk in these junk, or below investment grade, bond funds. An economic recession, or shrinking of the economy, will have a severe effect on bond issues that barely have enough current cash flow to cover their interest payments.

This is not to say that some investors who are willing to assume the risks involved shouldn't take advantage of the higher interest rates available from junk bonds. However, investors should always be aware of the higher risks they are taking. The old adage is still true, "You don't get something for nothing." The market for bonds is dominated by *institutional* investors. So it is a very *efficient* market. In other words, usually it will accurately represent the proper rate of return for the amount of risk assumed.

The third consideration regarding risks associated with bonds is the call feature. The "call feature" is written in the bond's indenture and specifies when the bond issuer may opt to pay back principal before the maturity date. Virtually all municipal bonds issued since 1987, and most recent corporate bonds, will contain a call feature. The purpose of this feature is to protect the bond issuer from having to continue to pay a higher than market rate of interest on its bonds should interest rates come down.

Most mortgage-backed municipal bonds are callable on any semiannual coupon date, and even less severe call features will typically offer only 10-year call protection on a 25- or 30-year bond. The call features will vary on every individual bond, but typically it will be worded in such a way that at the earliest call date it will pay a slight premium to par value, say 102, and the call price will be reduced by ½ a point each year for the next four years, and be callable at par thereafter. (Bond prices will be explained in the next section.) So, for example, a bond that matures on July 15, 2025 may be callable at 102 on 7/15/05, at 101½ on 7/15/06, at 101 on 7/15/07, at 100½ (par and a half) on 7/15/08, and at 100 (par) on 7/15/09 and any year thereafter.

The risk, of course, to the bondholder is that the bond will not be called if interest rates go up. He or she will be locked into a rate with a lower than market yield, and if rates go down, the bondholder will receive back the principal at a time when he or she can only invest in lower-yielding bonds or be forced to invest in something of lower quality to get the same yield.

How Do You Buy Bonds?

Because bonds are usually sold in $1,000 denominations, the dollar price of a bond is expressed as a percentage of $1,000. So, if you see a bond quoted at "95" in the newspaper, that quote represents 95 percent of $1,000, or $950 per bond. Bond prices will change, however, in increments on ⅛th of a point. This unit of change is meant to be analogous to stock price changes. However, one tick, ⅛th of a point, for a bond quote represents $1.25 per bond, but one tick, ⅛th of a point, for a stock quote represents $0.125. In other words, the incremental change in the price of one bond is ten times that of the incremental change in the price of one share of stock. A bond quote of 95¾ will represent 95.75 percent of $1,000, or $957.50. A bond quoted at 95⅛ will cost $951.25. Quotes on Treasury notes and bonds and government agency issues are expressed in ½₂ of a point, or $31.25 per $1,000 bond. In the newspaper, a government bond quoted at "95.24" would be 95²⁴⁄₃₂ or 95¾.

Those examples of bond quotes are all for bonds selling at **a "discount," a price below par value ($1,000). However, a bond that is selling for more than $1,000 is said to be selling at a "premium."** A bond that would be selling at a premium is one whose coupon rate of interest is higher than that which other comparable bonds are currently paying. So, if a bond is quoted at 105½, that bond would cost $1,055.00 (105.5 percent of $1,000). The equivalent quote for a government bond at this price would be 105.16.

Whether you should consider investing in a discount bond or a premium bond depends on your investment objectives. A discount bond will appreciate faster if interest rates fall, but the current yield on these bonds will be lower. A premium bond, on the other hand, will pay a higher current rate of interest, but the bond price will not rise as fast as a discount bond and the bond will repay only $1,000 when it matures. So, if you invest in a bond that costs $1,055, you will lose $55 of principal at maturity. Essentially, the higher interest you receive is your compensation for not getting all of your principal back at maturity. In fact, you could consider the higher rate of interest you receive from a premium bond as an early prepayment of principal.

Bonds may also be quoted in terms of their yield-to-maturity, or *basis price*. In other words, if a bond is selling at a price that would return 6.8 percent if held to maturity, this bond would be said to be selling at a 6.8 percent basis. **One "basis point" represents 1/100th of a percent, that is, 0.01 percent. One hundred basis points is equal to one percent.** So, as the dollar price of the bond changes, you can also observe how the basis price of the bond changes. Obviously, as the dollar price of a bond moves higher, the yield on the bond expressed in basis points will move lower. If the price of the bond moves up to a point where the yield-to-maturity changes from 6.8 percent to 6.7 percent, then the bond has dropped ten basis points. If a bond moves from a 6.8 percent basis to 6.85 percent, it has moved up five basis points. Since Treasury bills usually fluctuate very little in value because of their short-term nature, they are quoted at a basis price expressing their *yield*, rather than at a dollar price. A newspaper quote on a Treasury bill may show "4.57 bid, 4.55 ask." This means that if you were to invest in the bill, you would receive an annualized rate of 4.55 percent if you held the bill to maturity. If you wanted to sell your bill before maturity, that quote would indicate that a dealer is offering to buy it at a 4.57 basis. The "bid" is obviously at a slightly lower *dollar* price than the "ask." A higher yield indicates a lower price. However, the actual dollar quotes for T-bills are not printed in the newspaper.

Also, when you buy a bond, you must be aware of **"accrued interest."** Since bonds pay the same amount of interest every six months, **if you invest in a bond in the middle of an interest-rate period, you will have to prepay the amount of interest that would have accumulated since the last payment date.** Then on the bond's next regular interest payment date, you will get the full six months' interest. Essentially, you are simply refunded the accrued interest you paid at the time of purchase, and you net out only the amount of interest you would have earned on the bond for the period of time you owned it.

"Accrued interest" is the amount of interest that the bond would have paid since the last interest payment. It represents an additional expense to the bond investor, even though that amount will be refunded with the next interest payment. Accrued interest is calculated with a very simple formula. It assumes that every month is exactly 30 days— even February. So, since each month represents an equal amount of time, each month will accrue exactly ⅙th of the bond's regular six-month payment, and each day within the month will always be ¹⁄₃₀th of that month's interest.

Obviously, the seller of a bond receives the accrued interest that the purchaser of the bond paid. So, the owner of the bond at the time of the sale receives the amount of interest he or she is entitled to (for the period of time he or she owned the bond). The buyer nets out the amount of interest he or she is entitled to (for the period of time he or she owned the bond).

You may be thinking that what bonds are and how they are traded is not particularly important to an individual investor. However, the total volume of bond investments dwarfs that of stocks. It is a market dominated by institutional investors. Most individuals are not aware of just how large is the market for debt securities. In the next chapter you will see how corporations record their debt and equity securities. We will take a look at how companies organize their capital structure on their financial statements.

Do You Know What You Need to Know?

To check up on what you learned from this chapter, answer the following questions in your own words, then compare your answers with the answer key.

1. Why do bond prices go up when interest rates go down? Explain what factors cause this inverse relationship.
2. What is the difference between a collateralized bond and an uncollateralized one? Which type of bond is less risky?
3. Why do municipal bonds generally pay lower rates of interest than debt obligations issued by other borrowers?
4. Explain some of the key differences between the interest and principal payments of government agency issues such as Ginnie Mae (GNMA) and quasi-government sponsored organizations such as Fannie Mae (FNMA), Freddie Mac (FHLMC), and those of other bond issuers.
5. What is a convertible bond? Why is it more difficult to analyze than other types of bonds?
6. What is the dollar value of one *tick*, regarding a bond's price? What is the value of one basis point? What is the relationship between ticks and basis points?
7. Regarding bond prices, what is meant by the terms *discount* and *premium*? What are the advantages and disadvantages of investing in bond trading at discounts or premiums?
8. Explain *accrued interest*. How is accrued interest usually calculated when a bond is purchased?

Answer Key

1. Bonds pay a fixed-dollar amount of interest each year. If rates go up, the market value of a bond will drop to a point where those fixed-dollar interest payments represent a higher rate of interest. Thus, the yield on the bond will be in line with current rates on other comparable bonds.

2. A collateralized bond has assets pledged that will be given to the bondholder if the company defaults on its interest payments. An uncollateralized bond, called a debenture, does not. Collateralized bonds, if the coverage is sufficient, are usually less risky.

3. Municipal bonds pay lower rates of interest because their interest payments are exempt from federal income tax and from state income tax to residents of that state.

4. Ginnie Mae and Fannie Mae debt instruments make monthly payments of interest and principal because those issues represent individual mortgages. Most other bond issuers pay interest only and pay back the full amount of principal at maturity.

5. A convertible bond is one that can be exchanged for another security, such as common stock. An analysis of these types of bonds would include a review of the bond itself and a review of the underlying investment into which the bond could be converted.

6. A bond tick is equal to $1.25 per bond. A basis point is equal to $1/100$ of 1 percent. A tick represents the incremental change of the price of a bond. A basis point represents the incremental change of the bond yield. If bond prices are up-ticking, their yields are going down by basis points.

7. Bonds selling at prices below par value, $1,000, are at a discount. Bonds over par value are at a premium. Bonds selling at a discount will appreciate to par value at maturity. Bonds selling at a premium will decline to par value at maturity.

8. Accrued interest represents the amount of interest since the last semi-annual interest payment. Accrued interest is calculated on the basis of a 30-day month.

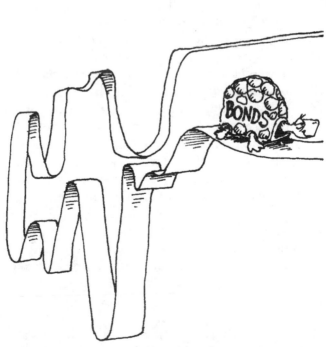

Bonds go up and down, but end up where they usually start—at par value.

— Chapter 5 —

How Do You Read Financial Statements?

Most of the information about a company's financial status is contained in two basic financial statements— the balance sheet and the income (or earnings) statement. The fact that two different words may be used to describe one type of statement—income or earnings—is indicative of the problem that most individuals will have when they first begin trying to read them. Different accountants use different words to describe the same thing. Several entries on financial statements do not have universal terms to describe them. So it is important to understand them not by the terms used, but by the order in which the entries are made. If you understand the order, then no matter what someone else may call the entry, you will know what it is.

The balance sheet is often referred to as a picture, or snapshot, of the company's financial position at one point in time. The income statement, by similar analogy, is referred to as a motion picture of the company's financial position over a period of time. Financial statements are filed after the end of each quarter of the company's fiscal year and then combined into an annual report. The quarterly reports, called 10Q reports or 10Qs, and annual reports, 10Ks, must be filed with the Securities and Exchange Commission.

The balance sheet summarizes the company's assets, liabilities, and equity. It follows the formula "assets

equal liabilities plus equity" (assets = liabilities + equity). This formula is another way of stating "assets minus liabilities equal equity" (assets – liabilities = equity), which probably looks more familiar and is a more logical way of expressing the same mathematical formula. A balance sheet is called such because it *balances* the total of the company's assets with the total of the liabilities and equity. The traditional way of organizing a balance sheet is to put the assets on the lefthand side of the page and the liabilities and equity on the righthand side. Today, however, you are more apt to see balance sheets organized with the assets, liabilities, and equity presented vertically on one page. You may still hear people describe entries on a balance sheet as either left-hand or right-hand entries, whether or not they are actually organized on the left or right side of the page. If, for example, a company sells some assets and puts the cash in equity, this would be described as changing left-hand entries into right-hand entries.

The sum of the liabilities and equity of a company make up its "total capitalization." Companies can either borrow capital, by issuing bonds or taking out loans (liability), or they can sell more shares of stock in the company (equity). You can quickly see by looking at the right-hand side of the balance sheet how the company has chosen to finance its operations. Generally speaking, the less debt the company has, the more conservative the financial structure. Illustration 5.1 is an example of how a typical balance sheet would be structured. It represents a snapshot of Unique Inc.'s current financial position.

"Current assets" are those assets that can easily be turned into cash, such as cash on hand in liquid bank accounts, marketable securities, and accounts receivable. "Fixed assets" would include property, plant, and equipment, or other similar assets that are not readily liquid.

```
UNIQUE INC.
                    CONSOLIDATED BALANCE SHEET
                          (In thousands)

Assets                            Liabilities
  Current Assets:                   Current Liabilities    $ 1,585
    Cash on hand      $ 1,782
    Marketable securities   64
    Accounts receivable    320      Long-term Liabilities    4,877
                       2,166                                 6,462
  Fixed Assets:
    Property,                      Shareholders' Equity
    Plant & Equipment    11,863
                                    Preferred Equity            21
  Other Assets:                     Common Equity
    Intangible             97         (11,740,000 shares)    5,870
    Goodwill               71        Retained Earnings       1,844
                         168                                 7,735
           Total: $14,197                    Total: $14,197
```

Illustration 5.1

"Other assets" would usually include illiquid invest-ments, intangible assets, such as the value of patents or trademarks, and goodwill. "Goodwill" is the accounting term for the amount that a company pays for acquired assets that exceeds the appraised value of those assets. In other words, when one company acquires another and the value of the company being acquired is smaller than what the acquiring company has paid for it, that excess is considered "goodwill." This is contrary to the popular belief that goodwill represents that magic number that allows accountants to balance the balance sheet, the number that can make the total of the assets add up to the total of the liabilities and equity.

Preferred stock is carried on the balance sheet as equity, but from an investor's point of view it is more like a bond than it is like a stock. It is a fixed-income investment.

The company issues preferred stock at a stated dividend payment rate. It differs from a bond, however, in that it does not have a maturity date and it is not a loan from the investor. The company is not legally obligated to pay the dividend as they are with a bond, and the board of directors must declare the dividend as they do dividends for common stock. However, the dividend rate is fixed by the terms of the preferred issue, and the company cannot pay common stock dividends until they have paid all preferred stock dividends, including those that have been omitted in the past if it is a "cumulative" preferred issue.

"Current liabilities" are those debt obligations that are due within the upcoming year after the date of the balance sheet. "Long-term liabilities" are those debt obligations that will come due in more than one year. Also included in the liabilities section of the balance sheet will be any other debt that the company must fund, such as deferred income taxes.

Common stock is carried on the balance sheet at **"par value,"** abbreviated PV. **This is simply an arbitrary value that is assigned to a share of stock for the purpose of determining an equity value for the stock on the balance sheet.** For example, if the common stock has a par value of $1 and the company has 10 million shares outstanding, then the common stock will show a value on the balance sheet of $10 million dollars. If it has a par value of $.50, as it does in the example for Unique Inc., the balance sheet will show the 11,740,000 shares of common stock at a value of $5,870,000. New investors sometimes get upset when, having just bought a stock for $23 per share, they get a certificate showing a par value of $0.50, but you should realize the par value has no relationship to the market value. Shares will frequently be issued with no par value, which allows the company to change whatever par value it is using on the balance sheet, without having to change the certificates.

"Retained earnings" is the running total of previous quarters when the company had net income after paying its fixed-income obligations and dividend requirements. Additions to the retained earnings will come from the bottom line of the company's income statement. Illustration 5.2 is an example of the organization of an income statement.

UNIQUE INC.	
CONSOLIDATED INCOME STATEMENT	
(In thousands, except per share amount)	
Net Sales (or Revenues)	$17,985
Cost of Sales	9,436
Gross Profit	8,549
Administration & Operating Expenses	1,722
Operating Income (Earnings Before	
Interest & Taxes, or EBIT)	6,827
Interest Expense	23
Earnings Before Taxes (EBT)	6,804
Taxes	2,040
Net Income (or Earnings)	$ 4,764
Earnings per Share (EPS)	$ 0.41

Illustration 5.2

The **"income statement" represents the total revenues and expenses of a company's business over a period of time and is organized from top to bottom according to the order of priority by which the company's financial obligations are paid.** So, the first item on the income statement is the total sales, or revenues, for the period covered. The entries after that are a prioritized list of the company's creditors. First, the company must pay the suppliers, the employees' salaries, the rent, and so on. Then it must pay the interest on its bonds and loans. Then it must pay taxes on whatever is left over.

The last line is **the "earnings per share," often abbreviated EPS. This is the net earnings divided by the number of shares outstanding.** The number of shares will usually be found in the common stock entry of shareholders' equity on the balance sheet. Unique Inc., for example, had 11,740,000 shares outstanding, and it earned $4,764,000 for that quarter, so its EPS is $0.41. Some investors obsess on this "bottom line" number, and their analysis usually stops there. However, an understanding of the company's "cash flows," the net cash receipts minus the net cash expenses over a period of time, can reveal much about a company's earnings. Illustration 5.3 is the Statement of Cash Flows for Unique Inc.

UNIQUE INC.
CONSOLIDATED STATEMENT OF CASH FLOWS
(In thousands, except per share amount)

Operating Activities:	
Income	$4,764
Accounting Adjustments	(395)
Depreciation and amortization	1,204
Deferred income taxes	1,370
Net cash from operating activities	6,943
Investing Activities:	
Purchase of Property	($757)
Sale of securities	548
Net cash from investing activities	($209)
Financing Activities:	
Payments on debt	($435)
Proceeds from common stock	215
Net cash from financing activities	($220)
Cash and cash equivalents at beginning of year	$1,794
Cash and cash equivalents at end of year	$6,514

Illustration 5.3

So, if you are reading an annual report, take a look at another very important financial report, **the statement of cash flows.** It begins where the income statement leaves off, with the net income for the company. Then it **shows the adjustments to income that resulted from cash and noncash accounting activities over a period of time.** Typical accounting activities include depreciation, amortization, or changes in accounting principles. If you are an individual investor with no accounting background, you don't have to be too concerned about how these numbers are determined. However, if you observe that a company is losing money from its operating activities, its core businesses, and making up for these losses through its financing activities, you could have a legitimate concern over a company's future earnings ability. The statement of cash flows can help you determine the *quality* of earnings.

The statement of cash flows is organized to show the positive and negative cash flows from (1) operating activities, (2) investing activities, and (3) financing activities. It reveals the net amount of cash "provided by" or "used by" these different segments of the company. The operating activities section of this statement will reveal the net difference between the income from sales of the company's products or services plus investment income, and the cost of those sales, such as employees' wages, payments to suppliers, taxes, and so on. The investing activities section will reveal information on the capital gains or losses on investments or on purchases and sales of assets related to the company's business. The financing activities section will include information on cash flows from the company's debt or equity.

A quick review of this statement can reveal a wealth of information about how a company uses and creates cash flow. You may be surprised to discover that even though a company may have little or no net income, it may still have hundreds of millions of dollars of cash flow. If some of these negative items are one-time expenses, or short-term in nature, this could indicate the possibility of very dramatic earnings growth in the future.

The resulting total of all cash flow activities is the net increase or decrease in cash and cash equivalents from the beginning of the fiscal year to the end. So you can easily see whether the net cash flow is increasing or decreasing from previous years. You are likely to observe that companies in industries showing generally declining cash flows from one year to the next will sell at much lower market prices relative to their earnings (that is, PE ratios, discussed in the next section) than companies showing increasing cash flows.

The entries made on the statement of cash flows will depend on the various activities in which the company engaged over that period of time. There may be many entries or only a few. The entries are itemized as to the specific activity. They are not standardized like the entries on a balance sheet or an income statement. The entries on the statement of cash flows for Unique Inc. are typical examples of what you might see on statements for other companies.

In addition to the three financial statements already mentioned, annual reports will also include a statement of shareholders' equity. This is simply an itemization of the entries included in the equity portion of the balance sheet. It is designed to give readers a clear presentation of the changes in shareholders' equity from year to year. The statement, like that for cash flows, reveals trends. Hopefully, the equity will be trending upward, since this represents the real *net worth* of the company.

What Can You Learn from Financial Statements?

If you are intimidated by the stock market, you'll probably be absolutely paranoid about financial statements. Most individual investors, even when they receive quarterly and annual reports from a company that they own, do not bother to look at the balance sheet and income statement. Many people have "math anxiety." If you are one of them, it's okay. You don't have to make any mathematical computations from the financial statements if you don't want to. All of the important information has already been computed for you by other sources and is readily available from your local library or from many of the online computer services (discussed in Chapter 12). Research reports from major financial publishers such as Standard & Poor's, Moody's, or Value Line are available in most libraries or through computer databases. These reports will provide you with a breakdown of important information from the financial statements. Their authors have already done all the mathematical calculations for you.

However, you should realize that, whether you are mathematically challenged or not, you can make a few simple computations from the financial statements. It is not nearly as complicated as most people think, and your results, assuming they are correct, are going to be the same as if a professional analyst had made them. In other words, there is nothing esoteric about financial statements, and it is not true that only high-powered analysts or accountants can understand them.

There are dozens of financial ratios that could be calculated, but you are going to learn how to compute only six of them. These are the ones that will be the most helpful to you in understanding how the company has financed its operations and how profitable it is. The three ratios that will help you understand how a company has structured its finances are the debt-to-equity ratio, the book value, and the current ratio. The three ratios that will help you understand how well the company's business is doing are the net profit margin, the return-on-equity ratio, and the price earnings ratio.

The "debt-to-equity ratio" is simply the company's total liabilities, both current and long-term, divided by the total shareholders' equity. The debt-to-equity ratio will let you know at a glance how much of the company's total capitalization is funded by debt and how much by equity. The more debt the company has, the greater the financial risk associated with it. The company must pay interest on that debt, whether or not it has any income. So, generally speaking the lower the debt-to-equity ratio the more conservative the financial structure of the company.

There are some notable exceptions to this rule, however. Most utility companies finance their operations with much more debt than equity. This is not usually viewed as risky because the utilities business of utility companies (keep in mind utility companies can be in *non*utilities businesses also) is regulated by state authorities. So these companies have regulated earnings (on their utilities business), regardless of their debt. In other words, a high debt-to-equity ratio for a utility company is not usually a cause for concern. For a company whose earnings are less predictable, however, this could be considered a problem.

Look at the balance sheet for Unique Inc. In order to compute the debt-to-equity ratio for this company, you will have to divide the total of the current liabilities and long-term liabilities by the shareholders' equity. So, that would be $6,462, total debt, divided by the total shareholders' equity, $7,735. The debt-to-equity ratio is about 6.5:7.7. It can be written as a ratio like that, as a fraction, 6.5/7.7; or as the result of that division, 0.84, or 84 percent. Another way of looking at this result is to say that the debt represents approximately 84 percent of the equity. A company that had a debt-to-equity ratio of 100 percent would have the same amount of debt as equity. If the figure is greater than 100 percent, then the company has financed its operations with more debt than equity.

The "book value" is the total shareholders' equity divided by the number of shares outstanding. Most accountants will also adjust the shareholders' equity by taking out the value of intangible assets, since such assets would not be considered marketable. The theoretical conclusion drawn from this calculation is that if the company went bankrupt and all of its assets had to be liquidated and all of its liabilities paid off, then this is what would be left to the shareholders on a per share basis. This is obviously a theoretical value only, because if the company really did go bankrupt, its assets would probably not be sold at the values at which they are being carried on its books. In most cases, however, if the company has a book value close to its current market value, there is little downside risk to the investor.

To compute the book value for Unique Inc. you would divide the total shareholders' equity, $7,735,000, by the number of shares outstanding, 11,740,000. This equals about $0.66. Assuming Unique Inc. is a growth company, book value wouldn't be too important. The primary purpose of investing in a growth stock is for future earnings. However, this low book value does emphasize the high risk of growth companies. If the company went bankrupt and its assets were liquidated, there wouldn't be much left for the shareholders.

The "current ratio" is simply the total current assets divided by the total current liabilities. So, for Unique this would be $2,166,000 divided by $1,585,000, which equals 1.37. The only significance of the current ratio is that it tells you is whether or not the company has enough liquid assets to pay its liabilities for the coming year. You'll very seldom find a company that will report in its public financial statements the fact that it won't have enough current assets to cover its current debts. However, if you do, that could be a glaring sign of impending trouble.

So far Unique Inc. looks healthy. It has a very conservative financial structure. In other words, it doesn't have very many liabilities. Even though the book value may be low when compared with larger companies, it probably isn't a major concern if the company's earnings are growing. So, let's look at how the company is doing. Is this a profitable company? To answer this question you will mainly need to look at ratios from the income statement.

The "net profit margin" is computed by dividing the net profit by the net (or total) sales, that is, the bottom of the income statement divided by the top of it. For this period, Unique Inc. kept $4,764,000 after paying all of its obligations out of the $17,985,000 in total sales. So, the net profit margin is $4,764 divided by $17,985, which equals about .265, and would be written 26.5 percent. In other words, for every $1.00 in sales that Unique Inc. reported, the company kept about $.26. This is a very high profit margin and a sign of a very well financed company. You could also compute the gross profit margin if you wanted, which would be the gross profit divided by the net sales. This would tell you what percentage of its sales the company kept before it paid its fixed liabilities and taxes. You can do this for Unique Inc. if you are interested.

Also, the net profit margin is usually evaluated by professional analysts according to whether the company would be characterized as *labor intensive* or *capital intensive*. A labor-intensive business is one whose largest expense would be employee wages. A capital-intensive company, on the other hand, would be one that finances its business primarily with capital, such as bond issues or bank loans. Generally speaking, as sales increase, the net profit margin of a capital-intensive company will increase faster than a labor-intensive one. This is the case because, once the fixed expenses are met, that is, the interest on the debt, almost everything after that is profit. However, with a labor-intensive business, the company must hire more employees to produce more goods to sell. Thus, their expenses go up at a rate corresponding to their increasing sales. High-tech companies are usually treated as if they were in a category of their own, neither labor-intensive nor capital-intensive. However, you needn't worry about that at this point.

The next ratio we will consider, the **"return-on-equity ratio" (ROE), is probably the most important one. It would be computed by dividing the net income from the income statement by the total Shareholders' Equity from the balance sheet.** For Unique this would be $4,764 divided by $7,735, for a whopping 0.62, or 62 percent. The significance of the return on equity is that it allows you to compare the return that this company is making on its shareholders' equity compared to alternative investments.

The return on equity ratio is often compared to **the "return-on-assets ratio" (ROA). This ratio is computed by dividing the net income by the total assets.** Note that ROA will always be a smaller number than ROE, unless the company has no liabilities. In that case, the return on assets will be the same as the return on equity.

Remember that U.S. Treasury bonds were used as the "riskless" money rate. So, if T-bonds are yielding 5 percent, then an investment that is higher up on the risk-reward scale should be yielding more. Another way of looking at this would be if a company's return on equity is below 5 percent, then the shareholders could theoretically make more money if this company were dead than if it were alive. If the company were only making a 4 percent return on equity, theoretically the shareholders would be better off if their company liquidated all of its assets. It could then pay off all of its liabilities and invest the remaining shareholders' equity in T-bonds paying 5 percent. The shareholders would be getting a higher return on their investment and would be assuming less risk.

The last ratio was first mentioned in "How Do You Read Market Quotes in the Newspaper?" in Chapter 1—the PE ratio. **The "price earnings ratio" is simply the current market price of the stock divided by last year's earnings per share, that is, the total EPS of the last four reported quarters.** The market price of the stock doesn't appear on any of the financial statements. It changes daily and is included in the market quote information in *The Wall Street Journal*. If we assume that the closing price of Unique Inc. is $23, then the computation of the PE ratio would be $23 divided by $0.41, which equals 56.

The PE ratio is also referred to as the "market multiple," for it is the number that, if you multiplied it by the EPS, you would get the current market price of the stock. In other words, Unique Inc. is selling at about 56 times earnings. The $23 share price is 56 times its current earnings of $0.41. The significance of the PE ratio may be overemphasized because it has such a high profile with the daily stock quotes in the newspapers. Generally speaking, a low PE would mean that the stock is currently selling at a relatively low price to its current earnings. A high PE would mean that the stock's price is not much of a bargain right now. "High" and "low" are relative terms, however. PE ratios will fall into different ranges for different industry groups.

For instance, high-tech companies with rapid earnings growth potential will generally sell at much higher PEs than low-tech or mature companies with limited growth potential.

From an investor's point of view, the *current* PE ratio is not as important as what it will be a year or so from now—or at the time in the future when you plan to sell the stock. So, if a company's earnings grow at a rate of about 25 percent per year, then the PE ratio will decline by 25 percent per year, assuming the stock's price remains the same. Just because a company may be selling at a low PE based on its current earnings does not mean that it is a bargain. That company may not be selling at such a low PE based on its projected earnings for next year. Some companies that maintain a high popularity with the investing public consistently sell at high multiples. If you waited for them to come down before you invested in that company, you would probably never buy the stock. In order for the PE ratio to be really significant to an investor, much more information is required than just the number itself.

Many times investors are quite surprised when a company reports higher earnings, and instead of causing the stock to rally, they see its share price drop. Normally one would expect that when a company reports higher earnings, it indicates that it is becoming more profitable or expanding its business or both. Such good news does usually cause the stock to appreciate in price. However, sometimes positive earnings don't translate into a positive reaction on the stock. This could be because some analysts were expecting even higher earnings, or it could be because the *quality* of the earnings was poor.

The "quality of earnings" is a term analysts use to describe the breakdown of the sources of that income. If most of the growth of the income came from an industry sector that is viewed as being in decline, this would not be a good sign. Analysts are always looking at future growth, not at the current situation. So, if a growth stock came in with a good earnings report, but the source of those earnings was primarily due to sales of a product with outdated technology, most investors would not be very impressed. *A good investor is always looking around the corner.* The current situation for a company is not as important as its outlook for the future.

Why Are Financial Ratios Important?

None of these ratios from the financial statements is very important by itself. The ratios become significant only when they are compared with the ratios of other similar companies. If Unique Inc. is a book publishing company, then you could compare its ratios with other similar book publishers to see which ones operated the most efficiently, had the highest profit margins, and the best return on equity. It would be meaningless to compare Unique's financial statements with those of companies in other industries.

Most financial statements will include last year's results side by side with the current year's. This way you can easily see how the company has improved, or weakened, year to year. Many companies even include the last three years, or more. Thus, you can interpolate a pattern of growth or shrinkage. Of course, the same pattern may not continue for the next few years. However, financial statements give you a basis for making future projections.

This process of comparing side-by-side numbers from corporate financial statements is called *horizontal analysis*, sometimes referred to as trend analysis. An investor can compute the percentage change in all of a company's entries on its financial statements by subtracting the previous year's entry from the current year's, and then dividing by the previous year's entry. Since this process can be done for every item on the financial statements, an analyst may detect not only trends in sales or earnings of a company's business, but also trends in such items as taxes.

Vertical analysis, on the other hand, involves computing the percentage difference of each entry on the financial statements for the same year. On the income statement, for example, an analyst would consider the total sales and revenues for one year as 100 percent. Then, by subtracting the cost of sales and dividing by the total revenues, he or she would be able to compute the percentage of the total revenues that the cost of sales represents. None of these computations for either horizontal or vertical analysis involves very complex mathematical calculations. However, the insight an investor will gain by taking a little time to do them can be very worthwhile.

You will find the financial statements toward the end of the company's annual report. The first part of the annual report will be the message to the shareholders from the chairman of the board or the CEO (chief executive officer) of the company. This will usually be followed by the description of the company's products or business. Then you will find the financial statements. Following that will be *footnotes* on the statements. **The "footnotes" are an integral part of the statements themselves.** They will explain any unusual or irregular entries on the statements and will also add very valuable information to the financial data.

Professional analysts will use the financial ratios they compute as the primary reason for recommending or not recommending that security. Usually, analysts will follow most or all of the companies in the same industry. This is why they can compare the ratios of several companies in the same report and explain why they prefer one company over another.

You can also compare the financial ratios of various companies within the same industry. If you were considering investing in Unique Inc., then you could also compute similar financial ratios for other book publishing companies: Barnes & Noble, McGraw-Hill, Dun & Bradstreet, Dow Jones & Co., and so on. The most significant ratios would be the *profit margin*, to see which company is the most efficient, and the *return-on-equity ratio*, to see which company is making the most money.

At no other time has there ever been so much research information available to individual investors. In fact, whether through computer databases or from published and publicly available reports, the individual investor today has more information at his or her fingertips than did institutional investors a decade ago. So, if you don't feel comfortable computing ratios yourself, read the reports of other analysts who have already done the work for you. With this information on financial statements, you should feel more comfortable reading that part of a company's annual report and have a better understanding of what the ratios mean.

The information presented in this chapter is not meant to be all-inclusive. There are many more ratios and much more information that you can get from financial statements that are not included in this discussion. However, individual investors should realize that they do not have to be accountants to compute a few ratios and draw some logical conclusions. With a few clicks of a calculator you can evaluate the degree of risk a company has assumed as it structured its capitalization. You can draw some conclusions about its financial stability, analyze its profitability, and so on. The results of your computations, assuming you punched in the right numbers, will be the same as those punched in by a professional analyst.

The information in this chapter is not intended to turn everyone into accountants. It is simply meant to demythologize financial statements and show you the knowledge that can be gained from a few simple calculations. If you are inspired to go further, take some accounting classes. There is much more information and many more ratios that you can use to add to this foundation.

Do You Know What You Need to Know?

To check up on what you learned from this chapter, answer the following questions in your own words, then compare your answers with the answer key.

1. How would you describe the two main financial statements? What is the Balance Sheet formula? What does the Balance Sheet balance? How is an Income (or Earnings) Statement organized?

2. What differentiates current assets from fixed assets or other assets, such as intangibles?

3. What is the difference between current liabilities and long-term liabilities? With which do you think companies would most often like to finance their business operations? Why?

4. Is it possible for a company's total assets to equal its total shareholders' equity? If so, explain why. Would you consider a company a good investment if its total assets equaled its total liabilities?

5. Describe a Statement of Cash Flows. What useful information does it reveal to investors about a company's earnings? What is meant by *quality of earnings?*

6. Which of the financial ratios mentioned in this book reveal information about how a company finances its operations, that is, its capital structure? Which ratios identify a company's profitability?
7. Return on equity (ROE) is probably the most important financial ratio. Why? Under what circumstances might a financial analyst conclude that a company may be worth more to an investor if it were dead than if it were alive?
8. What can an investor learn about a company by applying the principles of vertical and horizontal analysis to financial statements?

Answer Key

1. The Balance Sheet is a snapshot of a company's finances; the Income Statement is a motion picture of those finances. The Balance Sheet balances a company's total assets with its total liabilities plus equity. The Income Statement is organized from top to bottom in the order of priority for payments of the company's debt obligations.
2. Current assets can be turned into cash quickly. Fixed assets are frequently called "property, plant, and equipment." Other assets include goodwill and intangible assets, such as the value of patents and trademarks.
3. Current liabilities are those debt obligations that will come due within the forthcoming fiscal year. Long-term liabilities come due after that fiscal year. Interest rates are usually lower for short-term (current) debt.
4. The only reason why a company's assets would ever equal its equity would be that the company had no liabilities. Having no liabilities means that the company has no financial risk. However, some analysts might argue that management should leverage its assets.

5. The Statement of Cash Flows is organized to show the positive and negative cash flows from the company's (1) operating activities, (2) investing activities, and (3) financing activities. Quality of earnings often refers to the income from the company's operating activities because they usually represent the company's core business.

6. The way that a company finances its operations would be measured by the debt-to-equity ratio, the book value, and the current ratio. The company's profitability would be measured by the net profit margin, return on equity, return on assets, and the price earnings ratio.

7. The return-on-equity ratio shows how much money the company earned with the shareholders' equity. If that rate of return is below the riskless rate, the interest rate paid on U.S. Treasury bonds, you could theoretically conclude that the company would be better off investing in those bonds than in continuing with a more risky investment that is less profitable.

8. Horizontal analysis compares the entries on a company's financial statement from one year to another; it measures a company's progress over time. Vertical analysis describes most of the financial calculations in the book, a calculation derived from numbers on the financial statement for the same year.

The bottom line is you've got to know how to read financial statements.

— Chapter 6 —

What Is Fundamental Analysis?

There are two schools of thought regarding securities analysis: fundamental and technical. **The basic premise of "fundamental analysis" is that the most important consideration for selecting a good stock for investment is the future earnings potential of the company.** To forecast a particular company's earnings, however, you must also take into account the outlook for the economy as a whole and the outlook for the industry in which that company is involved. Most fundamental analysts would say that to select a good investment you must first start with macroeconomic analysis. You should begin by studying the general economic trends, and then narrow that study down to the outlook for particular industries. Finally, you narrow down that study to microeconomic analysis and examine a particular company within that industry and a particular investment in that company. This is referred to as a "top-down" approach.

Technical analysis, on the other hand, is a method of selecting good investments primarily on the basis of supply and demand factors. Technical analysis also relies heavily on interpreting chart patterns of the past performance of the stock's price. This method of analysis will be discussed in greater detail in the next chapter. Reading and analyzing financial statements and studying economic cycles and industry trends are disciplines of fundamental analysis.

**By far the single most important factor in funda-
mental analysis is the direction of interest rates.** *If you
want to be a good student of the stock market, you must
first be a good student of interest rates.* As is the case with
bonds, there is a direct cause-and-effect inverse relationship between interest rates and stock prices. As interest
rates rise, stock prices drop. This is due in part to the fact
that a rise in interest rates will generally result in a
decrease in many companies' earnings. Illustration 6.1
charts the stock market index for a recent one-year period
and the yield on the 30-year Treasury bond for the same
period of time. It shows that as interest rates moved up,
the market generally moved down, and as interest rates
moved down the market usually went higher. Since you
realize that bond *prices* move inversely with interest rates,
you could also say that bond prices will move in direct
correlation to stock prices.

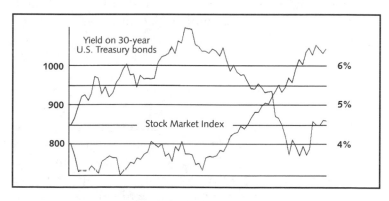

Illustration 6.1

There are several fundamental reasons for this inverse
relationship. Since most companies finance part of their

capitalization with debt, and since some of this debt is often tied to adjustable-rate bank loans, as rates go up, the company's interest expense goes up. In other words, the more money the company has to pay on its debt, the less money it will keep on its bottom line. The company will have to increase its earnings at a rate equal to its increased interest expense just to keep the same net income. Even if the company doesn't have adjustable-rate loans, investors anticipate that the company's borrowings will be coming due and will have to be refinanced at the higher rate in the future. So, you may see a reaction from investors even if there isn't a direct cause-and-effect relationship.

Also, many institutions follow a discipline of moving their investment portfolios between debt and equity, depending on the relative projected returns. So, as interest rates move down, some institutional investors are inclined to sell bonds and buy stocks. The opposite is also true. If interest rates move up, they will sell stocks and buy bonds. Thus, even though only a few institutional accounts may be following this strategy, they influence many other investors to follow suit. In other words, even individual investors who do not normally move their portfolios between stocks and bonds will follow what they believe institutions are doing. To some extent you could say this becomes a self-fulfilling prophecy.

It is much easier to anticipate interest rate changes or economic cycles than it is to accurately predict how one particular company will do. Although you have some valuable tools for drawing some conclusions about the future earnings potential of a company, being able to do in-depth analysis to predict earnings per share for a particular company is beyond the scope of this book. There are, however, many sources of information available through local brokerage firms or your local library for getting a professional analyst's opinion and forecast of earnings for a company.

Value Line is probably the most accessible resource for finding earnings forecasts. It can be found in most libraries.

What Are Economic Cycles?

Fundamental analysis deals primarily with forecasting economic trends and cycles. **An "economic cycle" is a period of either sustained inflation or recession. "Inflation" means that the price of most goods and services is rising and the size of the total economic base expanding.** So, you could say that if your total net worth isn't also expanding at that rate, your percentage of the economy is shrinking. This is a simplistic way of looking at inflation, but consider the total value of the economy as a pie and your net worth as your slice of the pie. If the pie gets bigger but your slice stays the same size, your slice has become a smaller piece of the pie. Unless your net worth can grow as fast as the economy is growing, you are losing buying power.

Most economists, however, will say that some inflation is healthy. A growing economy usually grows because it is producing an increasing quantity of goods and services. This means more people are employed producing those goods and services. However, the negative side of inflation is that because people are generally making more money, the cost of goods goes up correspondingly. If people have more money to spend, the prices on the items they want to buy most will go higher. This is due to supply and demand. So, the ideal economic situation is one of high employment and low inflation, a state that usually doesn't last very long.

If near *full employment* is achieved, then prices of most consumer items will begin to move up. Most economists define full employment as the state achieved when all qualified laborers are employed. However, when the unemployment level reaches about 2 percent, the anticipated scarcity of laborers tends to put pressure on increasing wages. As wages rise, more of the wage earner's salary becomes "disposable income," and this causes greater inflation. So, for practical purposes most investment analysts refer to **"full employment" as the state achieved when any further increase in the employment level would be considered inflationary. Usually this state is achieved at about the 5 percent unemployment level.**

When the economy reaches full employment, it is likely that the rate of growth of consumer prices will begin to outpace the individual's ability to increase his or her earnings. When the economy reaches a point where too many individuals no longer earn enough to be consumers of products at those price levels, then those prices will start coming down. This begins a recessionary cycle.

"Recession" means that the size of the economic base is shrinking. Yes, this does mean that the economic pie is getting smaller. So, if you are one of the lucky ones whose earning power is going up during a recession, your slice would be getting bigger. However, for most people, as the pie gets smaller, their slice of the pie gets smaller as well. During a recession many people are unemployed due to the fact that fewer goods and services are being produced. Thus, for many individuals the fact that the pie is shrinking doesn't benefit them. They don't have a job and don't have disposable income to capitalize on lower prices. **Most economists define a recession as two consecutive quarters of declining gross domestic product.** Gross domestic product (GDP) will be explained in the next section, "How Do You Measure Inflation?"

The main weapon in the government's arsenal to combat inflation and recession cycles is interest rates. **The Federal Reserve Board, the U.S. government agency that regu-**

lates the banking industry, sets domestic economic policy. It is generally referred to as "the Fed." Although the Fed only *directly* controls the policies of banks that are members of the Federal Reserve System, the influence of this board extends far beyond that. Its ability to control interest rates affects virtually all companies in the United States. To some extent the Federal Reserve Board also affects many of the economies of the world, since countries are becoming more and more economically interdependent.

One of the most followed interest rates by business reporters is the "Fed Funds Rate." This is the rate at which *banks* will lend money to other *banks*, usually for the purpose of meeting deposit reserve requirements, set by the Fed. These are *overnight*, or one day, loans. Business reporters frequently quote the Fed Funds rate because it is so volatile, changing continually throughout the day. Since it changes so quickly, the assumption is that it could forecast the direction of other less volatile rates. **The interest rate that the Federal Reserve Board charges its *member* banks for loans is called the "discount rate."** The fact that the source for most Fed Funds loans is money borrowed at the discount rate from the Fed illustrates one of the ways the Federal Reserve Board can influence bank policies, even of nonmember banks. The Federal Reserve Board can raise or lower the discount rate to indicate to other banks where they want them to set other loan rates. This is their main tool for setting economic policy, controlling inflation, or stimulating the economy out of a recession.

If the Federal Reserve Board is primarily concerned about inflation, it can raise the discount rate, triggering a rise in other bank loan rates, such as the prime rate, consumer loan rates, or even to some extent mortgage interest rates. **The "prime rate,"** also broadly followed by business reporters, **is the rate at which banks will lend money to**

their best corporate customers. Although individuals may not borrow money from a bank at the prime rate, this rate is important because it is used to gauge other business and consumer loans. For example, some adjustable-rate mortgages (ARMs) use the prime rate as a benchmark.

Rising interest rates have the effect of slowing down the rate of growth of the economy. Higher rates mean that consumers will probably be less willing to purchase items that would normally be bought on credit. Expensive items such as houses and automobiles are the most obvious consumer products that are usually purchased on credit. The volume of sales of these high-priced items is obviously affected by the higher costs of financing, but inflation has the same effect on less costly items as well. During periods of high interest rates, people generally consume less—even of items that are not bought on credit. The high rates of returns consumers can receive on their savings make it more advantageous to invest rather than to spend.

Higher rates of interest usually stimulate a higher percentage of saving by individuals. During periods when interest rates are well ahead of inflation projections, investors are more inclined to put their **"disposable income," that part of their income that is not needed for necessities,** into investments. This has the effect of taking that money out of circulation, at least for a while. **The terms used by the Federal Reserve Board for measuring *money supply* are M1, M2, and M3. The "money supply" is the total amount of cash and liquid investments in circulation.** M1 is the total amount of coins and paper currency in circulation plus the amount of money on deposit in such liquid accounts as checking accounts (called demand deposit accounts, or DDAs), savings accounts, and travelers' checks. M2 includes the total of M1 plus other savings deposits such as money market funds and small certificates of deposit (called CDs, or time deposits). M3, the broadest measure of money supply, includes the total of M2 plus slightly less liquid accounts such as jumbo CDs (of $100,000 or more) and institutional money market funds. *The most watched measure of money supply is M2.*

If the Federal Reserve Board is more concerned about recession than inflation, the board of governors will most likely lower the discount rate. When other interest rates are lowered following that reduction, this should have the effect of stimulating consumption. Savings accounts should become less desirable because of the low interest rates available, and the interest expense of purchases made on credit is lower.

The Federal Reserve System is a very interesting organization. It was created by an act of Congress in 1913. Prior to that, each bank operated independently. Originally, the intent of Congress was to create a central bank that would be large enough to bail out banks in financial crises. Having a "run" on banks, where a large number of depositors attempted to withdraw their money all at once, was not uncommon during those tense economic times. Although the Fed was created by the U.S. government, it is not a government agency. It is actually a corporation owned by its member banks. Every federally chartered bank must purchase shares of stock in the Fed. Although state-chartered banks do not have to be members, they are nonetheless under the control of the Fed.

The Fed is one of the most powerful and least public organizations in the world. No outside organization has ever audited its financial statements, which gives rise to frequent criticism as to the motives for its actions. The chairman is frequently asked to testify before Congress to explain the intentions of his actions. This testimony is also meant to be a check on the Fed's power, reminding the bank regulator that his authority was granted by Congress, even though it is an independent body.

The Federal Reserve board of governors is composed of 7 members, appointed to 14-year terms by the president of the United States. The chairman of the board serves a 4-year term, but may be reappointed. The presidents of the 12 district Federal Reserve Banks are appointed for 5-year terms by the bank's directors, but they are usually reappointed indefinitely.

Aside from influencing the levels of interest rates, the other main weapon used by the Fed for controlling economic cycles is **"open market operations." The Federal Open Market Committee (FOMC)** is composed of 5 of the 12 Federal Reserve Bank presidents and the 7 members of the board of governors. The FOMC **meets monthly to decide whether it wants to buy or to sell securities to member banks on the open market.** If the Fed purchases securities, such as T-bills, government bonds, and so on, it will be expanding the money supply by pumping more money into the banking system and increasing banks' excess reserves. This also reduces banks' need to borrow money at the Fed Funds rate and will cause that rate to drop. If the Fed wants to tighten the money supply, it will sell securities to member banks in its open market operations. Frequently, the days prior to an upcoming FOMC meeting can be very volatile ones for securities, especially bonds, as traders attempt to position their portfolios by second-guessing what the FOMC will do.

You should realize in reading about these methods of controlling and manipulating the economy that as you go through these cycles of inflation and recession, you never come to a point when you can say, "Stop. We've reached a state of economic perfection. Don't change a thing." Obviously, the economy is a dynamic system. There is never an ideal economic situation, where everything is rosy and will stay that way for a long period of time. *Every solution to every economic problem creates another problem.* Low interest rates can fuel inflation, causing your slice of the pie to shrink. High interest rates can send the economy into a recessionary cycle, creating high unemployment.

There has never been any time in the history of the stock market where you could not find someone forecasting economic disaster. Because of the very nature of the economy, disaster is always just around the corner. Every prophet yelling, "The end is near," can usually give a believable rationale for that statement. There is never going to be an ultimate solution to all the problems of the economy. Every solution will create another problem. However, if you understand how the economy functions, you will be less likely to buy into the extremist "doom and gloom" philosophy.

In addition to inflationary and recessionary cycles, another frequently mentioned business cycle is the **"industrial life cycle."** Illustration 6.2 shows this **three-stage graphic representation of the typical growth patterns of most industries.** The industrial life cycle simply means that at the beginning of a new industry a company involved in this business is likely to move up only moderately. During this phase, the company will be *developing* its new product, and the product may not be recognized or readily accepted by most consumers. This is a time in the company's cycle for high-risk venture capital.

Then, as the new technology or product becomes more accepted, the company will grow very rapidly. It will usually broaden its *marketing* approach to a wider range of consumers. Finally, the company will enter the maturity phase of this cycle. Increased *competition* will narrow the previous profit margins, and the company will enter a period of slower revenue growth. The industrial life cycle is not meant to predict the length of time that a company will go through these various stages. Depending on the industry, it could represent decades, or for some fad products it could represent only a few months.

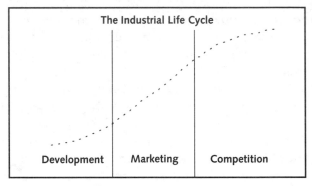

Illustration 6.2

Also, keep in mind that the industrial life cycle is not a chart of the company's stock price. It is a representation of the expected growth of the size of the company and of its revenues. Sometimes the stock price may appreciate most significantly while the company is still in the development phase, as speculators attempt to capitalize on the anticipated earnings growth resulting from increasing revenues.

How Do You Measure Inflation?

To qualify as a noteworthy measure of inflation, the name of the indicator must be easily reducible to a three-letter acronym, such as GDP, CPI, PPI, LEI, or CRB. **The broadest measure of inflation is GDP, which, as you already know, stands for gross domestic product. The gross domestic product is the total output of all goods and services produced within the geographical bound-**

aries of a country. It is the total of all the personal spending, government spending, and gross investing within a nation for a given period of time. The GDP for the United States is reported quarterly and compiled by the Commerce Department. However, the report is revised two times after its first release. For each quarterly report there will be *an advance report, a preliminary report,* and *a final report,* each one following the other by about one month. Sometimes even the accuracy of the final report is questioned by scrutinizing economists. Investors need to be aware of the way the GDP numbers are released. It is significant because, even though the GDP is a quarterly number, its reporting can affect the stock market every month.

Statistically more important than the actual GDP is the *Real GDP*. This is computed by adjusting the GDP numbers to exclude price increases, and thus show a net number that would more accurately reflect volume increases only. This adjustment is expressed in percentage form as the *GDP Deflator*. In other words, Real GDP measures the actual increased amount (or decreased amount) of money spent or invested in terms of an adjusted dollar value. The amount of this adjustment each year is based on the previous year's prices and is called a "chain price index deflator." Such an adjustment shows the net percentage increase in spending and investing, without including increased prices due to the declining purchasing power of the dollar. How the dollar loses purchasing power will be explained next, in the discussion on the CPI. The reason why more emphasis is placed on Real GDP is that it represents the actual amount of *inflation*, or expansion of the economy, for that period of time.

Most economists today would say that in a healthy economy the GDP should be growing at about 1 percent to 3.5 percent. This would indicate moderate inflation levels.

It means that the economy is expanding, but most wage earners still have the ability to increase their income at the same, or a higher, rate. By most standards, the ideal state is to have the GDP growing at about the same rate as the more volatile *CPI*.

The CPI is the "consumer price index." It is the measure of price changes in a market basket of goods and services purchased by most consumers. It measures inflation at the retail level, the level at which most people are concerned. It tells you, on an ongoing basis, how much the cost of frequently purchased items is increasing. Therefore, it is referred to as *the cost-of-living index*. Many government programs, such as retired federal employee pensions and social security benefits, use this index as a basis for adjusting payments to inflation. The components of the CPI include the prices of food, gasoline, clothing, medical care, automobiles, housing, public transportation, reading materials, laundry and cleaning products, and so on. There are about 400 components that make up the index.

The CPI is reported on a monthly basis, and each monthly figure will also be adjusted to show what the rate would be if it were compounded annually. The figures are released about two weeks after the end of each month. They are compiled by the government's Bureau of Labor Statistics, which is part of the Labor Department. Information on the CPI can be found at the web address *www.bls.gov/home.htm*.

CPI statistics are divided into two reports: CPI-U and CPI-W. The CPI-U is the one that is usually reported in the media. It represents the spending pattern of urban consumers. CPI-W is a compilation of price fluctuations associated with urban wage earners and clerical workers. More than 30,000 individuals and families provide information on their spending habits to compute the CPI. Price comparisons from the previous month are made on items in more than 200 categories of goods and services. These categories are divided into eight groups: food and beverages, housing (rent and other costs), apparel, transportation (including gasoline), medical care, recreation, education and communication, and other goods and services.

Contrary to popular belief, the CPI is not the same as the cost-of-living index. Although both measure price fluctuations of a market basket of goods and services, the Labor Department adjusts the cost-of-living index to represent a more accurate method of measuring the real costs of maintaining the existing standard-of-living. This includes many intangibles such as public safety, education, and health.

The two most volatile sectors of the consumer price index are gasoline and food prices. These are also the most heavily weighted components of the CPI. When the CPI is reported, a separate computation, with the changes in food and energy prices *excluded*, will be released. The result of the report without those two volatile sectors is called the "core rate" of inflation.

Closely related to the CPI is **the PPI, which is also reported by the Bureau of Labor Statistics. The "producer price index" is the measure of the rate of inflation at the wholesale level. It reports on the changes in prices of raw materials and wholesale goods.** The PPI will be reported one or two days before the CPI. It is generally viewed as a forecaster of what the CPI is likely to be. Wholesale prices usually go up before retail prices do.

The "index of leading economic indicators," or LEI, is a private-sector compilation of economic statistics, designed to predict future economic activity. It is supposed to forecast what the economy will be doing in about one year. Like the CPI and PPI, it is reported monthly, but the data are released about four weeks after the end of the month to which the figures apply. It was first reported in 1938 when Henry Morgenthau asked the National Bureau of Economic Research, a private organization, to compile a statistical indicator to predict when the Great Depression would end. There are also indexes of lagging indicators and coincident indicators. Their function and significance are to verify the accuracy of the leading indicators.

The list of leading economic indicators includes: (1) weekly hours worked in manufacturing, (2) new unemployment claims, (3) new orders for consumer goods reported by the Institute for Supply Management (ISM), (4) manufacturers' backlogs of durable goods orders, (5) the consumer confidence index, (6) growth of M2, the measure of money supply, (7) the Standard & Poor's 500 Index of common stocks, (8) building permits issued for new homes, (9) the performance of vendors' deliveries to factories, and (10) new plant and equipment orders. Individual components of the LEI have often been emphasized by the press or by financial strategists during certain economic periods.

Most of these indicators have an obvious reason for being there. There is a direct relationship between low unemployment, an increasing rate of new orders, a rising number of building permits, and so on, and an increase in the future level of the economy. The one component that gets the most attention, however, is the one that surprises most people as a *leading* economic indicator. That is the S&P 500 Index. Why would higher equity prices be an indicator of economic expansion in the future?

As you already know, stock prices go up when demand for them increases. However, most people don't invest in stocks just to sell them the next day, the next week, or the next month. They invest in stocks to sell them at some future date—perhaps in a year or so. In other words, investors think that the stocks they are buying now will be worth more in the future. Thus, stock prices are an indication of investors' expectations for the future, and that is why they are included in the list.

The monthly indicators become statistically more important when they show a consecutive trend for three months. Because of the volatile nature of the indicators, a one-month report that departs dramatically from other recent reports would probably be considered an aberration. However, if the trend is verified for three months in a row, one quarter, then economic analysts would be more concerned. For example, if the leading economic indicators were lower three months in a row, this would indicate the likelihood that the economy could be heading into a recession. A single month's statistical data are not as significant as the trend verified by several monthly reports.

Perhaps the most watched inflation indicator by _institutions_ is the Commodity Research Bureau index, or Reuters/CRB index, of commodity prices. The Commodity Research Bureau is best known for its research and analysis on commodities markets, but many professionals consider the CRB index one of the most important inflation forecasters. The Federal Reserve Board has often cited increasing commodity prices as a key indicator of future inflation, even when other economic indicators were not rising as fast. The index includes the price changes on the futures markets for oil, soybeans, cocoa, coffee, sugar, cotton, gold, platinum, silver, and so on.

Since inflation is so important in predicting future economic developments (particularly interest rates), many economists or

financial analysts look for indicators that will predict inflation before the inflation indicators. In particular, analysts
look for indicators that will predict a rising CPI before it
actually rises.

The media is constantly trying to second-guess which
economic indicators are most important to the Federal
Reserve Board. Trying to decipher the mind of the its chairman has become a national pastime. At one time or
another, the media has focused on the money supply, the
employment cost index, the unemployment rate, the consumer confidence index, changes in consumer savings and
consumer spending, and so on. Sooner or later every economic indicator, obscure or not, will take its time in the
media spotlight. In recent years, more emphasis has been
placed on geopolitical influences on the economy than on
economic indicators. Whatever the "economic indicator du
jour" bear in mind that it may be more media hype than
substance. Economics is an art, not a science.

Other important economic reports that affect investors'
perceptions of inflation or interest-rate movements are the
U.S. merchandise trade deficit and the fluctuating value of
the U.S. dollar versus other foreign currencies. The U.S.
dollar index by J. P. Morgan is a good indicator of how
much strong foreign currencies could add to rising consumer prices in the near future. This index should be given
greater emphasis by business reporters.

What Is the Biggest
Economic Problem Today?

The biggest problem facing the economy today will
also be the biggest problem facing the economy long after
this book is out of print. At the time of this writing it is in
excess of a $6 *trillion* problem. It is the national debt. No

one knows what the national debt will be at time you read this, but it is still probably going to be the biggest economic problem of that time.

About three quarters of the national debt is in the form of U.S. Treasury bills, notes, and bonds. The remainder is primarily in U.S. Savings Bonds. There has never been a time in history when a country has faced this amount of debt. Because it is unprecedented, no one can predict what will happen. A standard formula for selling a lot of books today is to write a "doom and gloom" scenario, that the U.S. government debt ultimately causes total economic collapse. On the other hand, some economists point out that in spite of the size of the deficit, it is shrinking as a percentage of the gross domestic product. Everyone agrees that if the elected *public servants* in the U.S. government could control spending costs, they could reduce the deficit and ultimately solve the problem. However, an inherent conflict of interest puts most elected officials in a position where their political future depends on pleasing their constituents rather than the whole body. Not until both the elected and the electorate realize that their futures depend on solving macroeconomic problems, not just micro ones, will real progress be made in reducing the deficit.

There are only two ways to reduce this deficit, and both of them are unpopular—raise taxes and reduce spending. To date the problem has been compounded because every time tax revenues have increased, spending has increased at about the same rate. Politicians are not much different from most everyone else. There is always something else they need to buy, or another project to fund, whenever the money is there. What is desperately needed to confront this problem is fiscally responsible elected representatives. No real progress is likely to be made toward reducing the government deficit until our elected public servants can fight as vehemently for the common good as they do for the good of their own constituents.

The national deficit creates economic problems because all other bond issuers—corporations, municipalities, or even foreign governments—must compete with the U.S. government for investors' dollars. So, if the government must raise interest rates to attract investors to buy Treasury bonds, then all other bond issuers must raise their rates to remain competitive. There is a legitimate concern that the deficit could grow larger than the potential pool of investors. In other words, there simply won't be enough investors who will want to put their money in government bonds to finance the debt. Also, many economic analysts are concerned that the U.S. government will have to raise interest rates to such high levels in order to attract enough investors to fund this debt that other competitors for these investors' dollars, such as state or local government agencies or corporations, could be forced into bankruptcy by having to pay much higher rates of interest on their debt.

All investors should be very concerned that those responsible for managing the debt do their job. The solutions to the problem are deceptively simple, and as a result many of those responsible for government spending do not take the situation as seriously as they should. So, this has turned a relatively small problem into an extremely large problem, likely to extend into future generations. Let's hope that rational judgment will be able to diffuse it before it becomes a catastrophe. This problem will be solved either by greater fiscal responsibility or by great economic hardship.

Do You Know What You Need to Know?

To check up on what you learned from this chapter, answer the following questions in your own words, then compare your answers with the answer key.

1. How does *fundamental analysis* differ from *technical analysis?* How is each approach helpful to investors?
2. In spite of the fact that the stock market is described as having the best inflation-adjusted rate of return, why does high inflation usually have a negative impact on securities prices? What is a recession, and what are its effects on securities markets?
3. Explain the Industrial Life Cycle. At which stage of the life cycle would investors be most likely to see the greatest amount of growth? Name some industries or companies that would currently fit each phase of this cycle.
4. How is the measurement of money supply recorded? What is the significance of money supply to economic cycles and to the securities markets?
5. How does the Federal Reserve Board control the growth of the economy? What are its main inflation-fighting techniques and tools?
6. What is the difference between nominal Gross Domestic Product (GDP) and Real GDP? Explain the GDP deflator. What is the significance of the GDP as an inflation monitor?
7. Why is the consumer price index (CPI) referred to as the cost-of-living index? What is its relationship to other inflation measurements, such as the PPI, LEI, and the CRB?
8. What is the effect of the national debt on interest rates and on inflation? How large is the current national debt? If the average rate of interest paid on the national debt is 5 percent, how much do interest payments alone add to the total debt each year?

Answer Key

1. Fundamental analysis is the methodology used to predict market expectations based on future earnings. Technical analysis is designed to do the same using supply and demand indicators. Fundamental analysis will help you determine what to invest in; technical analysis, when to invest in it.

2. High inflation—that is, rising prices—generally portends lower corporate earnings. A recession—two successive quarters of declining GDP—generally means less consumption and less production. Both are bad for most equity markets. Most investors want growth without higher prices, that is, a rising GDP and stable CPI.

3. The three stages of the Industrial Life Cycle are: (1) development, (2) marketing, and (3) competition. The most growth generally comes during the second phase.

4. The Federal Reserve measures money supply using a three-tiered method based on levels of liquidity. M1 measures coins and currency in circulation, checking and savings accounts, and travelers' checks. M2 is equal to the total of M1 plus most money market funds, CDs, and treasury bills. M3 is M2 plus institutional money funds and jumbo CDs over $100,000. There is also a fourth measure of money supply, L, which includes M3 plus other government securities such as savings bonds and treasury notes.

5. The Federal Reserve regulates the growth of the economy primarily by using three methods of regulating the availability of credit. The highest profile of these methods is setting the Discount Rate, to which most other lending rates are pegged, and regulating bank cash reserves through "open market operations." The Federal

Open Market Committee (FOMC) can require member banks to buy or sell U.S. government bonds, thus expanding or depleting bank cash reserves. Also, the Federal Reserve has the power to regulate bank reserve requirements, that is, the percentage of a bank's deposits that it must keep on hand.

6. Gross Domestic Product is the total output of all goods and services in a country. It is the broadest measure of inflation. Real GDP is computed by adjusting the actual GDP numbers for price increases. This adjustment is expressed in percentage form as the GDP Deflator.

7. The Consumer Price Index is the relative price change of a market basket of goods and services. It is called the cost-of-living index because many government and private compensation and retirement benefits are pegged to the CPI. Other inflation indicators—the PPI, LEI, and CRB—are forecasters of the CPI.

8. The total national debt is about $7 trillion. Because the government refinances much of this debt each year, it competes with other bond issuers for investors' dollars. Thus, if the government must raise interest rates to attract more investors to its bonds, all other bond issuers must do the same. Five percent of $7 trillion is $300 billion.

If you want to be a good student of the stock market,
you must first be a good student of interest rates.

Chapter 7

What Is Technical Analysis?

As previously stated, **technical analysis involves methods of studying indicators that are intended to predict whether the supply of shares of stock that will be offered for sale will be satisfied by the expected demand for those shares. A "pure technician" is one who doesn't care what a company's future earnings may be.** This type of analyst would only be concerned with interpreting chart patterns and other supply-and-demand-related indicators. Most analysts, however, are not really "pure technicians," even if they claim to be technical analysts. They are usually somewhat eclectic. Most technical analysts would admit they take into account the earnings forecasts for a company as well as their own technical indicators.

Most investors use fundamental analysis to select *what* **to invest in and use technical analysis to help them decide** *when* **to invest in it. Technical analysis is most valuable for offering guidelines on investment timing.** In addition to some typical methods of technical analysis, some mechanical market-timing techniques will be discussed at the end of the chapter.

"Market efficiency" is the term used to describe the concept that the market, and the price of any stock at any time, is always fully valued. In other words, the market is always selling at exactly the right price at any

given time. The market continually and quickly adjusts to reflect all of the factors that would go into evaluating the price of any security. Market efficiency is one of the main criticisms of technical analysis. It implies that there is no such thing as an undervalued or overvalued investment, since the price of all securities would be fully valued all the time. Technical analysts, however, would point out that though a security may be fully valued at any point in time, that value will change as circumstances change in the future.

Some critics of technical analysis take the extreme approach of market efficiency and have proposed what is called the random walk hypothesis. **The "random walk hypothesis" states that the direction of any particular stock is no more predictable than the steps of a drunken man. Just as there is no logical way to predict where a drunk's next step will fall, there is no basis for predicting where the price of any given security is going.** Whether the market truly follows a random walk or a predictable path is a debate that will probably never be solved to the complete satisfaction of all concerned. However, you can draw your own conclusions from these descriptions of some of the methods of technical analysis.

Technical analysis can be separated into three areas of study: charts, supply and demand factors, and contrarian indicators. Probably most people associate technical analysis with the study of charts. Interpreting chart patterns, however, is one of the most difficult areas to understand because every technical analyst will have a slightly different method of interpreting charts. A few standard methods will be discussed next.

How Do You Read Stock Charts?

The most commonly used chart pattern for stocks is the bar chart. It consists of a vertical line showing the range of the stock's price for that day, with a small horizontal mark to show where the stock closed. A mere glance at a bar chart will often reveal a normal trading range for a stock. The line that you could draw along the bottom of the range is called the support level, and the line along the top would be the resistance level. Illustration 7.1 is an example of a typical support and resistance range.

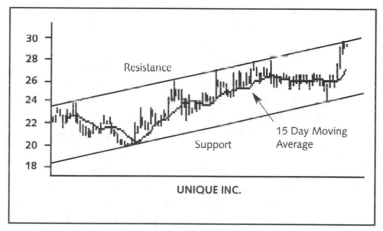

Illustration 7.1

The "channel" is that area of the chart between the support level and the resistance level. Usually, stocks will trade within a channel that will be running up, down, or sideways. **An upward channel would be a bullish indicator, a downward channel bearish, and a sideways channel neutral.** To a technical analyst, the best investment to buy would be a stock that is trading in a channel running sharply upward and is currently trading near the low end of that channel. If a stock is trading in an upward channel, it would be hitting higher new highs and higher lows following each pullback. Probably the type of chart pattern that would scare most technical analysts away would be one in which there are no discernible patterns, no channel showing a normal trading range for the stock. Of course, a stock that is trading all over the place would probably scare away more than just the technical analysts.

To a technician the channel in which a stock trades represents the price at which there is overhanging "supply," the resistance level, and pent-up "demand," the support level. In fact, you may even hear the terms demand and supply lines used to describe the support and resistance levels. **A short-term sideways channel would be called a "consolidation period."** This would mean that the price of the stock had run up to an area of resistance, and the stock isn't likely to go any higher until enough buyers move in to reduce the oversupply of stock at that level.

Support and resistance levels are open to some interpretation by different technical analysts, but generally most chartists would agree at least in general terms where the support and resistance levels would be. There can be major disagreements, however, between chartists on other esoteric areas of interpretation. You will hear some chartists talk about flag formations, pennant patterns, head and shoulder patterns, tea cups with handles, and so on. These are simply chart patterns that can be interpreted differently by different chartists, and they do not lend themselves to universal interpretation. Most chartists would admit that reading patterns is an art, not a science.

Some basic rules, however, are generally accepted. If a stock had been trading in a sideways channel and it finally trades over its resistance level, most chartists would then say that would be a buy signal and that the stock should now establish a new trading range within the bounds of a new channel moving upward. The same rule would apply if a stock's price goes below a support level. A chartist would consider that a sell signal. Many times you will notice that once a stock hits a new high, it continues briefly moving upward. Technical analysts might say that proves their theory. Their critics might say this proves that enough chartists are following these guidelines so as to drive the price of the stock up themselves, so this is nothing more than a self-fulfilling prophecy.

Also, to most chartists, it is very important that any gaps be filled. **A "gap" in a chart is created when a stock opens at a price well away from the previous closing price and never goes back to trade at that price—to "fill the gap."** A gap like this can happen overnight, the difference between the previous day's closing price and the next day's opening price, or it can happen when trading is halted on the stock because of some pending news announcement or development that radically changes the current status of the company. Gaps can occur either when the stock goes higher or lower. Most chartists would say that trading gaps need to be filled, either the stock must come down to fill a breakaway gap or move back up to fill a panic gap.

Bar charts will also usually contain a "moving average." A 200-day moving average is the arithmetic average of all the closing prices over the last 200 days. So, at the end of each trading day, that day's closing price will be added to the average, and the first price on that list, which would now be 201 days back, will be dropped. Because of the speed of home computers today, anyone can generate almost any moving average they want on any stock. Two hundred days would represent 40 weeks, or almost one year. That would be a standard measure for a long-term moving average. A 15-day moving average would represent three weeks, a standard short-term moving average.

A common interpretation of moving averages is that when the short-term average crosses the long-term, a trend reversal is forecast. In other words, if the long-term average had been moving downward, but the short-term average just went above it, then many chartists would say that signals the long-term average will now begin moving upward. That would be a buy signal. The short-term average crossing below the long-term average would be a sell signal.

In addition to bar charts, point and figure charts are very popular with technical analysts. **A "point and figure chart" is one in which an "x" is made on a grid every time a stock moves up one point and an "o" is made every time it moves down a point. The point and figure chart is not organized on the basis of serial time.** Whether it takes the stock one hour or one week to move up a point will not be reflected on the chart. The chart will only show that the stock moved up one point. The days of the month are recorded on the point and figure charts to give the reader some reference point for determining how long it takes the stock to move. The purpose of the point and figure chart, however, is to clarify a trend without concern about how long that trend will be, or has been, in effect.

Technical analysts are often referred to as chartists, but there are many other technical indicators that are just as important.

What Are Some Other Technical Indicators?

Perhaps one of the most popular technical indicators used today is the Put/Call Ratio. The meanings of the terms "put and call" will be discussed in detail in Chapter 9, but they represent contracts to sell or to buy a particular security or market index. A put contract gives the owner of that contract the right to sell a certain amount of a security or index at a specified price within a given period of time. A call contract, on the other hand, gives the owner the right to purchase a certain amount of a security or index at a specified price within a given period of time.

The owner of a call contract will make money on that contract if the price of the underlying security rises. If an investor owns the right to purchase a stock at 30 and the price of the stock goes to 40, the value of that call option will be worth at least 10 points. The higher the price of the security rises, the more the call contract will be worth. The put owner, on the other hand, will make money if the underlying security drops in value. Since a put holder owns the right to sell a security at a set price, if the value of that security drops, the put becomes more valuable. The right to sell a stock at 30 will be worth at least 10 points if the price of the stock drops from 30 to 20. The more the stock drops, the more valuable that put contract will become.

Technical analysts use this ratio differently; however, generally the Put/Call Ratio is simply the total number of puts that investors have purchased on any given trading day divided by the number of calls purchased on that same day. Usually this ratio is around 0.70-to-0.75. That means that there are usually about 70 to 75 percent as many put contracts purchased as there are call contracts. Usually, more investors expect the equities markets to go higher than to go lower. A number below 70 percent would mean that there was a larger number of call contracts than usual bought on that day. A number above 75 percent would indicate that there was a larger number of put contracts bought than normal. These numbers usually are smoothed out by a moving average, such as a ten-day moving average. That eliminates the difficult-to-interpret daily spikes in the ratio.

The Put/Call Ratio usually is considered to be a contrarian market indicator. If the ratio rises above normal expectations, that would be a bearish indicator. If the number is below normal, it is bullish. Although most investors may not have much interest in Put/Call Ratios themselves, this is the number that is usually used to report on market sentiment. If you read or hear a business reporter mention that the technical indicators are forecasting a bullish market sentiment, they are likely basing that on their Put/Call Ratio indicator.

Other technical indicators deal more obviously with supply and demand factors. Volume ratios, breadth of market ratios, and the tick figure are typical technical indicators with a more logical relationship to supply and demand than chart interpretation.

"Volume ratios" indicate the total volume of shares that traded at a higher closing price than the previous day's close and the number of shares that traded at a lower closing price. So, if there were more shares traded at prices that were going up than at prices that were going down, a technician would consider that a bullish indicator. Here the relationship to supply and demand factors is obvious. If buyers are more aggressive and willing to pay higher prices for a stock, then demand is high. Vice versa, if total volume is higher on stocks whose price is dropping, then demand is down and supply looks as if it is increasing.

The *breadth of market* is an indicator that compares the number of issues that are higher versus the number of issues that are lower. This is different from volume indicators, which measure the number of shares. **"Breadth of market" indicators, also called the advance-decline line, compare the total number of different companies that are up to the total number of companies that are down.** For example, considering all the companies on the NYSE, if 1,257 closed at a higher price than the previous day's close, 604 companies were lower, and 320 were unchanged, you might hear this reported as, "Stocks were 2-to-1 on the upside today." A technical analyst would obviously consider this a bullish indicator.

The tick figure is used as a very short-term indicator of the market's direction. One tick, as you will recall, is the smallest unit at which a stock's price will change—usually ⅛th of a point. **Throughout the trading day, computers will record which stocks traded on an up-tick and subtract the ones that traded on a down-tick. The net result is the "tick figure."** A tick figure that moves to a large plus number, such as +300, would indicate that the market is turning bullish, at least for the immediate trading session. A negative figure, such as –300, would indicate a bearish market.

The total number of different technical indicators could probably never be calculated. Every technician attempts to formulate his or her own unique approach, looking for that magic formula that will always forecast the direction of the stock market. The motivation for this never-ending search is not only to make money by predicting the market, but also to make money by selling more newsletters and books.

Insider trading sentiment is probably one of the most popular of these indicators. It is the net number of insiders who purchase shares of stock versus the number who sell. Insiders generally must register their transactions with the SEC. Keep in mind that insiders could be institutional investors, as well as employees or affiliates of a company. Also, the historic relationship between dividend yields and money market rates has become frequently mentioned in recent years. Market price to book value, dividend payout ratios, and the relationship between PE ratios and earnings growth projections are other common indicators taken from financial statements. These, however, begin to infringe on fundamental analysis.

What Is a Contrarian, and Should You Be One?

If you remember the section "How Do You Know When to Buy and Sell?" in Chapter 1, you will probably anticipate the answer to this question. Yes, you should be a *contrarian*. **A "contrarian" is likely to be an investor who is buying when the majority is selling and who is selling when the majority is buying.** That is a good position in which to be. The contrarian indicators that will be discussed in this section are the mutual fund liquidity theory, the short interest ratio, and the odd lot trading indicator.

The "mutual fund liquidity theory" measures the percentage of mutual fund assets that are not invested in equities, but are kept in money market funds. At first glance one would probably draw the conclusion that if mutual fund managers are not investing a large percentage of their fund's assets, then they must have a very bearish outlook on the market. So, the logical conclusion to high mutual fund liquidity would be that this represents a bearish outlook. However, it is a contrarian indicator. To a technical analyst, the higher the percentage of mutual fund liquidity, the more bullish the indicator. The reason this would be a bullish indicator lies in the basis for all technical indicators—supply and demand. To a technician, the more investments mutual fund managers have in cash, such as money market funds or Treasury bills, the more money they have that is going to be invested some time in the future. So, it simply means that high mutual fund liquidity represents pent-up demand.

The "short interest ratio" operates on the same premise. Short interest **is the percentage of the outstanding shares of stock that have been sold short.** The short interest on most major companies is reported weekly in *The Wall Street Journal* and in *Barron's*. If a large percentage of a company's shares have been sold short, you would assume that a large number of speculators believe that the stock is going lower. Logically, this sounds like a bearish indicator. A short seller, if you remember, would make money when the stock dropped. To a technician, however, this is a contrary indicator, and a high short interest would be a bullish indicator. The rationale is that the more speculators who have sold a stock short, the more investors there are who will have to be buyers of that stock in the near future. The short sellers arc all going to have to cover their short sales. So, like high mutual fund liquidity, high short interest also represents built in demand for that stock.

The third contrarian indicator is **the "odd lot trading theory."** In Chapter 1, an odd lot was defined as a block of stock less than 100 shares. One hundred shares represent a *round lot*, which is the most common increment for trading. This theory has already been disproved by more than one study. Nevertheless, it is still one of the staples of technical analysis. **The theory states that an increased number of odd lot buying on a stock would be a bearish indicator, and an increased number of odd lot selling would be a bullish indicator.** The basis for this theory is that the small investor is usually wrong. Small investors usually trade in odd lots because they don't have enough money to buy a round lot.

The New York Stock Exchange recently commissioned a study of small investor trading, and their study disproved the odd lot trading theory. In fact, the study showed that the small investors were correct in their investment decisions more frequently than institutional investors were.

How Do You Use Market Timing Techniques?

There are two basic market timing techniques used by some investors: dollar cost averaging and fixed

amount investing. If you are investing in individual stocks, these timing techniques may not be practical for most individual investors. These plans, however, can be very useful for timing mutual fund investments. Mutual funds will be explained in detail in the next chapter. They are professionally managed portfolios of securities.

"Dollar cost averaging" is a strategy of investing the same dollar amount in the same investment at fixed time intervals. Investors usually have the option of investing in mutual funds in relatively small dollar amounts. So, sometimes they will make an agreement with a fund to send in a fixed dollar amount every month to that fund. This adds discipline to their savings strategy, but it also could help the investor establish a better cost basis for the fund. Illustration 7.2 demonstrates the benefits of this strategy.

Dollar Cost Averaging			
Date	Price per Share	Number of Shares	Amount of Investment
1/30	$10.00	100.00	$1,000
2/28	$9.50	10.53	$ 100
3/31	$8.75	11.43	$ 100
4/30	$7.25	13.79	$ 100
5/31	$7.50	13.33	$ 100
6/30	$8.00	12.50	$ 100
7/31	$8.125	12.31	$ 100
8/31	$8.50	11.76	$ 100
9/30	$9.375	10.67	$ 100
10/31	$10.00	10.00	$ 100
11/30	$10.50	9.52	$ 100
Totals	$9.375 (avg.)	215.84	$ 2,000

Illustration 7.2

In this example, the individual invested $1,000 initially and added $100 per month over the next ten months, making a total investment $2,000. If, however, the individual had originally put in the whole $2,000, rather than invest half of that amount and cost averaged the other half, he or she would have had a total of 200 shares at $10 per share. Then, as the price of the shares declined, the shareholder probably would have been very worried. At the lowest point in this price decline, 4/30, the $2,000 investment would have had a market value of $1,450 (200 × $7.25). That $550 decline in market value would represent a 27.5 percent loss if sold. But by cost averaging, in this scenario the investor ended up purchasing a total of 215.84 shares, at an average price of $9.375. Because of the price decline after the initial purchase, the investor in this case benefited by cost averaging. That strategy reduced the price per share and increased the number of shares.

When you send in a fixed dollar amount every month, you will buy fewer shares when the price of the shares goes up and more shares when the price goes down. So you end up dollar cost averaging your price per share. If the investment goes through a down cycle, you will be buying more shares while it is down, reducing your average cost per share over that time. If it goes up, you will be buying fewer shares at the higher price. You should note that if the price of the investment had only gone up after the initial purchase, you would have ended up cost averaging a higher price per share. But, of course, you would still be profitable.

"Fixed amount investing" is simply the strategy of keeping a constant dollar amount invested at certain time intervals, such as six months or a year. Using this strategy, you would *sell* shares if the total amount of the investment went over the original amount you put in, and you would *buy* more shares if it went down. For example, consider that you invested $25,000 in a mutual fund. When you review the fund at the end of the year, you find its value has risen to $28,000. So, you sell $3,000 worth of the fund, leaving in only the original amount of your investment. If your original $25,000 dropped to $22,000, you would add $3,000 to the fund, buying new shares at a lower price.

A variation of fixed amount investing is fixed ratio investing. This is a strategy often used by institutional investors to keep the same ratio of stocks to bonds in a portfolio at all times. Typically, someone who uses a fixed ratio investing strategy will keep 50 percent of his or her investment capital in stocks and 50 percent in bonds. If the stock portion of the portfolio rises, he or she will sell stocks and buy bonds to keep the ratio at 50–50. Vice versa, if the stock portion drops, the investor would sell bonds and buy stocks to keep the 50–50 mix.

Do You Know What You Need to Know?

To check up on what you learned from this chapter, answer the following questions in your own words, then compare your answers with the answer key.

1. What is the main focus of technical analysis? Why?
2. Explain market efficiency random walk theory? Why does the concept of an efficient market cause some to become random walk theorists?
3. What does a chart of security prices reveal about how supply and demand factors affect prices? Explain what causes resistance and support lines.
4. How is a *moving average* computed and why is it important to a chartist?
5. Describe a point and figure chart. How does this type of chart clarify trends? How does it differ from bar charts?

6. Describe three contrarian indicators. Why are they called contrarian and what is their relationship to supply and demand?

7. If an investor is trying to decide whether to invest the whole amount that he or she has available now or to "dollar cost average," what would have to happen to the price of the investment in order for the individual to benefit from averaging?

8. How does fixed amount investing and fixed ratio investing attempt to improve investor timing? What are the drawbacks of this type of investing to most individual investors?

Answer Key

1. All technical analysis has its roots in forecasting market prices based on supply and demand indicators.

2. Market efficiency means that the market, at all times, represents the fair price that investors assign to any investment based on all the available information at that time. The random walk theory states that the future course of the market is unpredictable. Pure random walk theorists would say that there is no cause-and-effect relationship between market prices and economic indicators.

3. Support lines on a chart are sometimes called demand lines; resistance lines are sometimes called supply lines. Those price areas indicate where, in the past, investors have shown increased demand for a stock or have increased the supply due to an influx of sellers.

4. A moving average is the average of the closing prices of a stock over a given period of time. A short-term moving average may cover 10 days; a long-term average, 100 days. Different technical analysts use different averages. The significance to a chartist is that when the short-term line moves above or below the long-term line, it will be a bullish or a bearish indicator.

5. Point and figure charts use an "x" to mark every time a stock moves up one full point and an "o" every time it moves down one point, regardless of how long it takes to make that move. It is generally used to indicate long-term trends.

6. The contrarian indicators mentioned in this chapter are the mutual fund liquidity theory, short interest ratio, and the odd lot trading theory. They are called contrarian indicators because, while they would seem to indicate one thing logically, they indicate the opposite thing to a supply and demand theorist.

7. The only way that an individual who invests using a dollar cost averaging approach will benefit from that strategy is if the price of the investment declines.

8. Fixed amount and fixed ratio investing involves keeping a set amount in one investment and the same amount or ratio in another. The investor will sell enough of one investment when it goes up and buy the one that has the lower amount or ratio to maintain the predetermined mix. For individual investors, the main drawback to this type of disciplined strategy is the fees for such frequent transactions.

Technical analysis will help you determine when to buy.

— Chapter 8 —

What Is a Mutual Fund?

In recent years the popularity of mutual funds has skyrocketed. The number of mutual funds has grown from about 500 two decades ago to about 11,000 today. The mutual fund quotation section of *Barron's*, which took up a little over one page back then, has expanded to nearly 30 *full* pages today. Looking at this another way, you could say that probably only about one out of every 20 mutual fund portfolio managers working now has been managing a fund for over 20 years.

The effect of this mushrooming growth has been to turn many *individual* investors into *institutional* investors. The growth of mutual funds accounts is a major reason why the number of investors in corporate stocks has not been growing at the same pace as the amount of shares being traded. To understand what a mutual fund is, you must first understand the meaning of the broader term *investment company*.

An "investment company" is a company whose sole business is to make investment decisions regarding funds that have been entrusted to it by other investors. One of the main differences between an investment company and a corporation is that in order to qualify as an investment company it must pass through at least 90 percent of the net income and capital gains it receives from its investments to its shareholders. By so doing, it qualifies under Subchapter M of the Internal Revenue Code to be exempt from paying income tax as a corporation. The taxes on the income and capital gains that the investment company makes from its portfolio are paid only by the shareholders who receive the distributions.

Since one of the main differences between investment companies and other companies is their tax status, you should note that dividends paid to investors by corporations that are not investment companies are subject to double taxation. The corporation pays taxes on its net income, then the shareholders pay taxes again on the portion of the company's earnings they receive as dividends. Some legislators and shareholders' rights groups periodically bring to public awareness the inequity of having the same dollar in earnings taxed twice, but so far these campaigns have always come to naught. It remains a legal quandary in the tax structure that has never been rectified.

Investment companies fall into two categories: open-end funds and closed-end funds. A "mutual fund" is a regular open-end investment company. It is called open-end because it has an unlimited number of shares that it can issue. So, its capital structure is open ended. Its total capitalization and number of shares outstanding can change daily. **A "closed-end fund," on the other hand, has a fixed number of shares that it is authorized to issue, and thus has a relatively fixed capitalization. Shares of closed-end funds are classified as "shares of beneficial interest," or SBI, as opposed to the common shares issued by corporations.** Closed-end funds trade on an exchange or on the over-the-counter market, and their price is subject to supply and demand fluctuations like common stock. An open-end mutual fund, however, may be redeemed anytime at the fund's closing *net asset value.* **The "net asset value" (NAV) is the total market value of the investments held by the fund, divided by the total number of shares outstanding.** In other words, it is the value of the fund expressed on a per share basis, net of any fees.

A few mutual funds have amended their charter to limit new investments in the fund only to investors who already own shares. This is usually motivated by a desire to keep the size of the fund within a more predictible limit. The management of the fund might feel that their success could cause too many new investors to purchase additional shares. This could stretch management's resources beyond their ability to handle the fund effectively. Such a move does accomplish that objective without jeopardizing their status as an open-end investment company. Funds that limit new investments to existing shareholders only will probably be able to maintain a much more stable capitalization than those funds that do not.

The share price of a regular mutual fund will always be expressed as the net asset value. The NAV is computed on the daily *closing* prices of the investments in the fund. So, when you invest in a mutual fund, the price you pay for your shares will be the net asset value computed at the *closing price* of the fund on the day you entered the order. The NAV price that appears in the morning newspaper is computed on the previous day's closing prices. You will also have to pay any fees associated with purchasing shares of the fund. The fees, or load, charged when you invest in mutual funds will be discussed next.

What Does It Cost to Buy Mutual Funds?

Although there have been several attempts made in the past to regulate the costs of investing in mutual funds, none of them has resulted in empowering the Securities and Exchange Commission with such controls. However, greater volume and keener competition has brought the fees down considerably from what they were a decade ago. The mutual fund industry is another example of how a competitive free enterprise economy, rather than government intervention, results in price benefits to the consumer. Today, every fund is fully aware that in order to attract new investors it must offer a competitive product at a competitive price.

Past mutual fund performance records are reported quarterly by Lipper Analytical Services Inc., and the raw data from the Lipper Report is processed by nearly every major financial periodical. So, whether you read *Barron's*, *Business Week*, *Money*, *Forbes*, *Fortune*, or any other financial periodical, you will be able to read articles on a regular basis about mutual fund performance records. Since higher fees will lower the total returns reported by the funds, this exposure of their performance generally has the effect of keeping the fees low. Also, the Morningstar Mutual Fund Rating Service is broadly available in libraries and brokerage offices and over on-line computer data bases. This service gives a complete and thorough disclosure of all fees charged by the funds. Funds are also rated and evaluated by Weisenberger & Co., but this research material is available only to subscribers.

In addition to these rating services, mutual funds must provide prospectuses to all investors. The prospectus, like the one for all new issues in the primary market, must represent full disclosure of the fund's business, including fees and expenses. Funds must provide a prospectus to all investors as a result of the Investment Company Act of 1940. Since mutual funds have an unlimited number of authorized shares, every share they issue is defined as being a *primary* (new issue) share. This legal definition was a result of the Investment Company Act. As with all other primary shares, all advertisements for mutual funds must contain the disclaimer that solicitation for shares is by prospectus only and must advise potential investors to read the prospectus carefully before investing.

The fee charged for investing in a mutual fund, as you already know, **is called a "load."** On the basis of the fee structure, funds will either be classified as front-end load, back-end load, or no-load. **A front-end load fund is one that charges a fee when the investor purchases shares.** This fee is expressed as a percentage of the net asset value. A typical front-end load fund may charge 4.5 percent when you invest in it. However, this fee may range anywhere from 1 percent to 8.5 percent. Read the prospectus carefully before investing. The front-end fee structure will also have breakpoints, that reduce the amount of the load if you invest larger amounts. Typically, breakpoints will follow a scale like the one shown in Illustration 8.2. Different funds will have different breakpoints. So, if you plan on investing a large amount of money in a mutual fund, check into the breakpoint structure.

Typical Commission Breakpoints	
up to $25,000	4.50 %
over $25,000	4.00 %
over $50,000	3.50 %
over $100,000	3.00 %
over $250,000	2.50 %
over $500,000	2.00 %
over $1,000,000	1.00 %

Illustration 8.2

Also, if you plan on investing in a mutual fund on a regular basis, such as by sending in a check each month as a disciplined savings plan, you can file a *letter of intent* (LOI) when you initially invest in a fund. An LOI will typically be included as part of the application for a mutual fund, that you will usually find in the back of the prospectus. If your letter of intent, sometimes worded "statement of intent," specifies that you will be investing a total amount that would go over a breakpoint within the coming year, then you will be charged the lower fees on each of your purchases, even though no single investment exceeded a breakpoint. For example, if you invest $15,000 in a fund and plan to send in an additional $1,000 each month, you could specify by LOI that you intend to invest over $25,000 over the next 12 months, and you would be charged 4 percent on each purchase, rather than the 4.5 percent that would normally be charged for investments under $25,000. In most cases a letter of intent can be backdated up to 30 days after your initial purchase. Also, if you fail to meet the breakpoint you specified by the end of one year, the mutual fund will deduct shares from your fund in order to make up the difference between what you paid in fees and what you should have paid.

The mutual fund quotation section of a newspaper will usually show the net asset value for the fund, based on the previous day's closing prices, and the offering price. The offering price will simply be the NAV plus the *maximum* load that that fund would charge. If you were to purchase enough shares to exceed a breakpoint for that fund, you will pay a price less than the offering price listed in the newspaper. This price per share would be computed by adding the lower fees charged by going over a breakpoint to the NAV. If the fund is a back-end load or no-load fund, the offer price column will show NL. Daily mutual fund quotes may also include other information, such as year to date net asset value change or historical rates of return.

A "back-end load fund" is one that charges no front-end load but that charges a fee if the shares are redeemed within a specified period of time. The technical term for this type of fee structure is "contingent deferred sales charge." A typical back-end load fund may charge 5 percent if you redeem any or all shares within the first year of your initial purchase. Then the fee would decline to 4 percent in the second year, 3 percent in the third, 2 percent in the fourth, 1 percent in the fifth year, and no charge for any redemption after that. Different back-end load funds will have different fee structures. So, again, read the prospectus to find out the specific fees for the fund you are considering.

Many mutual fund families today offer different classes of shares on the same fund, with each class representing a different fee structure. Typically, Class A shares will be subject to a regular front-end load, Class B shares will be back-end load, and Class C shares will be no-load. Also, investors will usually have the option of switching between other mutual funds at net asset value within the same fund family for a small transfer fee, or for no fee at all. However, investors should realize that if they switch funds, they should stay within the same class of shares. Investors could not, for example, invest in Class B shares that charge no front-end load but would charge for early redemption, and then switch to Class A shares that have no redemption fees, in order to avoid paying the regular front-end fees of the Class A shares. If you invest in Class B shares of one fund and then switch to Class B shares of another fund within the same family, the holding period for redemption fees will be carried over from the original investment. Investors do not have to begin a new holding period at the time of the switch.

A "no-load fund" will not charge any fees for investing in it, and usually it will not charge any fees for redemption. Some no-load funds, however, do charge a fee if you redeem the shares within a short period of time, such as six months or one year, of your initial purchase. This fee was initiated to curb the high turnover from short-term traders trying to use the no-load fund as a surrogate for playing relatively small market swings. This practice by no-load fund speculators can play havoc with the fund managers' strategies and goals.

After reading these fund descriptions, most potential mutual fund investors start wondering why anyone would select a load fund over a no-load fund. Why would anyone choose to pay fees if they had an option not to? The answer to that question becomes clearer, however, when they realize that the selection process has one more step involving fees and expenses. Mutual funds are a business, not a charity, and you should realize that investment companies are going to be making money somehow. If they are not making money on the load, they must be making up for it somewhere else. So, some no-load funds make up for not charging a front-end load by charging higher annual administrative and operating expense fees. Such fees vary widely between funds, but typically a no-load fund will charge between 0.25 percent and 1.5 percent in administrative and operating expenses. A front-end load fund, on the other hand, will usually charge significantly lower annual fees. It is difficult to broadly categorize the expenses of all funds, but you will frequently see front-end funds charging .25 percent to .75 percent annually.

To put this in perspective, if you bought a no-load fund that charges 1.5 percent in annual expenses, you would pay 15 percent to own that fund for ten years. Whereas, if you bought a 4.5 percent front-end load fund that charges .5 percent in annual expenses, your total cost of owning that fund for ten years would be 9.5 percent. Over that period of time, that represents a significantly higher expense for owning a no-load fund versus owning a front-end load fund. In this example, an additional 5.5 percent of your investment capital went to the mutual fund manager of the no-load fund and was *not* invested in securities.

Many investment companies now offer no-load mutual funds exclusively. This is by far the fastest growing area of mutual funds. For a fund to be called "no-load," the NASD requires that it charge no more than 0.25 percent in annual sales fees. However, as you just learned, there are many other types of fees that funds can charge that are not classified as "sales fees." No-load fund families are allowed to charge other fees to recoup administrative and operating expenses and other overhead. Such costs vary widely from fund to fund. Many, however, charge total annual fees well below the 1.5 percent used in the previous illustration.

So, in conclusion, read the prospectus and at least one other analytical report, such as *Morningstar* or *Value Line,* on the fund's expenses if you want a true picture of what owning that fund is going to cost you. More important than the expenses, however, select a fund with a consistently above-average total return. Although "past performance is no guarantee of future results," that performance does represent a track record for evaluating management. If the management of the fund has done well in a variety of market situations in the past, that management is likely to continue to do well in the future.

What Types of Mutual Funds Are Available?

All of the mutual funds that are managed by one company are called a "family of funds." Most *families* organize the list of the funds they manage from their most conservative to their most speculative. Typically, a family of funds might contain a money market fund, a U.S. government bond fund, a corporate bond fund, a global bond fund, a high-yield (or junk) bond fund, a balanced fund of stocks and bonds, a Blue Chip stock fund, a mid-cap fund, a sector fund, a leverage fund, a foreign stock fund, and small-cap and/or growth funds.

Money market funds are brokerage account surrogates for bank savings accounts. **The primary investment in these funds is commercial paper, that is short-term unsecured corporate bonds and U.S. Treasury bills.** These money market funds usually price each share at $1.00, and since there is little or no credit risk to these instruments and they are very short term, the share price should never deviate from $1.00. Most brokerage firms as well as mutual fund managers offer money market funds with no load and very low annual expenses.

Money market funds were designed by brokerage firms to be a competitive alternative to bank savings accounts. Because money market funds encroach on bank accounts, and because banks started offering mutual funds to their customers around the same time as money market funds were becoming popular, recent legislation has blurred the boundaries between the brokerage and the banking industries. The Glass-Steagall Act, which originally clearly defined the boundaries between banks and brokers, has been significantly weakened by legislation over the last decade. Many bank holding companies now own investment company subsidiaries and may participate in most areas of the brokerage business, except for investment banking. Banks are still excluded from participating in the primary (new issue) market. Both brokerage firms and banks now compete as full-service *financial* organizations, with brokerages offering traditional bank account services and banks selling stocks and bonds as well as CDs and checking accounts to their customers.

Mutual fund investors should also be aware that not all fund portfolios will be what they appear to be. In order for a mutual fund to be called a particular type of fund, it need only invest at least 65 percent of its portfolio in that type of investment. For example, a U.S. government bond fund could invest 65 percent of its total assets in U.S. government bonds and the other 35 percent in high-yield (junk) bonds or in foreign bonds. In spite of this portfolio mix, it could still call itself a U.S. government bond fund—with the highest yield available. Now, admittedly most government bond fund managers realize that investors who choose government bonds are very conservative, and they would probably not try such deception. Investors, however, should realize that portfolios are not always what they seem to be and should read the prospectus and current annual report to have a clear understanding of the fund's philosophy.

Stock funds are subject to the same principle—only 65 percent of the fund's assets need be invested in the area specified by the fund. So, a utility stock fund may have only 65 percent of its assets in utilities, a foreign stock fund may have only 65 percent of its portfolio in foreign stocks, and so on. Most funds, however, do keep much more than that minimum required percentage invested in their specified sector.

Another type of stock fund is a leveraged fund. It is called such because it can leverage fund assets to enhance performance. This may be done on margin, as was discussed in Chapter 3, but most of these types of funds use *options* as a means of leverage. Options will be discussed in the next chapter.

A less common type of stock fund is the dual-purpose fund. This is a fund that splits its stock portfolio

into two different classes of shares. One class of shares
gets all the income from the portfolio, but none of the
capital gains. The other class gets the capital gains, but
no income. The chief selling point for dual-purpose funds
is that each class of shareholders has nearly twice as much
invested for either income or gains than they would have
had if there were two funds instead of one. In other words,
the income shareholders received the income on a portfolio
nearly twice as large as the total market value of their
shares, the capital gain shareholders benefited in the same
way. These funds did not prove to be very popular, however,
because one class of shares always got slighted. If the portfolio primarily invested in growth stock, then the growth
class of shares benefited. The income shares, however,
didn't receive very much income, since growth companies
don't usually pay much of a dividend. On the other hand, if
the portfolio invested heavily in companies paying high
dividends, the growth shares didn't receive much growth.

The concept of dual-purpose shares, however, has been
resurrected a few times in recent years with a slight twist.
Some investment banking companies began offering what
amounts to a one-company dual-purpose fund. An investment banker would take a company such as International
Business Machines, General Motors, Exxon, or Philip Morris,
and offer two classes of shares on the one company. One
class of shares would receive all the income from the dividends paid by the company, and another class of shares
would receive all the capital gains. The dividends paid on the
income shares would be much higher than if a shareholder
owned an equivalent market value of shares in the company
itself, and the shareholders of growth shares would receive
greater capital gains than if they owned the company itself.

Shareholders of companies for which dual-purpose
fund shares were available could exchange their existing

shares for new income shares or growth shares. Also, *new* investors could purchase shares specifically designated for income or capital gains. These dual-purpose fund shares have finite terms, and at the time of this publication most of them have been closed. However, it is very likely that this type of investment structure will be revived time and again. The concept of a one-company dual-purpose fund may prove to be more popular than the original. With one-company dual-purpose shares, the investor doesn't have to worry about the portfolio structure. Income shareholders know exactly what their income will be. So, you may see some similar types of dual-purpose funds in the future.

Equity mutual fund portfolios can be distinguished by industry sectors, total capitalization, leverage policy, dual-purpose strategies, or any number of other objectives. The peculiarities of the management strategy for each fund and the cost of owning that mutual fund will be clarified by the prospectus. That is why investors are always cautioned to "read the prospectus carefully before investing or sending money."

Also, mutual fund stock portfolios are frequently described as either *value* or *growth* funds. Those words identify the specific investment philosphy of the portfolio manager. For a **"value fund" the main criterion for selecting investments would be a conservative financial structure.** Value funds would invest in companies with high book values relative to their market price. Well-capitalized companies with large asset bases make good choices for these types of funds. A **"growth fund,"** on the other hand, would be one that **invests primarily in companies selected on the basis of their future earnings growth.** Obviously, growth funds are more speculative than value funds. So, with your own investment objectives in mind, watch for these key words. Make sure that the investment philosophy of the fund you select is consistent with your goals and risk-tolerance levels.

How Do You Select a Mutual Fund?

To select a good mutual fund a common investment strategy is to compare the past performance of all the available funds with similar objectives. Even though (once again) "past performance is no guarantee of future results," a fund's past performance does represent the success or failure of that manager. So, it is a logical assumption that if a manager has done well in the past, the performance could be somewhat similar in the future. This, of course, assumes that the same fund manager is still at the fund; that is frequently not a valid assumption. Fund managers often transfer, get fired, or retire. So, an investor should check to see how long the fund manager has been there.

Usually an investor will choose a fund on the basis of investment objectives. If an investor wants safety of principal and reasonably high income, he may select a government bond fund, for example. If investors' goals emphasize overall growth and they are willing to endure some market volatility, they might select a Blue Chip equity fund or perhaps a balanced fund of both stocks and bonds. If investors are willing to speculate and to assume high risks for potentially high returns, they may choose a small-cap fund or a leveraged fund.

Since past performance is the primary basis upon which investors make their selections, you should note that most mutual funds' performances have been abysmal. In fact, most funds underperform the average rate of return of the overall market that would theoretically be achieved by random selection. Most mutual funds, and other institutional investors for that matter, compare their performance to the Standard & Poor's 500 Index. You may recall that this is the case from the discussion of stock indexes presented in Chapter 1.

The S&P 500 Index theoretically represents what a random selection of stocks would be expected to return; however, for almost any reporting period—one quarter, one year, five years, ten years—fewer than 10 percent of all equity mutual funds will outperform that index. In other words, less than one in ten professionally managed mutual funds actually has shown a better rate of return than would have been hypothetically attained by random selection.

Why can't these *highly paid professional managers* select a portfolio of stocks that would give investors a better rate of return than a portfolio selected by the throw of darts at the quote pages from the business section of the newspaper? This is the unenviable legacy of mutual funds. There has never been a year in which anything close to 50 percent of mutual funds has achieved returns equal to or exceeding the market average. This is overly simplified, but statistically any randomly selected portfolio should be able to beat the overall average at least half of the time. In addition, most people would assume that if *professional managers* are making the portfolio selections, they should be able to beat the average market more than 50 percent of the time.

There are, however, several logical reasons for this poor performance history. First, the S&P 500 is always considered to be fully invested; in other words, this index represents a value that assumes that all the securities in it are fully paid for and that there is no uninvested cash. A mutual fund, on the other hand, must always keep a certain amount of *prudent reserve* in cash (usually a money market fund) to meet withdrawal demands without having to liquidate any securities in its portfolio. So, a fund manager has to do more with less. The manager will have to beat the market average with only perhaps 95 percent of the equity invested in the market.

Secondly, mutual fund managers are vulnerable to the whims of their investors. They are not in control of the amount of capital they have to invest at any given time. New investors may flock to a mutual fund that has had above-average returns. But to the fund manager this possibly means that many of the securities in that fund might be selling at a higher price than the manager would normally want to buy them. The managers may 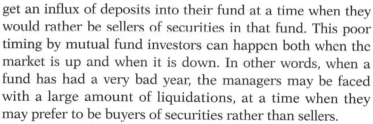 get an influx of deposits into their fund at a time when they would rather be sellers of securities in that fund. This poor timing by mutual fund investors can happen both when the market is up and when it is down. In other words, when a fund has had a very bad year, the managers may be faced with a large amount of liquidations, at a time when they may prefer to be buyers of securities rather than sellers.

Thirdly, the S&P Index is a moving target. If companies in the index are doing very poorly, they will be replaced with companies that are doing better. The index is not static, and changes may be made in the portfolio quite frequently. Now, it is true that mutual funds have this same capability. In fact, most mutual funds would make changes in their portfolio much more frequently than the index. Fund managers may change their portfolio whenever they like—sell the losers and buy some winners. However, you should note the index itself would not show nearly as much growth if the losers were left in it. In other words, the statistics of how well the market has done in the past are improved considerably by changes in the stocks used to represent the historical rate of return.

This discussion of mutual funds has obviously assumed an equity stock portfolio. It is not fair to compare the results of bond portfolios to those of stock portfolios. You should compare the results of funds with similar objectives. In the final analysis, a potential mutual fund investor would be well advised to select funds that have good long-term track records, but that might be coming off a bad year or selling at their lows at the current time. This is, by the way, a good strategy for selecting individual stocks as well.

A listing of the popular mutual fund family web sites seemed like a good idea. However, so many mutual funds exist that listing a few would be an inadequate way of presenting them. Such a list might be construed as a recommendation for those few funds included on it, while many more—some better—funds went unmentioned. So, it might be more practical to offer a list of web sites that present general information on mutual funds. Of course, there are many more web sites on that topic than are included on this list. However, this list should give you a good start at going through the process of selecting a fund that is right for you. Here are some sites you might find helpful:

www.lipperweb.com (Lipper)

http://money.cnn.com/funds (CNN)

www.mfea.com (Mutual Fund Education Alliance)

www.ici.org (Investment Company Institute)

www.morningstar.com (Morningstar)

www.mutualfundsite.com (Wall Street OnLine)

www.mutualfunds.about.com (About.com)

www.fundspot.com/main.html (Fund$pot)

This list presents some popular sites, but there are many more. To find others, use a web crawler such as *www.google.com,* and search using the words "mutual funds." To find information on a particular fund or fund family, use Google or another search engine, and search using the specific name.

What Are Closed-End Funds and Unit Trusts?

As previously explained, mutual funds are by definition open ended. **Closed-end funds are professionally managed portfolios of investments that will trade on an exchange or over-the-counter. Some popular types of closed-end funds are general stock funds, sector funds, government bond funds, corporate bond funds, municipal bond funds, foreign funds, country funds, royalty trusts, and real estate investment trusts (REITs).** Most mutual fund portfolio managers would probably say that they prefer managing closed-end funds over open-end ones simply because open-end funds have a volatile capitalization by their very nature, as discussed in the previous section. Portfolio managers of closed-end funds do not have to worry that they may be forced to sell securities in their fund at a time when they may not want to. Unlike their open-end fund counterparts, they do not have to worry about what will happen to the fund if a large number of shareholders want to redeem their shares. Also, closed-end fund managers do not have to worry about being in a position where they have to purchase securities in the fund at an inopportune time because a large number of investors have deposited money into the fund. Closed-end fund managers get to deal with a relatively fixed amount of investment captial.

Comparing the historical returns of closed-end funds with open-end ones, however, is not an easy task. Most closed-end funds have a narrow market focus. Very few of them are general stock funds. So, a comparison of similar portfolios with related investment objectives is almost impossible. There simply aren't enough closed-end funds with portfolios comparable to those of open-end funds to draw valid conclusions. However, most closed-end fund managers would tell you that they would rather not be in the position of having to buy investments at the top of a market cycle, when a large number of investors are sending them money. Also, they would rather not have to sell some of their holdings when many investors are redeeming shares at the bottom of a cycle.

With a closed-end structure portfolio managers know exactly how much capital they have to manage, and the managers don't have to worry about having enough liquidity. Generally, this should improve market timing and keep more money invested in whatever the fund is supposed to be investing in. The risk to the investor in a closed-end fund, however, is that the share price is now subject to increased market risk. **A mutual fund may be redeemed at any time at NAV, but the price of a closed-end fund is subject to supply and demand fluctuations. The closed-end fund will still compute its net asset value, but the actual share price may be lower or higher than the NAV.** As a rule, the market value of each share will stay close to the net asset value. In volatile market conditions, however, the share prices of closed-end funds can be much more volatile than the NAV. You could say that the share prices of closed-end funds can be as volatile as common stocks.

The types of investments of most closed-end funds is implied in the title of the fund. The number of bond funds, government, government agency, or municipal bond funds, has grown the fastest in recent years. Country funds, such as the New Germany Fund, Spain Fund, Greater China Fund, Malaysia Fund, India Growth Fund, Brazil Fund, Korea Fund, Taiwan Fund, and so on, have also proliferated.

Perhaps the oldest types of closed-end funds are REITs and royalty trusts. **A "REIT" is a real estate investment trust. It is an investment company that invests only in equity real estate and/or mortgages.** REITs can be structured either as all-equity investments that would primarily try to achieve capital appreciation with some income from rental receipts, as all mortgage investments, whose objective would be for high income only, or as a combination of equity and mortgage.

A "royalty trust" is an investment in oil or natural gas production, structured somewhat like a REIT. It is an investment in direct ownership of oil and/or natural gas wells. It may or may not be leveraged. Many times the income from royalty trusts will be tax advantaged. In other words, some of its distributions may be tax sheltered because of favorable tax laws on domestic energy production. Some natural gas royalty trusts even qualify to pass through Section 29 income tax credits that amount to a direct reduction of federal income tax owed. Keep in mind that all of these closed-end funds qualify as investment companies because they pass through at least 90 percent of their income to their shareholders.

There are several web sites where you can get more information on closed-end funds. Here's a brief list:

www.closedendfunds.org (Closed-End Fund Investors)
www.closed-endfunds.com (Closed-End Fund Center)
www.icefi.com (Internet Closed-End Fund Investor)

A related type of closed-end fund is **a "unit investment trust." This is a type of fund created by investment bankers that invests in a fixed and usually unmanaged portfolio. Once the portfolio of securities has been put into the trust, whether stocks or bonds, that portfolio usually cannot change.** Whereas most other investment companies are actively managed and the portfolio of

securities may change frequently, most unit trust investments do not allow changes in the portfolio once the trust
has been closed. Unit trust bond portfolios will pay back
principal as the bonds in the fund mature or are called.
Unit trust stock portfolios will usually have a stated term
and after that time all securities are required to be sold and
all proceeds distributed. The trust will then simply be dissolved. It does not have an infinite life as do most other
investment company funds.

Unit trusts do not usually trade on secondary markets.
Most investment bankers who create and market these
trusts, however, stand ready to redeem shares at NAV with
no sales charge. Some investment bankers also hold previously redeemed units in their own inventory and maintain
a market for those units. So, in some cases it is still possible for an investor to purchase units of a trust after it has
already been closed.

Do You Know What You Need to Know?

To check up on what you learned from this chapter, answer
the following questions in your own words, then compare
your answers with the answer keys.

1. What is the difference between an investment company
   and other types of companies? Discuss the tax liabilities
   faced by each type.
2. Explain the difference between a closed-end fund and
   an open-end fund? How does the structure of each of
   these funds affect the market price of the fund? How
   does it affect the way the fund's investments are managed?
3. How is the net asset value of a fund computed? Can you
   think of any assets that could create problems for a
   fund to accurately compute on a daily basis?

4. Explain the difference between a front-end load fund, a back-end load fund, and a no-load fund. What other expenses might an investor pay besides the load?

5. What is a letter of intent (LOI), and how might it benefit a mutual fund investor?

6. In order for a government bond fund to be labeled as such, what percentage of its assets must be invested in government bonds? Why is it important to look at the portfolio of investments of a fund rather than just its total return figures?

7. Mutual funds usually *underperform* the market indexes that are supposed to represent the rate of return of a randomly selected portfolio. This is usually an embarrassment to the managers, but what factors in the structure of mutual funds contribute to this performance? Does an investor in individual stocks have an advantage over an investor in mutual funds? Why, or why not?

8. If you were a fund portfolio manager, would you prefer an open-end structure or a closed-end one? Why? Describe some closed-end funds. What is a REIT? How does a unit investment trust differ from other closed-end funds?

Answer Key

1. Investment companies "pass-through" income and capital gains to their investors. Thus, they are not taxed as other corporations. The investors are responsible for the tax liability on the fund's distributions. Corporate earnings, on the other hand, are subject to double taxation. The company pays taxes on its reported earnings, and shareholders owe taxes again when their share of those earnings is received as a dividend.

2. A closed-end fund has a fixed number of shares and trades on an exchange, like shares of common stock do. An open-end fund can issue an unlimited number of shares. Closed-end funds may trade above or below the net asset value of the fund because of market volatility. An open-end fund may be liquidated at net asset value at any time.

3. Net asset value is the total market value of all the investments in a fund, divided by the number of fund shares outstanding. Funds that invest in securities trading on an illiquid market, such as emerging markets, may have to make some assumptions to determine an accurate net asset value.

4. Front-end load funds charge a fee when an investor makes a purchase. Back-end load funds do not charge a front-end load, but may charge a fee when the investor withdraws from the fund. The withdrawal fees usually will decline to zero after a few years. A no-load fund charges no fees to purchase or to sell shares. All funds, however, charge annual fees for administration and operating expenses.

5. For most front-end load funds, fees are reduced for an investor who invests an amount that exceeds a certain "break point." If the investor signs an LOI to purchase an amount over a period of time that would exceed a break point, he or she will get the lower fee charged even though no single purchase was over the break point.

6. All mutual funds are required to invest at least 65 percent of their portfolio in the area that identifies what type of fund they are. A U.S. government bond fund could invest 65 percent in U.S. bonds, but have 35 percent in junk bonds. Although it could still call itself a government bond fund, it may not be as safe as the title of the fund implies.

7. Mutual funds charge fees and must usually keep part of their portfolio in cash to meet client redemptions. That affects total return. The S&P 500 Index, against which

funds are measured, is considered to be 100-percent invested and charges no fees.

8. Generally, managers prefer the closed-end structure because they have greater control over timing investment decisions. A Real Estate Investment Trust is a closed-end fund investing in equity real estate or in mortgages. A unit investment trust is a finite-term, passively managed fund.

Mutual funds that outperform the stock market are difficult to find.

Chapter 9

What Are Stock Options?

A stock option is a contract that gives its purchaser the right to buy or the right to sell a fixed amount of stock, usually 100 shares, at a predetermined price and within a predetermined period of time. The contract that gives the purchaser of an option the right to *buy* the stock is called a "call" option. The contract that gives the purchaser the right to *sell* the stock is called a "put" option.

If you think this concept sounds simple, you will change your mind as you read further in this chapter. Trading options is complicated significantly by the use of terminology that is unique to these types of securities. Also, understanding how the options market works probably requires participating in that market. It is somewhat like learning how to use a computer. You have to work on a computer to understand it well. Reading this chapter, or for that matter any other material about options trading, will not result in the same level of comprehension that comes from experience. So, *do **not** invest in options until you have a thorough grasp of how the market works*. There are significant inherent risks in options speculation. The Options Clearing Corporation (OCC) has prepared a booklet, "Characteristics and Risks of Standardized Options," that the SEC requires to be distributed to all individuals before they invest in options. This booklet contains more complete information on options trading than this chapter.

The largest options exchange in the United States is Chicago Board of Options Exchange (CBOE). However, the American Stock Exchange (AMEX), the Philadelphia Stock Exchange, the Pacific Stock Exchange, and the New York Stock Exchange also make markets in options contracts. The Options Clearing Corporation is the primary rule-making body responsible for options trading. All exchange-traded options are issued by the OCC. However, as with other securities, the primary governing body of the options markets in the United States is the Securities and Exchange Commission.

Options originated as an idea to give stock investors a means of insuring their portfolios and limiting market volatility. Shareholders could sell a contract guaranteeing delivery of their stock at a predetermined price above what they paid for it. By so doing, they would receive additional income from the sale of that contract that would reduce their loss if the stock dropped and had to be sold at a lower than purchase price. The option contract in that case would, of course, not be exercised. However, if the stock went above the price at which the investor had guaranteed to sell it, he or she would not receive that excess profit. So, the investor would be limiting the upside potential from the stock, but he or she would also be reducing the downside risk.

Options quickly evolved, however, into a highly leveraged, short-term speculator's dream. You can still pursue either strategy—conservative hedging or outlandish speculation—using options. To understand why and how the speculators became the dominant options investors will be clarified when you understand what an option is. **The conventional method of describing an option contract requires four parts: (1) the name of the company to which the contract applies, (2) the month in which the** contract will expire, (3) the strike price at which the option contract can be exercised, and (4) whether the option is a call or a put. This complete four-part description is called an option "series." An option series on Unique Inc. would be written "Unique Inc. July 30 Call," for example. Note that "30" is the strike price in this option series, and not a date.

The price that the purchaser, or "holder," of the option pays or that the seller, or "writer," of the option receives is called the "premium." For example, a speculator who purchased a Unique Inc. July 30 Call option might pay a premium of $250. The premium is expressed in whole numbers and fractions like stock quotes, but a one-point move on an option premium is worth $100, not $1. So, if the premium is $250, that would be written as 2½ points. **Option premiums are quoted in $100 denominations because each option contract represents 100 shares of underlying stock.** A one-point price change in the option premium has the same dollar value as a one-point change on 100 shares of stock—$100.

The only time a listed option contract would not represent 100 shares of stock would be if the stock splits. In that case, the option would represent whatever number of shares the original 100 shares would change into after the split. Also, the strike price of the option would be adjusted to the equivalent price change after the stock splits. For example, on the ex-dividend date for which Unique Inc. splits 3-for-2, the Unique Inc. July 25 Call will be adjusted to a contract representing 150 shares at a strike price of 16⅔. In this case, the option will be identified with a new symbol, a ticker symbol different than the one for the stock. This symbol is assigned by the options exchanges. This way brokers, and investors as well, will be alerted that the contract does not represent 100 shares, and a one-point quote for this option premium would represent $150 (not $100). In other words, a one-point change in the stock price will still represent a one-point change in the value of the underlying shares for that option contract. If the stock splits 2-for-1, however, usually the number of option contracts is doubled and the strike price is reduced by one half. This way, each option still represents 100 shares, and there is less confusion with the premium. For example, if an option holder owned *five* Unique Inc. July 25 Calls and the stock split 2-for-1, after the split that holder would own *ten* Unique Inc. July 12½ Calls.

The expiration date for option contracts needs only to be identified by the month, and not the specific *day* of that month, because the day of expiration always follows a predetermined formula. **The last day of trading for options will always be the third Friday of the month.** So, the Unique Inc. July 30 Call will no longer be traded after the market closes on the third Friday in the upcoming month of July. Technically, the expiration date is defined as the Saturday following the third Friday of the month. This extra day is given to allow the Options Clearing Corporation (OCC), which is responsible for matching options that have been executed, enough time to process the paperwork.

When options were first introduced they always offered three different expiration months in three-month increments. The options that would be available for Unique Inc. would always follow the cycle January-April-July-October. So, if the three months that were currently available for Unique Inc. were January, April, and July, then after the January contracts expired, the options exchange would open the October contracts. On the Monday following expiration of the January contracts, the three options available for Unique would be April, July, and October. After the

April expiration, the cycle would go to July, October, and January of next year, and so on.

This simple expiration cycle, however, was changed by the exchanges for most options, because the traders found that the most actively traded contracts were the ones with the shortest terms. So, the exchanges changed the cycle to one that would always offer the nearest two months, as well as the next two months following the normal three-month cycle. As a result, most stocks have options with four different expiration months, even though many newspapers only show the quotes for the closest three months. If you think this sounds confusing, it is. The options exchanges are motivated by the volume of contracts traded, not by simplicity.

To illustrate this cycle, suppose Unique Inc. has options available for January, February, April, July. When the January options expire, the exchange will open the March contracts, so the cycle will be February, March, April, July. Then when February options expire, since the next two closest months are already available, the exchange will open trading on options for the next month that would follow the regular three-month cycle. This would be the October contracts. The cycle will then be March, April, July, October. The two nearest months and two months that follow the normal three-month cycle will always be available.

The "strike price" is the price per share at which the option contract may be exercised. There will usually be several strike prices available, near the current market price of the underlying stock. New strike prices will be added if the market for the stock moves away from the existing strike prices. The various strike prices on stock options used to follow a predictable pattern, but, like the expiration cycle, they have since changed to accommodate demand. For stocks trading under $25 per share, the strike price usually changes in increments of 2½ points. The exchanges will always make available several strike prices near the current market price of the stock. So, after Unique Inc.'s 3-for-2 split, the stock is now trading in the low 20's. The options that would now be available would have strike prices of perhaps 17½, 20, 22½, and 25. As you can see, an option investor has quite a variety of expiration dates and strike prices to choose from.

For securities trading over $25 per share, the strike price increments jump to 5 points. The increments will go to 25, 30, 35, and so on, if the underlying stock price moves close to that range. If the price of the stock is over 200, then the options will begin to trade in 10-point strike price increments—200, 210, 220, and so on. The exchanges, however, set the rules and can designate strike prices in smaller increments if they feel investors would actively trade them. For example, if a company has very actively traded options and the stock is trading around 60 and is not very volatile, the exchange may make available options with a strike price of 62½.

The last identifying factor of an option is whether the contract is a call or a put. As you already know, a call represents the right to *call*, or to buy, the stock from someone else, a put represents the right to *put*, or to sell, the stock to someone else. This shouldn't be very confusing yet; however, it will be when we discuss *writing*, or selling, options. You can either buy or sell a call or a put, and the "someone else" you will either be buying your stock from if you exercise your call, or selling your stock to if you exercise your put, is the writer of that call or put.

Like stock, every time an option is sold, someone else bought it, and every time an option is bought, someone else sold it. The options exchanges, however, function more like the over-the-counter market than they do like securities exchanges. When you buy **an option, you buy it from an option "trader," a member of the options exchange who maintains a market for that option.** The function of the option trader resembles that of the over-the-counter market maker more than that of the specialist on an exchange.

What Happens When You Buy Options?

Before answering this question, you need to understand one more term—*open interest*. The first transaction you make, whether buying or selling an option, creates an *open position*. If you purchase a contract, you are obligating yourself to make a decision to do something before the expiration date of that contract. You have three possible choices: (1) sell the contract itself, (2) exercise it, that is, buy the stock if you hold a call or sell it if you hold a put, or (3) let it expire. Keep in mind that you have a relatively short period of time in which to make this decision. If you understood how the option expiration cycle works, you should realize that the maximum amount of time you will have on most contracts is *eight* months. In most cases, you will have less than that.

The first transaction you make on an option contract, whether it is a buy or a sell, is an opening transaction. When you decide to sell or to exercise the contract you bought, or buy back or to exercise the contract you sold, you are creating a closing transaction. **"Open interest" is the total number of options contracts on a company at the same strike price and same expiration date that have been bought or sold as an initial transaction.** As these contracts are closed, either by trading them or exercising them, they will reduce open interest. Open interest is used as an indicator of the level of investor interest in the underlying stock. Keep in mind, however, that you cannot tell from the open interest number how many of those contracts have been bought from the option trader and how many have been sold to the trader.

Generally speaking, more speculators are attracted to buying options than to selling them. This is because of the tremendous leverage potential from these contracts. A speculator can benefit from the price movement of 100 shares of stock without having to invest the amount of money it would cost to buy that much stock. Consider the following scenario, assuming that Unique Inc. stock is trading at 29. If you purchase a Unique Inc. July 30 Call option for 2½ (a $250 premium), then as the stock goes over 30, your right to buy 100 shares of stock at a lower than market price will begin to have intrinsic value. Each point Unique Inc. moves over 30 will add $100 to the value of a contract to buy 100 shares of stock at 30.

However, it cost you $250 to make this speculation. So, the stock must not only go above 30, but also go up another $250 in market value to recoup the option premium. This would amount to another 2½ points on 100 shares of stock. So, if you were to buy this option, you should realize that the stock must actually go over 32½ before you make a profit from the intrinsic value. In other words, each point Unique Inc. goes over 32½, the strike price plus the cost of the option, would represent a $100 profit to the option speculator.

To put this in terms that perk speculators' ears and accounts for the reason why most option contracts are bought by speculators: If Unique Inc. goes up 4½, or approximately 16 percent (4½ divided by 29), the speculator who invested $250 stands to make $100, or 40 percent (100 divided by 250). In other words, if the stock goes from 29 to 33½, the option contract to buy 100 shares of stock at 30 will be worth at least 3½ points. This is the lure of leverage.

Instead of investing $2,900 for 100 shares of stock and making 16 percent ($450) when it went up to 33½, the options speculator could invest $2,500 in 10 option contracts and make 40 percent ($1,000) from the same stock movement. This is great temptation for speculators. If the stock goes higher, the returns on the option become even more inflated. If it went to 35, for example, the option would gain at least 100 percent; at 37½, 200 percent, and so on. **If the share price is above the strike price of a call option, that option is said to be "in the money."** When the stock went to 35, the July 30 Call was 5 points in the money.

The explanation of this option transaction has been overly simplified so far, because it has assumed that the option would have value only if the stock was in the money. Option traders usually describe the premiums as having two parts: intrinsic value and time value (or speculative value). When you originally bought the contract for $250, the stock was out of the money. Unique Inc. was trading below the strike price ($30). So, all of this premium represented time value (or speculative value); there was no intrinsic value whatsoever. If, indeed, there were several months left before the option expired when Unique Inc. ran up to 33½, then the option premium would be worth much more than just 3½. Depending on the amount of time and the whims of the speculators, the premium could be much higher. If the stock appeared from this recent run up that it could continue up to about 35 by the time the option expired, the market for that option may actually be 5 to 5½. Supply and demand factors affect options premiums as well as stock prices.

Before you get too carried away by the lure of leverage, however, look at the risks. Options are described as time-wasting assets. The expiration date of the option contract wasn't considered in this last discussion, and this is a very important component. Options have a very short life span. Let's say your Unique Inc. option had four months until expiration. What would that option be worth if the stock rallied up from 29 to 30 on the option's expiration date? If you owned the stock, you would have made $100, but if you owned the option, you would have just thrown away $250 per contract, or helped reduce your taxable income on April 15. The contract will expire worthless. Let's also say on the Monday after the contract expired, Unique Inc. reported fantastic earnings and the stock ran up to 35. How much money did you make on the option? Still zilch. You ran out of time. When you speculate on options, you not only have to be right about *how* the stock is going to do, you have to be right about *when* it is going to do it.

These examples so far have been about *call* options, but consider how the strategy changes when you are dealing with *put* options. A put gives you right to sell the underlying stock. So, if Unique Inc. is trading at 29 and you buy a Unique Inc. July 30 Put option for $250, you would make money if the stock dropped. Such a strategy would be similar to selling the stock short—only with greater leverage. If you own a contract that gives you the right to sell 100 shares of stock at 30, and the stock drops to 25, the contract will be worth $500. The option for which you paid 2½ points will now go to about 5 in intrinsic value, giving you a 100 percent return on your investment. A put option is said to be "in the money" when the price of the underlying stock is below the strike price. This is the exact reverse of the call option. To present this in terms of relative percentage change, a 4-point, or 14 percent, drop in the stock resulted in a 2½ point, or 100 percent, return on the put option.

One last note of caution before we leave option buying: Estimates are that about 80 percent of all option contracts expire worthless. So, the odds do not favor the speculator who purchases calls and puts. The premiums that the purchaser paid become free credit balances to the *writer* who sold the contracts. When the options expire, the writer's potential liability of having to buy back the options, or "cover the short position," is eliminated. So, let's look at how money is made by selling options.

What Happens When You Sell Options?

The most common strategy used by option writers is called "covered writing." This is the strategy of selling call options representing the amount of stock you already own. If you own 200 shares of stock, you could write two options on those shares. If you own 1,000 shares of stock, you could write 10. **If you write calls for which you do not own stock, this is called "naked writing,"** or establishing a naked position.

The holder of the contract owns the right to exercise that contract. So, the holder of a call option owns the right to buy the underlying shares of stock at the exercise price. If the holder decides to exercise the call option, whose stock will he or she be buying? The shares of the person who wrote the contract. Consider the consequences if an investor writes two Unique Inc. July 30 calls. If he or she wrote *covered* calls, that writer would deliver the stock that he or she already owns. If the writer wrote *naked* calls, he or she would have to purchase 200 shares of Unique Inc. on the open market to deliver them to the holder. The holder who exercised will, of course, have to pay the writer for those shares. So, if the holder exercises two call options at 30, he or she will pay the writer $6,000 for the 200 shares of Unique Inc. The holder will also have to pay brokerage commissions for the purchase, and the writer will have brokerage commissions deducted from his sale.

Because of this potential liability, the writer of naked call options must deposit an initial margin equity requirement in his account equal to 20 percent of the market value of the underlying stock plus the option premium, minus the out-of-the-money amount of the stock. There is also a minimum equity requirement for a naked option position, requiring 10 percent of the market value plus the current option premium. Whichever of these two formulas is greater will be the margin requirement.

If the writer was covered, and had originally purchased Unique Inc. at 25 ($5,000), he would make $1,000 on the sale, without deducting transaction costs. If the writer was naked, however, he or she would have to buy the shares at the current market price. The chances are very good that Unique Inc. would now be trading at a price higher than 30. The holder of the call would not make any money by exercising the call if the stock were not above the strike price. So, if the stock had gone to 35, the writer is going to have to pay $7,000 (200 times 35), and he or she is going to have to sell it to the holder for $6,000. If the writer were naked, he or she would lose $1,000 on this transaction, excluding commission costs. So, a relatively conservative position for a covered writer would be a very speculative position for a naked writer, who has virtually unlimited risk.

A bit more complicated is the scenario when a speculator writes a put option, or establishes a short position. *Long and short positions* are terms used to describe whether the speculator has bought or sold. **When you buy an option, you establish a "long" position. When you sell an option, you establish a "short" position.** The holder of a put, who is long the put, owns the right to sell shares at the contract's strike price. Who does the holder sell the shares to? The writer of the put. So, if you sell a put contract, you must stand ready to purchase the stock. If that put is assigned, you are going to be the buyer of the underlying stock. There is no such thing as a naked *put* option, for a short put must always be *covered by* sufficient equity. The term "naked" would properly be used to describe short *call* positions only.

Writing put options requires a margin account. You use the equity in your margin account to maintain enough credit should you need to buy the stock represented by the short put. The usual equity requirement for a short option (both puts and calls) is 100 percent of the current option premium plus 20 percent of the underlying stock's market value minus the out of the money amount. However, if the price of the stock is far away from the strike price of the option and out-of-the-money, the minimum equity requirement may be 100 percent of the current option premium plus 10 percent of the stock's market value. Whichever of these two computations is larger will be the initial equity requirement for a short option position. If this is unclear to you, don't write put options. If it is clear to you, you should already realize that the usual strategy for writing put options is to try to buy a stock at a lower than current market price. If the stock goes up and the put does not get assigned, your only consequence is that you get to keep the put premium as a reward for not being able to buy the stock.

What Are Some Other Option Strategies?

Speculators have been able to formulate several option strategies using various combinations of buying and/or writing calls and puts. The two most common strategies are straddles and spreads. **A speculator would establish a "straddle" by establishing an option position with both calls and puts on the same stock with the same expira-**

tion date and the same strike price. You could either buy a straddle, or you could write a straddle. If you establish a long straddle position, your hope would be that the stock will be volatile enough to go above the strike price plus the cost of the two option premiums, both the call and the put, or that it will go below the strike price minus the two option premiums. This would be a position a speculator might try if he were unsure whether the stock was going up or down, but it was definitely very volatile. Obviously, if you write a straddle, you will want the stock to stay within the area bounded by the strike price plus or minus the two premiums. A volatile stock in that situation would *not* be a good choice.

Another common option strategy is a spread. **A "spread" is a position whereby a speculator buys and sells calls on the same stock with different strike prices or different expiration dates.** Spreads can be established either at the same strike price with different expiration dates, at different strike prices on the same expiration date, or when both the strike prices and expiration dates are different. With each different spread position the speculator would profit from different stock price movements.

In addition to listed options with standard expiration dates, the CBOE has created long-term options called LEAPS. This is an acronym for **L**ong-term **E**quity **A**ntici**P**ation **S**ecurities. The options markets are known more for their creativity in designing new products than for their creativity with new names. LEAPS are options that expire one or two years out. They expire in the month of January, so they need only be identified by the year in which they expire.

Also, speculators who want to "bet the market," can buy or sell options on a wide variety of security indexes. Near-term "OEX" options are almost always the most actively traded calls and puts on any trading day. These are options on the S&P 100 Index, a shorter version of the S&P 500 created just for option trading. The "SPX" is the symbol for S&P 500 Index. The "XMI" is the AMEX option called the Major Market Index that is supposed to closely follow the Dow Jones Industrial Average. The New York Stock Exchange Index is "NYA." "RUT" is the symbol for the Russell 2000 Index options of small-cap stocks. There are also market industry indexes on such groups as biotechnology, computer technology, oil, pharmaceuticals, utilities, gold and silver, natural gas, securities broker/dealers, and others. Since index options cannot be exercised for delivery of shares of a security, they are assigned a cash value. This is usually $100 times the market value of the index. If the index were at 150, for example, that would have a cash value, if exercised at expiration, of $15,000.

Index options are often linked to **"program trading." This is a term for computer programs, usually of institutional traders, that monitor the changing market prices of the companies that make up an index option. The computer program will simultaneously compare the actual price of the index option with that of the prices of the underlying stocks.** Then the program will generate buy and sell orders to take advantage of any price disparities. This strategy is referred to as *risk arbitrage*. Programmed trading was blamed as one of the main causes of the market crash in 1987. As a result some restrictions were imposed on it. If the market is up or down over 50 points, program trading orders are subject to some restrictions. These will be discussed in the next chapter, "What Have We Learned from Previous Market Crashes?"

Also, the market tends to be unusually volatile on or near the third Friday in March, June, September, and December. Those four days are called "quadruple witching days," because on those days four different securities contracts expire: listed stock options, listed index options, and commodity index futures, and commodity stock futures. The unusually heavy volume on or near the expiration dates can cause larger than normal market swings. Because this volatility often occurs when there is no corresponding news event or any rational reason for that movement, they are referred to as quadruple witching days.

What Are Stock Rights and Warrants?

Stock rights and warrants are similar to stock options in that they are relatively low priced securities that can be converted into shares of stock, but there are significant differences between these securities and options. Stock rights are usually issued if a company is planning to issue more new shares in the primary market. Prior to the issuance of these shares the company will give its current shareholders the right to purchase additional shares of the stock. These **"stock rights" allow the owner to purchase enough new shares at a lower than market price to maintain the same percentage ownership of the company after the new shares are issued. By increasing the number of shares the company has outstanding, it is in effect "diluting" (or decreasing) the percentage ownership of the current shareholders.** If you owned 100,000 shares of a company with 10 million shares outstanding, you would own 1 percent of the company. But if the company increased its shares to 20 million, your 100,000 shares would then only represent 0.5 percent of the company.

About a month before the company's planned primary offering, it will issue one right for each share held by its current stockholders. If the dilution of the current shares will amount to about 5 percent, then each right will convert into ½₀th of a share. In other words, it will take 20 rights to purchase one more share. If the shareholder already owned 100 shares, his or her 100 rights would allow the purchase of an additional 5 shares. So, after the primary offering, the 105 shares will represent the same percentage ownership as 100 shares did before the offering. Admittedly, 100 shares of most companies is not a high enough percentage for most investors to be concerned about dilution. If you owned a million shares, however, you would probably hold a significant voting block of stock, and the dilution of that voting block would be of much greater concern to you.

The exercise price of the stock rights is always below the market price of the stock at the time the rights are issued because when the new shares are issued, the market price will drop by the approximate amount of the dilution. If Unique Inc. had 15 million shares outstanding, and the board of directors planned on offering an additional 1 million shares through the primary market, that would be a 6.25 percent dilution (1 million divided by 16 million). The total number of shares outstanding after the offering would no longer be 15 million; it would be 16 million. Assuming that the market price of Unique Inc. is 25, then after the offering the price will likely drop approximately 1⅝ points. So, in this scenario Unique Inc. would issue rights to its existing shareholders that would convert into ¹⁄₁₆th of a share each. These rights could be exercised at approximately $23.375. The rights themselves would have a nominal cash value and could be sold if the shareholder decided not to exercise them. In any case, the shareholder would have to decide within a couple of weeks, or within a relatively short period of time, whether or not to exercise.

Warrants, on the other hand, are more like long-term options. **"Warrants" are contracts that allow the holder to convert them into shares of stock of the underlying company. At the time they are issued, the conversion price of the warrants will be higher than the market price of the stock.** Warrants, like listed stock options, are highly leveraged contracts. For a relatively small investment, like the option premium, a warrant will rise in value dollar for dollar as the price of the underlying stock rises above the exercise price. Listed warrants will trade like stock, usually on the same exchange as the stock into which they can be converted. Not very many companies currently issue warrants. If you wanted to find some that do, you would have to look in the newspaper market quotes. The name of the company will be followed by the abbreviation "wts."

The leverage from investments in stock options or warrants, however, pales in comparison to the leverage from commodity futures contracts.

What Are Commodity Futures Contracts?

Futures contracts are similar to listed stock options in that they give the speculator the right to buy or to sell a specified quantity of a commodity within a certain period of time. However, there are many major differences between commodity futures and stock options. First, futures are contracts to purchase or to sell a specific amount of an underlying *commodity*, not an equity security. This underlying commodity can be precious metals such as gold, silver, or platinum. It can be consumable products such as wheat, corn, soy beans, cocoa, sugar, coffee, orange juice, live cattle, or pork bellies (bacon). There are several energy-related contracts such as crude oil, heating oil, or natural gas. There are foreign currency contracts in such denominations as British pounds, Swiss francs, German deutschemarks, or Japanese yen. There are even interest-rate and index contracts on Treasury bonds, Treasury bills, GNMAs, or the S&P 500 Index.

Each contract on these commodities represents a specified quantity that varies from commodity to commodity. The quantities are not standardized as they are with listed stock options. A T-bill contract is for 1 million of principal. A gold contract is for 100 troy ounces. A coffee contract is 37,500 pounds; sugar, 112,000 pounds. Wheat is 5,000 bushels. The quantities of the different futures contracts vary. A commodities trader must learn the quantity of a contract and the unit price at which it trades. Also, the time periods for commodities are not uniform as they are with listed options. Some commodity contracts offer terms for every month of the year and can go out two years. Others offer periods expiring in two- or three-month increments.

The actively traded short-term contract is referred to as the "spot contract." The "spot price," frequently quoted by business reporters, is the price of the spot contract and represents the market price for near-term delivery of the commodity. Usually traders who plan to take delivery of the commodity use the future's market for hedging. **"Hedging" is a strategy whereby the trader can lock in a fixed price for the commodity months in advance of taking delivery.** By doing this the hedger can work out a financial plan for the sale of his product based on that price for his raw materials.

A wheat farmer, for example, is able to estimate the total expenses of producing his crop before harvest. He is also able to estimate the approximate size of the harvest. Thus, he can presell his commodity by selling wheat futures contracts that will expire at the time of the harvest and will equal the total bushels of his estimated harvest.

He would sell these contracts at an acceptable profit margin. If the price of wheat drops between the time he sells the futures contract and the time he sells the wheat, the market value of the futures contract will appreciate enough to offset the shortfall in the sale of the wheat. If the price of wheat rises, he will be able to sell his harvest for more, but he will take an offsetting loss on his futures contracts. He has effectively locked in a certain profit margin. He cannot make any more than that net profit, but he cannot lose any more either. This is a proper hedging strategy.

On the other hand, the cereal company to which the farmer sells his wheat would *buy* futures contracts to hedge its risk. If wheat drops, the company benefits by buying the commodity at a lower price, but loses that net gain by taking a loss on the futures. If wheat goes up, the cereal company pays more for the commodity, but gains on the futures. Hedging is not a strategy limited to consumable products. Interest-rate futures are frequently used by financial institutions to offset the interest-rate risk on loan portfolios. A bank, for example, that has a portfolio of mortgages paying an average of 8 percent, could hedge that portfolio by selling GNMA futures contracts. If interest rates rise, although the value of the portfolio of mortgages will decline, the value of the GNMA contracts will appreciate at an approximately offsetting pace.

The main difference between commodities and stock options is that with an option you cannot lose any more than the option premium. **With a commodities futures contract, the speculator has undefined risk.** The speculator deposits a small amount of equity when he or she buys (or shorts) a futures contract. If the price of the commodity moves against that position, that is, if the speculator is *long* and the price drops, or *short* and the price rallies, he or she will have to deposit additional equity to meet margin requirements. The speculator will have to continue adding money to meet his or her equity requirement many times if the commodity keeps moving the wrong way. Some commodities exchanges have introduced trading in *options contracts*. Options are similar to futures, but they *do* limit the trader's risk to the amount of the investment. In this sense, they are similar to stock options.

The commodities exchanges are regulated by the Commodity Exchange Authority, which is part of the Department of Agriculture. The exchanges have been frequent targets of government sting operations and have a checkered history. Even though there is greater regulation of the exchanges today, such regulation doesn't seem to improve the trader's chances of profiting from these types of speculative investments. A frequently quoted statistic is that **nearly 90 percent of all commodities speculators have lost money in the futures markets.**

Do You Know What You Need to Know?

To check up on what you learned from this chapter, answer the following questions in your own words, then compare your answers with the answer key.

1. Define the term *option* and explain the difference between a call and a put. Name the four parts of a complete option description, or series. How many shares of underlying stock does each contract represent?

2. What is an option premium? Why is a one-point premium usually equal to $100? Under what circumstances might it not be?

3. What is the Options Clearing Corporation (OCC)? What are its functions and responsibilities?

4. On what day of the month do option contracts expire? What are triple witching days and why are they significant?

5. What is the *strike price* of an option contract? In what increments do strike prices change?

6. What is the significance of *open interest?* What assumption do most options speculators make from the open interest number?

7. What are the differences between a *stock right* and a *stock warrant?* Which type of contract is similar to stock options? Why?

8. Describe some of the differences between futures contracts and stock options. What are the limits of the investor's liability with each of these types of contracts?

Answer Key

1. If exercised, a call option obligates the holder to purchase 100 shares of the underlying stock at the strike price on or before the expiration date. A put option obligates the holder to sell 100 shares of the underlying stock at the strike price on or before the expiration date.

2. The premium is the price of the option contract. A one-point option premium equals $100, equivalent to $1 per share for 100 shares. Thus, ⅛ of a point equals $12.50. If a stock splits and each option contract represents a number of shares different from 100, the option premium for that contract will equal one point for that many shares. For example, one point on an option contract for 120 shares will equal $120, and a ½-point premium will equal $60 on that contract.

3. The Options Clearing Corporation (OCC) oversees options trading and matches exercised option contracts.

4. The last trading day for options is always the third Friday of the month specified in the contract. They expire the following day—for OCC matching purposes. Triple witching days are when stock options, index options, and index futures contracts expire on the same day. They fall on the third Fridays in March, June, September, and December. Frequently, there can be unusual market volatility around these dates.

5. The strike price is the price at which the option is exercisable. Below 25, the increments are 2½ points; over 25, usually 5 points; and expensive stocks, usually over 200, trade in 10-point increments.

6. Open interest is the number of speculators who have made an initial option transaction on a certain contract. Analysts usually assume that most open interest is from buyers.

7. Stock rights are issued to current shareholders when a company is planning a new stock offering. Shareholders who exercise their rights will maintain the same percentage ownership of the company after the new shares are issued. Warrants are contracts that trade like shares on an exchange and have terms similar to long-term options.

8. Futures contracts are for an underlying commodity. An important difference is that speculators' liability is not limited to the initial amount invested, as it is with options. Also, futures do not follow standardized strike prices and expiration dates as do options.

Watch out for unusual market activity on quadruple witching days.

— Chapter 10 —

How Are Your Rights as an Investor Protected?

All investments in accounts through brokerage firms that are members of the Securities Investors Protection Corporation or SIPC, are currently insured up to $500,000 for securities or $100,000 for cash. The Securities Investors Protection Corporation is an agency similar to the Federal Deposit Insurance Corporation, or FDIC, insures member banks' depositors. During the late 1980s and early 1990s, however, the FDIC had to periodically go before Congress to request additional government backing. Without such an increase, its resources would have been insufficient to cover the liabilities of the large number of failed banks. The SIPC, however, has not had to make such requests. Almost all brokerage firms are members of the SIPC and display a sign so stating.

Both the SIPC and FDIC are private corporations that function as quasi-government agencies. They can borrow money from the U.S. government if necessary to back up insurance claims. However, the reserve requirements of these two agencies and the insurance protection they provide are completely different. The FDIC insures bank accounts up to $100,000. This coverage limit would apply to the total of all accounts in one bank held in the same name. So, if you had a $75,000 certificate of deposit (time account), $35,000 in a passbook savings account, and $15,000 in a checking account (demand deposit account), the total amount you would have invested in that bank would be $125,000. Therefore, $25,000 of your deposits would not be insured. Also, if you invested in a $100,000 jumbo CD and the bank failed, any interest that you would have earned on that CD would be uninsured.

The insurance protection of both of the SIPC and the FDIC is designed to keep investors' funds or securities protected in case the financial institution is forced to declare bankruptcy. So, if your deposits in one institution under FDIC insurance exceed $100,000 and the bank mismanages its investments and is forced by its creditors into bankruptcy, that excess would be lost. The insurance limit for *cash* in brokerage accounts covered by the SIPC is also subject to this $100,000 limit. Only *security* investments are insured up to $500,000. For most accounts, however, money market funds are defined as securities. Since most brokerage firms keep free credit balances in money market funds, those balances are not subject to the $100,000 insurance limit for cash. In addition to the SIPC insurance, many brokerages purchase additional coverage from other insurance companies so that their large accounts will also be fully protected.

The Securities Investors Protection Corporation does not insure an investor against market risk. It will simply guarantee that you still own the same securities that you owned before the financial institution went bankrupt. Since traditional bank deposits do not assume market risk, if you do not exceed the limits, you will be fully covered. However, if you own a security whose market value drops from $100,000 to $50,000 and is covered by SIPC insurance, you are only guaranteed the $50,000 worth of the security. The market risk is not covered.

Since the modification of the powers of the Glass-Steagall Act in the early 1990s, most banks offer securities that are not covered by the FDIC. The Glass-Steagall Act of 1933 prohibited banks from being involved in the primary market for securities. It established a legal separation of the banking industry and the securities industry. In the 1990s, however, the Glass-Steagall Act was significantly weakened and allowed banks to offer brokerage services, although banks are still prohibited from participating in the primary (new issue) market. Many depositors may not be aware that some of their investments through banks are not covered by FDIC insurance. As a result, there have been some horrendous disasters. There were several highly publicized cases in the early 1990s in which banks were accused of diverting depositors' investments from FDIC-insured investments to uninsured junk bonds. The most notable case was that involving the officers of Lincoln Savings & Loan and its chairman, Charles H. Keating, Jr. The junk bonds into which depositors' funds were diverted were used primarily to finance risky real estate ventures that went bankrupt. Banks have also diverted some deposits in mutual funds that were not insured because they were not members of SIPC. When the financial institution failed, many depositors lost their life savings from these investments. Most never even knew that they were not insured until after the failure.

What Have We Learned from Previous Market Events?

Prior to, and for a few years following, the market crash of 1929, there were virtually no securities regulations. Public companies were under state security regulations only. **State security laws, known as "blue sky laws," var-**

ied widely from state to state and generally did not have much enforcement power. Companies were not required to file financial statements or to report their earnings on a regular basis. Also, many illegal securities trading practices went uncaught and unpunished because states did not have the ability to enforce the laws. Manipulation of some securities was commonplace because a few wealthy individuals were able to "corner the market" on certain commodities or in certain industries. By controlling all, or most, of a particular industry's business, the executives had the ability to set artificially high prices on their commodity or product. They had a monopoly. The railroad industry was an example of such a monopolistic industry. It was perhaps the major industry of that time, and it was controlled by only a handful of individuals.

Fictitious security trades were sometimes reported. These were called "wash sales." They were direct attempts to misrepresent current market prices or conditions. Wash sales were arranged transactions usually between two parties in collusion who would report that securities had been sold usually at a higher than market price. No money would actually change hands, however, and the parties would report this sale in an attempt to mislead other investors into thinking that the price of the security was moving dramatically upward. When other investors began buying the stock, these parties would begin selling their holdings at the inflated prices.

The term "wash sale" today has an entirely different meaning. It is used by the IRS to refer to the sale of a security to establish a capital loss, and then the repurchase of the same security within 30 days after the sale. If an investor does repurchase the same or an equivalent security within 30 days before or after the date of sales, the IRS does not allow that person to claim a capital loss.

A person may not use such a sale to reduce taxable income from the loss. In order for a person to deduct a capital loss, he or she must wait over 30 days to repurchase the same security that was sold.

Also, investors in 1929 could borrow up to 90 percent of the market value of securities. Margin requirements were only 10 percent. Ten thousand dollars could buy $100,000 worth of stock. So, when the market dropped *10 percent*, the investor had lost all of his or her money. If it dropped more than 10 percent, the brokerage firm or bank that had loaned the margin funds started losing its money. The casualties of that crash were not only investors, but many financial institutions as well. From peak to trough, the market crash that began on Black Thursday, October 24, 1929, and ended in 1933 was about a 70 percent drop.

Black Thursday was followed the next week by Black Tuesday, October 29, when the market went through another round of panic selling, even after six prominent New York bankers attempted to prop up the market with an infusion of about $40 million apiece. In spite of President Hoover's assurances that recovery was at hand, the United States entered the Great Depression, where unemployment hit 25 percent, the total output of goods and services dropped by over 30 percent, and one third of the nation's banks failed.

The first federal legislation to address the problems of the securities industry was the Securities Act of 1933. This act specified that companies that conducted business across state lines would be required to file a registration statement or prospectus for all new issue shares. Every investor in an initial public offering (IPO) of stock must be provided with **a "prospectus," that represents *full disclosure* of the company's business operations and finances.** This act also made corporate officers accountable for any misrepresentations or omissions in the prospectus.

The Securities Act of 1933 was followed by the Securities *Exchange* Act of 1934. It expanded rules governing new issues to securities trading in the secondary market. It also legislated the creation of the Securities and Exchange Commission. This act required companies to file **quarterly financial reports, called 10Qs, and annual reports, called 10Ks,** with the SEC. In addition, it authorized the Federal Reserve Board to set initial margin requirements, that, as you already know, resulted in Regulation T. Other provisions from the act included the requirement to send proxy solicitations to all shareholders, allowing each the right to vote on any material change in the structure of their company. **"Tender offers," that is, offers by an outside party to buy shares directly from current shareholders, usually with the intent of gaining a controlling interest in a company,** must also be filed with the SEC. Anyone who owns over 5 percent of the outstanding shares of a company's stock must file a letter explaining their intentions for that ownership. The SEC is particularly interested to know whether or not holding that much stock is the beginning of a takeover attempt of that company.

Perhaps the most important part of this legislation was defining and allowing for the prosecution of *insider trading*. **An "insider" is anyone who has information about a company that has not yet been made publicly available.** The Securities Act made it illegal for anyone who had nonpublic information on a company to profit from that information. Although there have been many scandals involving insider trading in securities, the SEC has been vigorously prosecuting them. For many years this type of "white collar crime" had gone largely unpunished, but in recent years many high-profile criminals have spent time in jail for attempting to profit on the basis of insider trading.

Several other legislative acts have followed these two milestones of securities regulation. **The Public Utility**

Holding Company Act of 1935 laid down regulations governing electric and gas utilities. The Trust Indenture Act of 1939 clarified the legal obligations of debt security investments. The Investment Company Act of 1940, amended in 1970, expanded the powers of the Securities Act of 1933 to include mutual funds. Several other pieces of legislation have expanded the prosecuting powers of the Securities and Exchange Commission and of the National Association of Securities Dealers. Most of these legislative actions were a direct result of the Crash of 1929.

The market went through another major correction in October 1987. The Dow Jones Industrial Average dropped about 500 points in one day, October 19, that came to be known as *Black Monday*. That was the largest one-day change in the history of the market. Although it is often referred to as the "crash of '87," the market drop was only about 36 percent from peak to trough. This was a relatively small correction compared to the Crash of 1929. Also, the year following this "crash," the market rallied back up to new highs. Following 1929, the market did not reach its precrash high again until 1952, 23 years later.

Most of the blame for Black Monday fell on *program trading*. If you remember from Chapter 9, this is a highly speculative system of programming a computer to simultaneously monitor stock index options and/or index futures and the prices of the individual stocks that make up the indexes. Most of the program trades generated are of the *risk arbitrage* type. The computer will automatically generate buy or sell orders on the option contracts or on the individual stocks when it computes a discrepancy between the prices of the two. On October 19, 1987, the computers apparently kept seeing huge discrepancies between the falling stock prices and the market values of the index options. As a result, they kept generating program sell orders. The more the market fell, the more panicky others became, and many individuals and institutional investors joined in the selling. The only policy changes to come out of this event were requirements to put restrictions on program trading. The real lesson of the "crash of '87," however, was buy when everyone else is *selling*. The trading activity of that period was a good object lesson, verifying what you already learned in Chapter 1—"buy low and sell high."

The NYSE defines *program trading* as "a wide range of portfolio trading strategies involving the purchase or sale of 15 or more stocks having a total market value of $1 million or more." According to Rule 80A, adopted as a result of the volatility of the market in October 1987, if the DJIA has changed 2 percent or more from the previous day's close, a program trade may not be executed unless there is a market *up-tick*. In other words, if the market is down at least 2 percent, it must up-tick before sell orders from program traders can be executed. This is called a trading collar and is similar to the up-tick rule on short sales discussed in Chapter 3. Likewise, if the market is up at least 2 percent, a down-tick rule would apply to program purchases.

There are also more restrictive rules on *all trading* if the market becomes extremely volatile. Rule 80B of the NYSE specifies that if the DJIA is down 10 percent from the previous day's close, the exchange will halt *all trading* for one hour. When the market is reopened after this hour, if it continues to drop and hits minus 20 percent, trading will be halted for two hours. The NYSE does have certain discretionary options with these time limits. For example, if there is less than two hours left in the normal trading day when the minus 20 percent "circuit breaker" kicks in, the market may be reopened sooner. Such discretion is based on the regulator's opinion that the exchange will be able to maintain fair and orderly market conditions. In the unlikely event that the market is down 30 percent, it will be closed for the rest of the day.

The imaginative activities of sophisticated program traders continue to advance faster than the capabilities of regulators to control them. In spite of the existing restrictions, abuses of program trading could still create abnormal volatility in the market. The primary deterrent to abuses of this nature is the self-control of the traders themselves, not the existing trade restrictions. The huge volume generated by program trading is very profitable to exchanges and brokers alike. The prevention of abuses of this type of trading activity relies primarily on self-control, rather than on clearly defined rules with severe penalties. The innocent victims of poorly regulated program traders could be individual investors who own stock affected by their activities. Investors should only have to be concerned about earnings or market developments that would affect their company's business. They shouldn't have to worry also about what a program trader is going to do to their company's stock.

There used to be a common saying among investment advisors about companies that achieved their earnings projections by manipulating the information on the financial statements: creative accounting. That term became a euphemism for anything from changing LIFO (last in first out) to FIFO (first in first out) to accelerating depreciation and amortization schedules, and so on. Accountants who offered the most creative advice to enable a corporation to meet or beat its earnings expectations were actively recruited and abundantly compensated. The practice of creative accounting was not illegal; it was just a different way of presenting the same information. Everybody did it. It was nothing more than robbing Peter to pay Paul. Of course, sooner or later Peter would need to be repaid, but that could always be later—much later. It could be later when we really made our numbers, later when we could find a better creative account, or later when I was no longer CFO and it was someone else's job to keep juggling the ball in the air.

The marketplace was a harsh taskmaster. It quickly and severely punished anyone who didn't live up to its expectations. The marketplace wanted results, not excuses. Most of the increased volume of trading was coming from mutual funds. So, institutional investors, holding the bulk of a company's stock, could wield significant power influencing managers. Corporate management came under extreme pressure to make decisions that satisfied shareholders' shortsighted goals to keep the share price inflated, and management buckled. Its future was tied up in the success of the company's stock, so management became all too willing to sacrifice the future for the present.

After decades of creative accounting that led to many cases of corporate mismanagement and abuse, a crisis finally came to a head in 2002. Several large corporations came crashing down and many others fessed up to accounting irregularities. The one that captured the most headlines was Enron Corporation, which at its peak was the fifth largest company in the United States by market capitalization. It had started out as an energy trading and brokerage company, and had expanded into trading several non–energy related commodities. Accusations of accounting irregularities finally caught up to it, and the company came crashing down, ruining many investors and most of its employees in the process.

You should note that Enron was not the only company that precipitated a financial crisis at that time. Other large companies that also became casualties of their accounting practices were WorldCom, Global Crossing, Calpine,

Kmart, and many more. However, the Enron situation had several peculiarities.

The management of that company allegedly worked in collusion with their supposedly independent auditing firm, Arthur Anderson, to misrepresent the company's fiscal position on its financial statements. This was done by creating a maze of limited partnerships related to certain areas of the company's business. The financing of these limited partnerships became a tool for off–Balance Sheet financing. The partnerships were another corporate entity and thus did not have to be included on Enron's financial statements. Many losing investments were siphoned off of Enron's statements and splattered onto the partnership's statements. Thus, Enron kept making money while all of its partnership investors were losing money. Also, as Enron's business began to completely unravel, some profitable ventures were allegedly siphoned off into limited partnerships that Enron insiders invested in.

The legislative response to this situation was penned in record time, coming less than 6 months after Enron's demise. It was called the Sarbanes-Oxley Act and has been called the most comprehensive reform of securities law since the Securities Exchange Act of 1934. First and foremost, Sarbanes-Oxley required CEOs and CFOs to personally certify the authenticity of their company's financial statements. They could no longer pass the buck—they had to become more intimately involved with the work of their auditors. They would need to know and understand accounting practices as well as the independent auditors did.

Although the Sarbanes-Oxley Act made a lot of CEOs and CFOs sweat, the heart of the act was in its increased stringency on accounting practices across the board. It required full disclosure of accounting methods that the firm used and ongoing investigations of anything that was deemed irregular. The act also shortened the allowable lag time between when the fiscal quarter ended and when the financial report was due. This increased acceleration of reporting meant that managers would have to maintain a hands-on approach to the accounting practices involved.

As a result, most companies showed drastically reduced earnings immediately following the implementation of the Sarbanes-Oxley Act. However, most investors were aware that they could put more trust in the numbers and rewarded companies for their honesty. Companies continued to sell at higher-than-normal price/earnings ratios because the decline in earnings was not due to lower sales, but instead to higher standards of accounting. The Sarbanes-Oxley Act did much to restore investor confidence in the stock market, and it came at a time when it was needed most.

What Is the National Association of Securities Dealers?

The National Association of Securities Dealers, or NASD, is a self-governing professional organization of securities broker/dealers established in 1938. The NASD sets legal and ethical standards of conduct for professional securities brokers. It is the agency that is responsible for administering brokers' tests and qualifying brokers for registration. Its authority in the securities industry is similar to that of the American Bar Association in the legal profession. The ABA is responsible for testing and granting membership to attorneys. The examination administered by the NASD that qualifies an individual to become a stockbroker is called the General Securities Exam, often referred to as the Series 7. It is copyrighted by the NYSE.

The NASD may discipline members who violate its rules of ethics by revoking their membership, making it virtually impossible for them to continue to conduct securities business. Also, the NASD establishes arbitration committees to hear investor complaints about broker/dealers. The NASD arbitration process allows for hearing investors' grievances outside a court of law. This is usually much less costly than the legal system, and the NASD specializes in securities law violations. Arbitration suits where the amount of money involved is less than $1,000 have only a $30 filing fee. The fee structure goes up to $1,800 for suits involving more than $5 million. These fees are significantly lower than the cost of an attorney to settle the suit in a court of law. Attorneys' fees can run anywhere from $125 to $600+ per hour. Also, if the amount named in the suit is less than $10,000, you can take it to "simplified arbitration." This is the security industry's equivalent of small claims court. Such suits are usually settled in five months or less.

The phone number for the **NASD is (212) 858-4400.** They also have a toll-free investor hotline—**(800) 289-9999**—with information on past disciplinary actions taken against securities firms and individual brokers. Their database covers the approximately 5,400 member firms and the over half million registered brokers. To contact the **NYSE,** call **(212) 656-2772.** Arbitration of disputes involving options trading are often settled by the **Chicago Board Options Exchange** at **(312) 786-5600.** Disputes over municipal bond trading may be settled by the **Municipal Securities Rulemaking Board** at **(202) 223-9347.**

Common investor complaints about their brokers include such things as executing unauthorized trades, churning, and recommending inappropriate investments. Unauthorized trading is the practice of brokers making investments on behalf of their clients without the clients' permission. **"Churning" is the practice of making frequent changes in securities that do not directly benefit**

the investor but that generate multiple commissions for the broker. Misrepresenting inappropriate investments, such as purchasing high-risk investments for a conservative investor, also often results in harsh penalties being assessed against brokers. This is usually prosecuted on the basis of what is known as the *Prudent Man Rule*. **The "Prudent Man Rule" has a somewhat vague definition, stating that all fiduciaries must make investment decisions as a prudent, or conservative, person would.**

No other industry is as highly regulated as the securities industry. Most brokerage firms conduct frequent internal audits of their employees' books. Brokers may also have their books reviewed or audited by the Securities and Exchange Commission, the National Association of Securities Dealers or the New York Stock Exchange. Even though you may read occasional articles on broker misconduct, this is a good sign that the regulatory bodies are doing their jobs. The environment in the securities industry today is becoming much healthier than it has been in the past. However, whenever there are large amounts of money involved, there is a potential for fraud.

The regulatory functions of the NASD and the SEC have frequently overlapped. Because of the lack of clearly defined jurisdictions, the work of one agency has frequently duplicated the work of the other. So, in the future you are likely to see the NASD function more as a watchdog regulator and the SEC function in more of a government legislative role. The power of the NASD to discipline violators of securities rules of trade will increase, while the SEC will focus more on clearly defining what the rules should be.

You must be aware of your legal rights and of your options for recourse if you are a victim of broker misconduct. However, better yet, if you are an investor who is well informed, you may be able to avoid the necessity for arbitration or legal action. Most broker-client conflicts arise from miscommunications or misunderstandings between the two parties. A knowledgeable investor, such as yourself, should know how to avoid inappropriate investments and how to judge imprudent advice. Ideally, you will not need to use the information in this chapter.

Do You Know What You Need to Know?

To check up on what you learned from this chapter, answer the following questions in your own words, then compare your answers with the answer key.

1. What is the Securities Investors Protection Corporation (SIPC)? What are the limits of its insurance protection? Compare and contrast it with the Federal Deposit Insurance Corporation (FDIC).

2. How has the securities industry changed since the infamous stock market "crash of '29?" Why is it unlikely that we will ever see a repeat of the circumstances that led to that crash?

3. Who is an *insider*, according to the SEC? What is an insider prohibited from doing? How is the SEC investigating reports of insider trading?

4. What is a *prospectus*, and when is it issued? What is a *proxy letter*, and when is it issued?

5. What is program trading? How has the introduction of stock index options resulted in the growth of this type of trading? How does program trading affect stock prices?

6. What trading restrictions resulted from the 500-point market drop in October 1987, the "crash of '87?" What lessons did investors learn from that drop?

7. What are the NASD and the SEC? What are some of the important functions of these organizations? How do

they differ, and how do they overlap? Explain the NASD arbitration process.
8. How has the increased emphasis on security industry regulations changed the nature of the business in recent years? How has this benefited the investor?

Answer Key

1. The SIPC is a government agency that insures brokerage accounts up to $500,000 in investments and $100,000 in cash. The FDIC insures bank accounts up to $100,000.
2. The "crash of '29" was due in part to a lack of enforceable legal disciplinary actions that could be taken against market manipulators. Many legislative acts regarding the securities industry were passed as a result of the crash. Today it is one of the most heavily regulated industries in the world.
3. Anyone who has access to nonpublic information about a company is an insider. It is illegal to profit from an investment based on insider information. The SEC actively pursues prosecution of insider trading.
4. A prospectus is issued to all investors in an IPO. It represents full disclosure of the company's business, including risks to the investor. A proxy solicitation letter is sent to shareholders prior to the annual shareholders' meeting. It allows your vote to be cast in absentia by a proxy at the meeting.
5. Program trading is computer-generated buy and sell orders usually tied to offsetting index option positions. Because of the increased volume due to program trading, unpredictable volatility can frequently result.
6. The 500-point market drop in October 1987 drew attention to the problems resulting from increased program trading. The NYSE has subsequently imposed restric-

tions on this type of trading if the market becomes too volatile.

7. The NASD is a self-governing organization that sets the standards of ethics and professional conduct for brokers in the securities industry. The SEC is a government agency empowered to regulate the industry.

8. Strict regulations have improved the standards for becoming a registered representative. Investors' interests have probably never been as closely guarded as they are now.

The National Association of Securities Dealers is the chief watchdog of the securities industry.

— Chapter 11 —

What Types of Investments Offer Tax Advantages?

Albert Einstein once quipped, "The hardest thing in the world to understand is the income tax." Over the last 50 years since he spoke those words, it hasn't gotten any easier. Understanding the Special and General Theory of Relativity is a piece of cake compared to complete comprehension of the Internal Revenue Code. Relativity altered our view of the universe just once; the Internal Revenue Service has altered it thousands of times. Einstein's book explaining the space-time continuum is 157 pages, written at a high school reading level. The Internal Revenue Code is about a 10,000-page tome, and it isn't written to be understood at any reading level. Relativity is a constant; tax code is in a constant state of flux. Relativity is an ephemeral theory; tax code is a concrete law. Something is wrong with this picture. Can you understand why trying to write about taxes in a short chapter of a paperback book is an impossible task?

Anything put into print about tax-planning strategies will not have a long shelf-life. Tax law is revised so frequently that anything written about this subject had better be written in morphing ink, or otherwise the information will quickly become obsolete and inaccurate. Whenever you read anything about taxes, the information is usually accompanied by a disclaimer that says something like, "Consult a qualified professional about your tax situation." So, be aware that the information presented here is subject to change without notice, and consider its applicability to your particular tax situation properly disclaimed.

Note that I have made every attempt to ensure that the information in this chapter is accurate and valid. Also, I have attempted to present facts on taxes in broad-enough terms that they will be useful and applicable for years to come. However, I cannot guarantee that all information will still be correct at the time you read this. In recent years, lawmakers have become increasingly more active at rewriting extant tax code.

This manipulation of tax structure is happening so rapidly because of the practice of using adjustments as political tools, as well as to regulate economic activity. Current political thought is that the regulation of the economy and economic activity is the most powerful political weapon. Tax cuts have been used to simulate consumer spending and thus economic growth. Tax hikes have been used to stem the inflation that naturally results from too much consumer spending.

Note that the problem of regulating the economy through the use of tax manipulation illustrates an inherent problem. High tax rates, by their very nature, can create recession. Because growth in the economy is usually achieved through consumer spending, anything that reduces the consumer's availability of cash reduces spending. With higher taxes, consumers have less money to spend.

However, does that mean that if taxes are lowered, consumer spending will increase? Although that is certainly the hope of those trying to regulate the economy, people do not always respond as expected. If the psychological motivation of most consumers is focused primarily on fears and concerns about the economy, most will still put a high priority on saving, rather than on spending. So, such simplistic reasoning that tax incentives can achieve economic results does not necessarily follow. Therefore, economists must ostensibly deal with a psychological problem to solve a materialistic one.

"Nothing in life is certain but death and taxes." Very few people would argue with that statement. However, although taxes may be certain, how much they are is anything but certain. In recent years nothing has been more *uncertain* than the amount of individuals' taxes. Even when your *tax bracket* remains constant, the changes in methods of computation and allowable deductions can dramatically change the amount of taxes owed.

As marginal tax brackets creep up each year, investors need to keep a watchful eye on the effects their investments have on their tax situation. You need to be aware of the levels of taxable income that will bump you into the next higher bracket. This is a moving target each year, so don't get complacent. Even if your income doesn't go up, your taxable income and your tax bracket very well might.

Because of the complexity of the income tax structure, several legislators have presented proposals for tax reform. These generally fall into two categories: a modified flat tax or a consumption tax, also called a national sales tax. Flat tax proposals usually involve repealing most, or all, deductions and charging all taxpayers a set percentage of income. A flat tax would probably be set at about 20 percent, and in theory would be revenue neutral. In other words, it would not increase or decrease the total amount of annual tax receipts by the government.

A national sales tax would be a tax paid by consumers at the time of purchase. Many states currently have sales taxes. Certainly, if all other taxes were repealed, the cost of most manufactured items would be reduced. The prices of most items you buy today include the costs of corporate income taxes, value-added taxes, import taxes, and so on. To do away with these tax burdens would greatly improve productivity. The net effect on consumer prices would probably be neutral. The tax burden would be more fairly paid by the wealthy. The greater the consumption, the greater the taxes paid. Certainly, you are not going to be much of a consumer if you do not have much of an income.

This is, of course, theory. It is impossible to imagine the dismantling of the IRS within the foreseeable future. But every action begins with an idea. Very few taxpayers dispute that an overhaul of the IRS is necessary. More and more individuals each year are overcome by the stress of filing. Many refuse to file, either in protest or out of a paralyzing incapacity to complete the task because of its complexity. As tax burdens continue to increase, so will the number of individuals who drop out of the system. Something is going to have to be done.

A prospect that is gaining popularity—and may very well be law by the time you read this—is to modify the tax status of corporate dividends. As was previously mentioned near the beginning of Chapter 8, earnings reported by publicly traded corporations are subject to double taxation: Companies pay taxes on their net income, and shareholders pay taxes again on their share of that income, their dividends.

Political sentiment is not so radical as to favor the elimination of this double tax inequity. However, there have been many recent proposals to grant a more favorable tax status to shareholder dividends. The most likely scenario is that corporations will be allowed to deduct dividend payments from taxable income and thus reap a tax savings on that part of their earnings. However, several political figures do favor the idea of making stock dividends exempt from federal income tax. That's definitely the most equitable solution.

So, the reality is you must deal with the current tax liabilities on your investments. Besides the taxes due on income and dividends you receive from your investments, you must be concerned about capital gains taxes. **A "capital gain" or a "capital loss" is the difference between what you pay for an investment, or another adjusted-cost basis, and what you receive when you sell it, or it is redeemed.** The capital gains or losses are reported on *Schedule D* of the *1040 Tax Form*. The net amount computed on Schedule D is transferred to line 13 of the 1040 Form. At the time of this writing, a long-term capital gain or loss is generated from investments held over one year.

At the time of this writing, an asset that is sold after being held for over one year would be taxed at a long-term capital gains rate. This is currently either 20 percent or 10 percent, depending on your marginal federal tax bracket. If investors are in an upper bracket (28 percent or higher) their long-term capital gains rate will be 20 percent. If investors are in a lower bracket, such as 15 percent, their long-term capital gains will be taxed at the 10-percent rate. Also, in the year 2000 these rates were lowered to 18 percent and 8 percent, respectively, for taxpayers who held investments for over five years. In other words, long-term was redefined to include two holding periods for determining tax liabilities—over one year, and over five years. As is the case with all tax questions, every individual's tax situation is different, and you should consult with a qualified tax preparer regarding your particular circumstances.

Also, investors may use any amount of capital loss to offset capital gains. However, they may only use $3,000 per year to offset ordinary income. If you have more than $3,000 in capital losses, you may use the remainder next year. In fact, you may continue to forward capital losses into the future, until they are used up. Keep in mind that this $3,000 loss does not apply to capital gains. If you have $6,000 in gains and $5,000 in losses, you may use the full $5,000 against the gain, thus netting out only a $1,000 taxable event. If, however, you have $5,000 in capital losses and no gains, you could only use $3,000 of that loss to offset income in that year. You could forward the remaining $2,000 in losses to offset capital gains or income next year.

Should You Have an IRA?

There are several investments directly aimed at supplementing retirement income that make excellent financial planning tools for helping individuals to meet retirement goals. Probably one of the most popular strategies is to set up **an "individual retirement account" (IRA). An IRA must be kept separate from other personal accounts. All income or capital gains received from investments in an IRA are exempt from current income tax.**

There are several different types of IRA accounts, including Traditional IRAs, Roth IRAs, Spousal IRAs, SIMPLE IRAs, Rollover IRAs, and Simplified Employee Pension Plans or SEP-IRAs.

The primary difference between a Traditional IRA and a Roth IRA is the tax status of contributions made to each. In both cases, individuals may currently contribute up to $3,000 per year of earned income. The maximum amount of this annual contribution will remain at that level through 2004. Then it will increase to $4,000 for years 2005 through 2007. In 2008, it will max out at $5,000 and then follow a schedule of indexed increases after that. However, there is a special "catch-up" provision for individuals over age 50. They can add an additional $500 to their IRA each year through 2005, and then after that an additional $1,000 over the regular $5,000 limit that will be in place at that time. With a Traditional IRA, this contribution may be tax deductible. In other words, individuals may contribute money on which they have not already paid income taxes— pretaxed earnings. Such funds are referred to as "qualified." The requirements to be met for deducting this contribution from taxable earnings depends on whether or not the tax-payer is covered under another retirement plan, such as a corporate pension plan, and on the taxpayer's income level.

With a Roth IRA, individuals may contribute up to the maximum amount listed above; however, these contributions are not tax deductible. Contributions to a Roth IRA are always considered to be with after-tax dollars, in other words "nonqualified." No one, not even the IRS, knows what the tax brackets will be at some future date; however, if they are on the high end of the current federal brackets, the total value of a Roth IRA will probably be greater than an equivalent Traditional IRA. If the taxpayer's liability is at a 15-percent rate at the time of retirement, the after-tax value of a Traditional IRA account will probably be greater than that of an equivalent Roth IRA. Another difference is that individuals may continue to make contributions to a Roth IRA after they reach age 70½. With a Traditional IRA, individuals must begin taking mandatory annual distributions once they reach age 70½. The minimum amounts of those withdrawals will be computed using life expectancy actuarial tables.

In order for individuals to be able to deduct their contributions to a Traditional IRA, they must meet certain income requirements. If they are already covered by another retirement plan, such as an employer's pension plan, individuals are not allowed to deduct IRA contributions unless their adjusted gross income (AGI) is below a certain threshold. This threshold for complete deductibility of Traditional IRA contributions is being raised each year and will top out in 2007 at $50,000 for singles or $80,000 for taxpayers filing jointly. Beyond these thresholds, some portion of your contributions may still be deductible if your AGI does not exceed $60,000 for singles or $100,000 for joint returns. So, unless you are a very good saver, or a better than average budget manager, you probably won't have enough money left over to make a deductible contribution to a Traditional IRA. This was probably the plan when the IRS revised this part of the tax code. Deductible IRA contributions represent a loss of tax revenue to the government. A chart published by the IRS that explains the limits and requirements for deductibility of IRA contributions can be accessed at *www.irs.gov/forms_pubs/graphics/15160x01.gif.*

A unique advantage of a Roth IRA over a Traditional IRA is the nonworking spouse contribution limits. A Roth IRA allows individuals to make contributions into a Spousal IRA, even if the spouse was not the one who earned the income. Spousal IRA contributions are currently subject to the same limits as those of the wage earner. In a family where only one spouse had income, the wage earner could currently put a total of $6,000 into two IRAs ($3,000 for the wage earner's IRA and $3,000 for the Spousal IRA). Only *earned* income can be contributed to an IRA. So, this contribution limit is predicated upon the wage earner's making over $6,000 for the year.

A SIMPLE IRA is one for which an employer is allowed to make pre-taxed salary reduction contributions currently of up to $8,000 per year into an employee's separate account. The term "SIMPLE" is an acronym for Savings Incentive Match Plan for Employees. The "Match" part of that acronym means that employers can match the amount that employees contribute. These IRAs can be set up for self-employed individuals or for any small business. The contribution limit will be increased by $1,000 over the next two years to $10,000 in 2005. Increases to contribution limits will be indexed after that. Also, SIMPLE IRAs offer more aggressive "catch-up" allowances for participants over age 50 than Traditional or Roth IRAs: $1,000 in 2003, then increasing by $500 each year to $2,500 in 2005. Subsequent catch-up contributions will be indexed beginning in 2007.

An IRA that is sponsored by a bank is usually structured like a certificate of deposit, or CD. That is why if you establish an IRA with a bank you are not able to add to your existing account. Each new deposit into an IRA requires opening a new account. You are not allowed to deposit additional funds into a CD once you invest in it. This is completely different from brokerage IRAs. However, because of bank IRAs, many people think that they also have to set up a new account each time they make a new contribution to their IRA at a brokerage firm. That is not the case.

Brokerage firms offer you two basic choices when establishing an individual retirement account. You can invest your IRA contribution in a mutual fund and in most cases the investment company that manages the fund will act as custodian for the account. Some mutual funds hire outside custodians simply because they do not have their own trust department, or they find it is more economical to hire out this service. Your choices with an investment company IRA will be limited to the funds within that family. You will also have to pay a relatively low annual custodian fee—usually about $5.00 per year. Most funds will also charge a $5.00 switch fee if you transfer from one fund to another.

The other option would be to set up a **"self-directed IRA." With this type of IRA, the brokerage firm will act as custodian (unless they hire an outside manager),**

and your investment options will include just about anything the broker offers. You could invest in individual stocks, bonds, mutual funds, or even U.S. gold and silver coins. Current IRS rules, however, do not allow you to invest in gold or silver bullion or coins from other countries in an individual retirement account. You could also invest in annuities or private investments, which will be described later in this chapter. The annual custodian fee will be higher—usually around $35.00. You will also pay regular brokerage commissions for your investments.

Individuals who own their own businesses or work for themselves should consider a simplified employee pension, or SEP-IRA. **A "SEP-IRA" allows a self-employed individual or business owner to contribute up to 25 percent of annual adjusted gross income (AGI) as a deductible contribution.** However, the contribution may not exceed 25 percent of compensation up to a maximum of $40,000. Self-employed individuals are allowed to reduce their compensation by the SEP-IRA contribution. So, in effect individuals who earned $200,000 per year could make the maximum $40,000 contribution. To illustrate:

$200,000	self-employed earned income
− $ 40,000	SEP-IRA contribution
$160,000	adjusted compensation
× .25	maximum percentage SEP contribution
$ 40,000	maximum allowable contribution

A Rollover IRA is created when an individual transfers a distribution from a corporate retirement account, such as a 401(k), or other retirement account. The key word here is *transfers*. If an individual takes a full distribution and then puts it into an IRA, the IRS will consider the distribution fully taxable. It must be *transferred* from one institution to another without ever going to the individual in order to avoid being fully taxed. This transfer can be either to a Traditional IRA or to a Rollover IRA. If the corporate retirement funds are commingled with other IRA contributions, then you may not transfer the funds back to another corporate retirement account if you decide to participate in another one in the future. You must keep your retirement funds in a separate Rollover IRA account if you want to transfer back out. Most people do not need to bother with a Rollover IRA; they should just transfer corporate retirement accounts to a Traditional IRA. The reason for this is that most people who retire don't plan on going back to work and establishing another retirement account. Even if they do, they generally have more investment options from their self-directed IRA than they would have from their corporate retirement account. About all that will happen if you transfer to a Rollover IRA is that you will pay two annual custodian fees— one for your Traditional IRA and one for your Rollover IRA.

All interest and capital gains earned in a qualified account accumulates free from income taxes while the funds are in the account. Roth IRAs also have the unique advantage of offering tax-free withdrawals after the participant reaches age 59½. For all the other accounts previously mentioned, withdrawals will be subject to income tax in most cases. However, if that money is withdrawn after retirement, presumably you will be in a lower income tax bracket. This is a very important benefit. Deferring taxation on your investments means that you will be able to earn interest on money that you would have otherwise sent to the IRS. Investing in tax-deferred accounts greatly increases your total return over investments made in taxable accounts.

If an investor in a 36 percent tax bracket (combined federal and state taxes) put $10,000 in a taxable account paying 7 percent and in a tax-deferred account paying

7 percent, after ten years the taxable account would be worth about $15,500, the tax-deferred account, $19,671. Over a 20-year period, these returns jump to $24,027 and $38,696, respectively. In other words, taxes took $14,669 from the return in this example. That's 147 percent of your original investment. Your account value will grow much faster in a qualified plan than it will in a taxable account. Besides retirement accounts, the only other popular investment that offers the benefits of tax deferral is an *annuity*.

Should You Participate in Your Employer's 401(k) Plan?

For most employees, the tax advantages and retirement benefits available to them through participation in employer-sponsored 401(k) plans outweighs most other alternatives. The equivalent of this type of account for non-profit organizations is identified as a 403(b) Plan. For employees of state and local government entities it is called a 457 Plan. Some organizations, such as education associations, may identify this type of plan as a TSA, a tax-sheltered annuity. Many features of these plans, such as the investment choices offered, are designated by the plans' sponsors. Consequently, some are better than others. However, as a general rule, employees will have more flexibility and more generous tax benefits by participating in their 401(k) or equivalent payroll-deduction program.

Almost all companies offer a 401(k) plan. If your company doesn't, talk to the Employee Benefits Department about it. There are many organizations that offer turnkey programs for a minimum expense. The federal regulatory oversight of these plans is the responsibility of the Pension and Welfare Benefits Administration (PWBA) of the U.S. Department of Labor. Some information on these plans is available on their web site at *www.dol.gov/pwba/*. Other information can be found with a Google search, or other web crawler or search engine.

Probably the most important benefit of these plans is that they offer a way for you to contribute pretaxed dollars to an account that will grow on a tax-deferred basis. This is done as a payroll deduction, so you will not be tempted to spend the money before it gets invested. To those of us who are tempted toward unbridled consumption, this can be an attractive feature.

Like contributions made to retirement accounts or pension funds, a withdrawal from this type of plan is subject to a 10 percent penalty if taken before age 59½. However, participants can take out a loan from their 401(k) account before that age. Typically, such loans can be taken for reasons such as economic hardship, disability, education expenses, and a home purchase. Participants are, in effect, lending the money to themselves with a commitment to pay it back with future payroll deductions.

By having pretaxed dollars taken out of their paycheck, employees reduce the amount of current income tax owed. For example, assume an employee's monthly paycheck is $4,000, and this employee has 10 percent, ($400) taken out as a 401(k) contribution. If this taxpayer is in the 35 percent tax bracket (combined federal and state), instead of owing $1,400 in taxes (35 percent of $4,000), he or she will owe $1,260 (35 percent of $3,600). That represents a tax reduction of $140 monthly, or $1,680 annually. Of course, employees will eventually pay taxes on that money when they begin taking withdrawals. However, the benefits of earning tax-deferred interest on tax-deferred contributions is extremely significant over many years.

The maximum amount of pretaxed dollars that can be contributed to a 401(k) is set by the Internal Revenue

Service. In the year 2003, that amount was $12,000. However, that maximum will grow each year as a means to counteract negative effects of inflation on retirement benefits. For the following 3 years, the maximum will grow by $1,000 per year, to $15,000 in 2006. After that, the forecast is it will grow by $500 per year. However, participants, in most cases, can also contribute additional taxed monies. The taxable funds that are contributed over this maximum amount will be put in a 401(a) plan. These plan numbers, 401(a) and 401(k), are sections of the Internal Revenue Code that define qualified retirement plans and payroll deduction plans.

Also, employees who are near retirement age and who do not have sufficient funds in their 401(k) to meet their financial needs at retirement are allowed to make "catch-up" contributions, similar to those offered with IRAs. If you are over age 50, you can put in another $1,000 over the regular maximum limits each year through 2005, bringing the total allowable tax-advantaged contribution to $13,000. Under current law, the catch-up amount will be reduced from $1,000 to $500 per year after 2006.

Another benefit of 401(k) plans is that many companies offer matching incentives. This means that if you contribute 10 percent of your salary and the company matches it 50 percent, the employer will add an extra 5 percent to your 401(k). Not all companies offer matching contributions, but if they do, this amounts to a raise in salary. If your company offers matching contributions, it is generally in your best interest to take advantage of it. Many companies might require you to remain employed by the company for a certain length of time before the contributions they make for you are completely vested—that is, before you can take possession of that asset. However, your payroll deduction contributions are considered 100 percent vested at the time they are made. In many plans, matching contributions are made with company stock, rather than cash. The two main reasons for this are: It is cheaper for the company, and management usually considers employee ownership of the company an incentive for a better work ethic.

Another advantage of 401(k) plans is what is called portability. If you leave the company you can transfer the vested amount in your account to your new company's plan or to another qualified account. Because the average employee changes jobs five or six times during his or her career, this is an attractive feature. Generally, you can transfer qualified (pretaxed) funds to a Traditional IRA and nonqualified (taxed) funds to a Roth IRA.

With all these benefits, is there a downside? Yes, there's always a catch. In recent years participation in 401(k) plans has been declining. Although this decline may be due to a cyclically weak economy, there have also been some sensational catastrophes. The participant's return on 401(k) contributions is only as good as the investment alternatives the plan offers. Most plans offer a variety of choices, such as a broad range of mutual funds, a fixed-rate account, and company stock. If the mutual funds lose value, the fixed account is paying a rate that doesn't outpace inflation, and the company's stock is down, you are going to be very disappointed. In sum, all the tax advantages of the 401(k) are not going to offset the large loss of principal.

This worst-case scenario was dramatically played out a few years ago when the largest energy trading company in the world filed for bankruptcy. That was, of course, Enron. The reasons for Enron's demise were unmitigated greed and compromised ethics. Some of the company's senior executives allegedly colluded with their financial auditors at Arthur Anderson to hide trading losses and to hype the market value of the stock. The whole scheme of off–balance sheet financing through numerous limited partnerships imploded in 2002. Enron filed Chapter 11, and Arthur Anderson changed names and management after losing many of its clients. The wrongdoers received justice. However, the innocent victims of this fiasco were the participants in the 401(k).

Enron had offered generous matching contributions to employees who kept their 401(k) investments in company stock. Corporate officers strongly touted Enron stock, and most employees took their advice. Some senior executives were allegedly selling large holdings of their stock at the same time they were recommending that their employees buy it. Then when the news broke that the whole company was really a house of cards, the assets of the 401(k) were frozen. Participants could not move out of the stock as they watched it plummet from over $50 to about 10 cents. Thousands of employees watched in agony as their life savings evaporated before their eyes, and there was nothing they could do about it.

That scenario was unsettling not just to Enron participants but to all 401(k) investors. Up until the time of Enron's collapse, it seemed inconceivable that corporate management could have gotten away with so much while so many regulatory authorities were watching. However, that situation, and the few others that followed, resulted in greater enforcement powers for those responsible for accounting oversight—the Sarbanes-Oxley Act of 2002.

In spite of the whirlwind of controversy over the casualties of Enron's 401(k), with the checks and balances that are in place now, you should be able to participate in your company's program with complete peace of mind. Current 401(k) plans will likely have more features than most other alternatives, and the environment that led to Enron's collapse has been completely overhauled. One key feature of the Sarbanes-Oxley Act is that it prevents the freezing of 401(k) assets in the event of bankruptcy. However, probably the hardest hitting component of the act is that CEOs (chief executive officers) are now required to sign off for their company's financial statements, making them personally liable for any misstatements or misrepresentations of the company's financial position. They are no longer able to make their auditors scapegoats for misrepresentations or mistakes.

What Tax-Advantaged Investments Can Be Used for Education Expenses?

Within the next few years the cost of a 4-year college education at a private university will likely be close to $150,000. At the rate at which college expenses are growing, that amount should double in about 14 years. The cost of an equivalent education at a state-sponsored school will probably run close to $50,000 within a few years and will also likely double by the time your child is ready to go if he or she is 4 years old now. College education expenses are rising much faster than the overall rate of inflation. If parents don't begin making provisions for their children's college education long beforehand, most will not be able to afford it.

Consequently state and federal government agencies have been created to help parents save for these expenses by offering tax-advantaged investments for such planning. The two popular methods of saving for educational expenses that offer tax advantages are a Coverdell Educational Savings Account (ESA) and a Section 429 Plan.

ESAs offer participants the opportunity to contribute $2,000 in after-tax dollars per year into a tax-free account, similar to a Roth IRA. The interest that is

earned will not be taxed while it is in the account, and the money can be withdrawn tax-free if it is used to meet qualified educational expenses. Such qualified expenses include college tuition, room and board for college, school textbooks, and so on.

Contributions to an ESA are considered to be assets of the student, not the person who made the contribution. Consequently, if the money in an ESA is not used for educational expenses, it will become the property of the designated individual and not revert back to the original donor. Also, funds in an ESA must be used for college expenses by the time the student reaches age 30, or else they will be subject to taxes and penalties. So, if you are a career student, don't count on living off tax-free withdrawals from your ESA after that age.

Another consideration is that Coverdell ESAs may negatively affect the student's eligibility for federal financial aid. There are many sources for student financial aid. For information and applications, check out the web site of the U.S. Department of Education Federal Student Aid at *www.ed.gov/offices/OSFAP/Students/*. To get to one of the many other sites on this topic, use a web crawler such as Google and search under the topic "student financial aid."

You should also be warned that you may still end up with some tax liability even if you use ESA withdrawals for qualified educational expenses, the reason being allowable income tax deductions from Hope or Lifetime Learning credits. If you are a parent and you pay for part of your child's education with ESA funds and claim a Hope or Lifetime Learning credit for some overlapping expenses, you will probably find that the overlapping funds are taxable. The IRS does not allow a double deduction for such expenses. You can get information on Hope or Lifetime Learning Credits from the IRS at *http://www.irs.gov/*.

Request publication 970 *Tax Benefits for Education*. Also, this is one of those areas where you should check with your professional tax consultant about your particular situation.

That said, let's take a look at what benefits you could expect from making annual ESA contributions. If you were to begin making a $2,000-per-year contribution the day your child is born and then on his or her birthday each year for the next 17 years (a total of eighteen contributions), that ESA would grow to about $56,000 (assuming it earns about 5 percent interest). That total includes approximately $20,000 in tax-free interest plus the $36,000 principle. Aside from the fact that your child may be disappointed in your choice of birthday presents ("But I wanted a video game!"), you better hope your child wants to attend a state school. It's going to cost at least another $100,000 if he or she wants a diploma from a prestigious private institution. In such a case, it would be advisable to look into a 529 Plan.

So, what is a 529 Plan, and how does it work? First, 529 Plans are created by and regulated by state, not federal, government agencies, and they are available in all fifty states. There are two kinds of state-sponsored 529 Plans: prepaid tuition plans and college savings plans. **Prepaid tuition plans allow you to pay for future college expenses at current prices with a guarantee that the funds will grow at the rate of inflation to meet actual higher education expenses at the time the student attends. College savings plans allow you to contribute monies within certain guidelines set by the state in which you live.**

Like ESA contributions, 529 Plan investments are made with after-tax dollars, grow tax-free while in the account, and can be withdrawn tax-free if they are used for qualified educational expenses. However, there are fewer restrictions on 529 Plans than on ESAs.

The prepaid tuition plan offers a guarantee that the student has sufficient savings to pay for however many semesters (or quarters) of college had been paid for, regardless of how high the cost may go. In other words, you "lock in" today's rates by paying for all or part of the education expenses up front. This would apply to any of your state's eligible colleges, as well as to out-of-state private or public schools. Some states may offer a discount from current costs if the student is very young. That feature is based on the expectation that the funds can be invested to grow at a faster rate than college expense inflation.

By far the most popular 529 Plan is the college saving plan. Although this type does not guarantee that you will have the exact dollar amount necessary to meet education expenses, it allows you to invest large enough sums to cover everything (even the frat "keggers" and resulting repair costs—room and board). Each state sets its own contribution limit, but most states have maximums over $200,000. Also, each individual may contribute up to $55,000 (or $110,000 for married couples) for the benefit of each student without incurring federal gift taxes, so long as more gifts are not made within the next 5 years.

Contributions to 529 Plans, unlike those to ESAs, are not considered part of the student's assets. So the person who made the investment still maintains control of the funds, and monies not used for college expenses can revert back to the original donor or can be given to another family member to pay for education expenses with tax-free funds. Obviously, taxes will be owed on the funds withdrawn not used for college. Also, while these funds are in the 529 Plan, they are considered to be outside the contributor's estate, and thus would avoid estate taxes upon the owner's death.

Most financial institutions have master 529 Plans that comply with the applicable state laws. The amounts being contributed to these plans have been growing exponentially. These plans offer more benefits and more flexibility than the alternatives. The sponsoring state will maintain income tax records. When students make withdrawals for college expenses, they will receive a 1099 Form itemizing the amount that they need to report.

For more information on 529 Plans check out the site *www.collegesavings.org/*, which is sponsored by the College Savings Plan Network and affiliated with the National Association of State Treasurers. Also, many financial institutions maintain web sites with a wealth of information on 529 Plans.

What Is an Annuity?

From a tax point of view, an annuity functions much like a nondeductible IRA. **An "annuity" is a contract issued by an insurance company that allows the returns on the investments within the contract to accumulate tax deferred until withdrawn. Like the IRA, it also has a 10 percent IRS penalty if withdrawn before age 59½.** However, there are no limits on the amount you may contribute, except those set by the insurance company due to the age of the participant. Some insurance companies, for example, will not allow individuals over age 80 to invest in annuities. This age limit is set because of the life insurance benefits that are part of the contract.

Also, your tax liability when you take distributions from an annuity will only be on the *capital appreciation* of the value. Since you had already paid taxes on the original amount that you invested in the annuity, that part of your distribution is considered return of principal. You will not have to pay taxes on your principal twice. In most cases, the percentage of tax-free income from your annuity distributions will be the same percentage that your original principal represents of the current total market value. This is not as complicated as it sounds. To illustrate, assume you put $50,000 in an annuity, and in ten years it grows to $100,000. The annuitized distributions that you take at this point will be considered 50 percent taxable income and 50 percent tax-free return of principal. So, if you are in the 28 percent bracket, you would be paying an equivalent of 14 percent in taxes on the total distribution—only 50 percent of the income would be taxed at 28 percent. Annuitized withdrawals from your annuity will be assumed to be part income and part principal in the same ratio as the capital appreciation amount and original principal, making up the current total market value. The tax deferral of earnings in an annuity is possible because life insurance companies do not have to pay taxes on investments they make for their policyholders. This tax benefit for the insurance companies is passed through to the annuity contract owners.

When you set up an annuity contract, there are three designated individuals: the owner, the annuitant, and the beneficiary. The "owner" of the annuity is the individual who purchases the policy and has the authority to make the investment decisions. Usually, this is also the annuitant. However, it can be different. **The "annuitant" is the individual who will receive any distributions from the contract and on whose life the insurance policy applies.** If the annuitant dies, or in some cases the owner, the beneficiary will receive the cash value or death benefit value of the annuity, whatever is greater. This transfer to the beneficiary avoids probate and is accomplished relatively easily and in a short period of time compared to most estate transfers.

There are two ways to withdraw from an annuity. The annuitant can either take systematic (or periodic) withdrawals or he or she can annuitize. The systematic withdrawals have limits set by the insurance company. Usually, these limits will be 10 percent of the account value or the amount of interest earned. However, different companies put different wrinkles in their withdrawal requirements. You will have to read the prospectus for a complete explanation. Also, for tax purposes, systematic withdrawals will be treated as if the first dollars taken out were from the last earnings. Thus systematic withdrawals will not usually get as favorable a tax treatment as annuitized withdrawals. Most companies will have penalties for early withdrawals from deferred annuities. Typically, this is a declining penalty such as 5 percent in the first year, 4 percent in the second, 3 percent in the third, and so on, with no penalty after five years. Keep in mind that this penalty would be in addition to the 10 percent IRS penalty if you withdraw from it before age 59½. *Immediate annuities* allow immediate withdrawals with no penalties.

When the contract is *annuitized*, the annuitant will begin receiving regular periodic distributions. These distributions can be set up with a wide variety of options. You can receive a fixed dollar amount for life, jointly for your life and the life of your spouse, for life with a fixed number of years certain, or for various periods of time guaranteed. Once you annuitize, however, the terms of your distribution cannot be changed. Often the owner and the annuitant are the same individual. However, they don't have to be. The owner can be a trust, such as a living trust, or the owner can name someone else the annuitant if he or she wants the distributions to go to that person.

The investment options offered for annuities are also different from those of IRAs. Annuities can either be fixed or variable. A fixed annuity will guarantee a certain rate of interest for a predetermined period of time. Most insurance companies offer several options for fixed annuities: typically one-, three-, five-, or ten-year terms. The interest rate you would receive would depend on the term selected.

A variable annuity does not offer a fixed rate of return. It is usually set up with an investment company, frequently offering a variety of portfolios that will closely resemble the portfolios of some of the mutual funds of that manager. In other words, this will be a separate portfolio of investments from the mutual fund that the manager controls, but it will invest in the same or similar securities and the investment decisions will be made by the same fund managers. The annuity investor is allowed to transfer between funds or to change the percentage mix of the funds as frequently as the annuity contract allows.

Another popular investment that many insurance companies are now offering are *life insurance* contracts designed primarily as investments. Such contracts offer portfolios similar to those managed by investment companies for annuities. One of the more noteworthy differences between life contracts and annuities is that the insured may borrow money from the insurance policy, subject to certain restrictions or expenses established by the issuer. The actual insurance benefits may not be as high for these types of policies as they are for more traditional policies, but the potential for growth of value may offset that. The beneficiary inherits the value of the policy free of federal income tax, as with any life policy.

A third type of investment that is frequently used for tax strategies is a limited partnership. Probably because many of these partnerships were designed primarily for tax benefits, many of them have been investment disasters. Indeed, the term "limited partnership" has taken on such a negative connotation that it is no longer in vogue.

What Are Limited Partnerships?

Limited partnerships are usually referred to by euphemisms, such as "private investments" or "direct investments." The term "limited partnership" is usually intentionally avoided because most people associate it with a negative connotation. In recent years, many limited partnerships have had very poor track records, and many general partners or brokerage firms have been defendants in class action lawsuits over partnerships they represent. In the past, there have been an unusually high number of limited partnerships that have given grossly substandard returns. These include real estate partnerships, oil and gas partnerships, equipment leasing partnerships, and so on. The fact that there are many euphemisms for limited partnerships illustrates the sorry state of the industry. The SEC appears to be trying to make the requirements for offering new partnerships so restrictive as to be prohibitive.

There is nothing wrong with the legal structure of a limited partnership per se. In fact, it offers many advantages over a corporate structure. **A limited partnership is, in the legal sense, a partnership. It will be managed by a "general partner" who will make all the investment decisions, but the "limited partners" will have "limited" liability.** As with equity ownership in a corporation, the limited partner's liability is limited to the amount of the investment. The limited partner is also very limited as to the influence he or she has in making partnership investment decisions, as is the case with equity ownership of a corporation. However, because of poor performance by some general partners, the limited partners in some partnerships have attempted to exert much more influence over the management of their investments.

One obvious advantage of a partnership structure over a corporate structure is the avoidance of the double taxation of distributions. You may remember that corporations pay taxes on their earnings, and the shareholders pay taxes again on the share of earnings that they receive as dividends. A limited partnership functions as a passthrough agency. In this sense, it is similar to an S corporation. It does not have to pay taxes on the income it receives. Therefore, if a partnership and a corporation both have the same earnings, the partnership will be able to distribute more to its investors than would a corporation. Only the limited partner who receives those distributions will pay income taxes on them.

Probably the most notable negative feature of this structure, however, is that it is very difficult to transfer ownership. Limited partnerships are considered illiquid investments. If investors wish to sell their interests in a partnership before it liquidates its assets, they are very likely to lose money. You should note, however, that all partnerships have finite terms. They will eventually dissolve, and the partners will receive the proceeds from liquidation. Typically, real estate partnerships, for example, have 30-year maximum holding periods, though the general partner may state that the partnership intends to sell the investments within about a 10-year period. Many problems with limited partners have arisen in the past because properties were not liquidated within the anticipated 10-year period, usually because of poor market conditions at the time. If the limited partner holds the partnership to completion, however, he or she will receive the cash flow from the real estate, if any, plus the capital gains or losses at the time of sale. However, if the limited partner wishes to sell the units of the partnership before that time, he or she will probably have to sell at a loss. This is the case not only because past partnerships have frequently had such a poor performance, but because the only buyers of partnerships in this illiquid market are usually opportunists who assume that since an investor wants to sell, he or she must be desperate for money and is likely to accept a low bid. Such buyers realize that partnerships are illiquid investments and try to capitalize on that fact.

Since these are long-term investments, the commissions and fees paid to invest in them are relatively high. Many general partners charge 15 percent to 30 percent in total expenses for managing your investment in their partnership. If that seems high to you, imagine how you would feel if they not only charged you that much in fees, but also invested in carefully scrutinized deals that managed to lose 90 percent in market value, or even to go completely bankrupt. This has been the unfortunate legacy of many past partnerships. General partners will of course tell you that they did not know that the commercial real estate market was going to plummet or that the cost of drilling was going to go up while oil and gas prices were coming down, but that doesn't change the fact that they profited very handsomely while the limited partners lost their shirts.

Not all partnerships have turned out to be bad investments, but the bad ones have frequently been utterly disastrous. The SEC couldn't, of course, change the direction of the market, but they did manage to require general partners to disclose fully their past records and to put enough negative disclaimers into partnership statements to scare away most of the potential investors. Actually, most of them had already been scared away by the time the SEC stiffened the disclosure requirements.

Some general partners, however, do have consistently good track records. It is unfortunate that the bad ones have tarnished the attractiveness of the good ones. The best structure for a limited partnership is when the general partner puts up its own capital at risk in the investments and shares equally with the limited partner according to the amount of the investment. Generally, a fair fee structure is a good indication of a good general partner, and these partnerships are less likely to perform poorly.

An increasingly popular alternative to the types of partnerships previously mentioned is called an MLP (master limited partnership). MLPs offer the liquidity of being able to transfer ownership by buying or selling shares on an exchange. They avoid the double taxation of corporate structures by acting as a pass-through agent. Consequently, most are designed for income-oriented investors, usually paying dividends or making distributions at much higher rates than their corporate counterparts. You can follow the daily price fluctuations of an MLP just as easily as you can any other share of stock. Many businesses in natural resource industries offer MLPs, including natural gas, oil, timber, and so on.

A variation of a limited partnership is a private placement. A "private placement" is a partnership investment that is offered to a small number of accredited investors. The SEC defines an accredited investor as one who has a net worth of at least $1 million or who has an annual income of over $200,000 ($300,000 for joint income). The laws defining accredited investors vary somewhat in different states. Private placements are generally offered on investments that have a very high degree of risk. Many biotech companies financed the early stages of development of pharmaceutical products with private placements.

Do You Know What You Need to Know?

To check up on what you learned from this chapter, answer the following questions in your own words, then compare your answers with the answer key.

1. Can you explain why the amount of tax that most individuals pay has been rising even when their tax brackets have not gone up?
2. How do you compute and report capital gains and losses? What are the tax consequences of capital gains and losses? Are they different from the consequences of taxes on ordinary income?
3. How does tax deferral increase the amount of your investment? Is this a good reason to invest in a retirement account of some kind?
4. Who qualifies to make contributions either to a Traditional or a Roth Individual Retirement Account? Under what circumstances are contributions to a Traditional IRA tax deductible? At what age can you begin to take IRA distributions without an IRS penalty?
5. What are the key differences between a Traditional IRA and a Roth IRA? In what ways are they similar?
6. What are the differences between a self-directed IRA and a mutual fund, or a bank, IRA? Can you explain the advantages and disadvantages of each? What is a SEP-IRA and how do contribution limits to it differ from those of other IRAs?
7. Who are the principals involved in an annuity contract? How does an annuity differ from other retirement accounts? What are the differences between a fixed annuity and a variable annuity?
8. What are the drawbacks of investing in limited partnerships? Why are these investments disappearing? Why are there so many euphemisms for limited partnerships?

Answer Key

1. Tax liability has been rising because many tax-deductible items have either been reduced or eliminated. Thus, in

many cases, taxpayers' adjusted gross income has been rising even though their income from salary and wages may not have been.

2. Capital gains and losses are reported on Schedule D, which is attached to the IRS Form 1040. Short-term capital gains are currently taxed at the taxpayer's marginal rate. Investments held over one year (long-term) are taxed at either 20 percent or 10 percent, depending on the taxpayer's marginal rate.

3. By investing in a tax-deferred investment—such as an IRA, another retirement account, or an annuity—the investor will earn interest on money that would have otherwise gone to pay taxes. Thus, the compounding effect of earning interest on more money increases the investor's total return.

4. In most cases, anyone who has earned income qualifies to make a contribution to either type of IRA account. Contributions to a Traditional IRA can be tax deductible if the individual is not covered by another retirement fund or if his or her income is below certain thresholds. One can begin taking withdrawals from either type of IRA without a penalty when he or she reaches age 59½. For a Roth IRA, penalty-free distributions can also be taken before that age if the funds are used for college expenses, first time home buyers, disability, and so on.

5. The most important difference between IRA accounts probably is that Roth IRA contributions are always with nonqualified funds, that is, dollars on which taxes have already been paid. Traditional IRAs allow for pretaxed, qualified funds in some cases. Also, Roth IRAs allow for Spousal Roth IRA, even if the spouse had no earned income.

6. A self-directed IRA allows individuals to select their own investments—stocks, bonds, mutual funds, and so on.

Mutual fund or bank IRAs allow for a limited selection of investment choices. In most cases, investors are limited to choices within the mutual fund family or to the bank's investment choices, usually a Certificate of Deposit (CD). Only self-employed individuals may contribute to a SEP-IRA. The contribution limit is 25 percent of annual adjusted gross income (AGI) up to an inflation-adjusted maximum.

7. The principals in an annuity contract are the owner, annuitant, and beneficiary. An annuity is a contract issued by an insurance company, the features of which are similar to retirement accounts. There are no limits to annuity contributions except for those set by the issuing company. Annuity account values compound at a tax-deferred rate.

8. The primary drawback to limited partnerships is illiquidity; however, there are many master limited partnerships (MLPs), which offer the same liquidity as shares of stock. The number of limited partnerships has declined dramatically because of the many past class action lawsuits over the poor management or poor performance of some partnerships. That is why there are so many euphemisms for these types of investments.

Tax strategies can help you keep more of your investment profits.

— Chapter 12 —

What Changes Are Coming to the Securities Markets?

Many people like to read a book by skimming or skipping most of it and going directly to the last chapter to find out how it ends. If you are one of them, stop here. Go back and read the rest of the book. Only math texts have the answers in the back. You will not find many answers here, and the conclusions drawn may not satisfy you. The answers that you are looking for are in the body of this book, not at the back. I am not a fortune teller, and I do not believe in fortune tellers. The conclusions I draw about the outlook for the future of the securities markets are my own opinions. They are not facts. Quite frankly, that is all that anyone knows about the future. No person can predict what has not yet happened on the basis of insider information. So, here are some personal thoughts about where I believe the industry is headed.

Since the securities markets reflect the economy and the economy is in a constant state of flux, the financial services industry must be constantly changing as well. The most discernable development in this industry today probably is the trend toward financial "supermarkets." Within a decade you will likely find far fewer choices of full-service stockbrokers. Instead, you will likely find only a handful of financial supermarkets offering banking, insurance, and brokerage service products to their customers. A wave of mergers and acquisitions will likely continue for the next few years, until the financial services industry has been reduced to a few megastores that can offer everything that a consumer of financial products could want.

Smaller, specialized companies will likely be priced out of existence as multi-hundred-billion dollar companies are able to offer products and services at more competitive prices than less well-capitalized companies. These large companies will also cross domestic borders. They will be multinational, multi-hundred-billion dollar companies. Although at first this will appear to benefit the consumer with lower prices and more competitive products, I think this will eventually be a detriment to the consumer. The goal of the companies that are part of this trend is to become more monopolistic in their approach to business. Of course, they do not want to become so large that they violate antitrust laws; however, they do want to become legal monopolies. Consumers should take advantage of the price benefits they will receive due to more competitive pricing as this state of affairs takes shape. Once the competition has been limited to only a handful of companies, the consumer will not likely benefit.

At the time of this writing, a long-lasting debate has been going on about the privatization of Social Security. This is becoming a more significant issue as the aging "baby boomer" population reaches retirement. This segment of the population, born in the decade following World War II, is the largest age group. They have been paying into the Social Security system all their wage-earning years and hope to reap the benefits of that in the near future. The original idea behind Social Security was that the younger segment of the population would help subsidize the cost of retirement for the older segment. However, for the past 60 years, a large part of the population has been paying to supplement the retirement of a small part of the population. When the baby boomers retire, there will be a small part of the population trying to pay for the retirement benefits of a large part. That is not going to work. Unless there is some change in costs or benefits, the Social Security system will be bankrupt by about 2040.

Some legislators and others have advocated allowing Social Security funds to be invested in the stock market. This is referred to as "privatization." In other words, it would allow the individuals who will be the recipients of Social Security benefits to decide what they want their retirement funds invested in. Initially, only a small portion of Social Security funds would be privatized. As it is, all Social Security funds are invested in U.S. Treasury bills, notes, and bonds (so-called riskless investments). The argument for this is that long-term stock prices have averaged around a 12-percent annual return as measured by almost any standardized index, while long-term U.S. government debt securities have averaged around 5 percent. Of course, the stock market can be very volatile and even though long-term results have always been there, short-term results are far less predictable.

If the Social Security Administration allows its funds to be invested in the stock market, it would be a great boost for equities prices. Such an event would almost certainly guarantee that the market would go up, even if only a small portion of Social Security were to be invested, because there would be billions—perhaps even trillions—of new dollars going into the market. The law of supply and demand would indicate that demand would greatly increase, and there would be no particular offsetting increase in supply. The problem would come, of course, years later, when many securities would have to be sold to meet Social Security pay-out benefits. Then politicians would have to come up with some new plan to fix that problem.

I think allowing some stock market investments with Social Security funds would be an excellent idea. It would certainly help solve the impending problem of the bankruptcy of the system; however, I also believe that there is a very compelling reason why this is not going to happen.

Since the largest single investor in government bonds is currently the Social Security Administration, the loss of this buyer would have to be replaced by other buyers. Managing the government debt has far-reaching ramifications beyond what most people realize. The privatization of Social Security may save that system, but it would have negative consequences on U.S. government debt securities. The government would have problems financing its $7 trillion debt if it lost its chief customer, the Social Security Administration.

I've said it before, and I'll say it again: The biggest problem facing the economy today is the national debt. The size of the national debt, which will be over $7 trillion at the time this book goes to print, has been growing faster in recent years than at any time in history. For the current status, check out the web site *www.publicdebt.treas.gov/*. There are many reasons for this, not the least of which are the geopolitical uncertainties and the threat of a global economic recession. Interest payments to the national debt alone add about $350 billion every year. Additionally, annual U.S. government budget overruns have cost another $100 billion or so in recent years.

The largest single investor in U.S. Treasury debt securities is the Social Security Administration. The FICA tax deductions from your paychecks currently fund about half of the U.S. government debt. The next largest group of purchasers of U.S. Treasury debt securities is foreign investors, primarily Japanese and Chinese banks and private citizens. The Japanese invest heavily in U.S. government bonds because their culture encourages saving, and the interest rates being paid by Japanese banks is virtually nil. The population of China is about one-third of the world's total. It is the largest emerging economy in the world and, having tasted the fruits of free enterprise, the Chinese are beginning to invest heavily in U.S. Treasury debt securities.

Sooner or later, even if Social Security continues to fund this debt, the U.S. Treasury will not be able to attract enough buyers. This problem needs to be addressed if there is ever to be stability in the economy or in the securities markets.

The unprecedented growth of the *NASDAQ* market has forced the older stock exchanges to modify the traditional manner in which most of their business is conducted. **"NASDAQ," as you previously learned, stands for National Association of Securities Dealers Automated Quotation. It is a computer system connecting all the market makers for those stocks that qualify to trade on the NASDAQ.** As a result of its success, the New York Stock Exchange has been forced to embrace many changes brought on by computer technology.

In the past, once a company met the listing requirements for going on the "Big Board" (the NYSE), it usually did. It meant prestige for the company and was perceived as an event that would attract more investors. Today, however, many companies, even after they grow to sufficient size to qualify for listing on the NYSE, prefer to continue trading on NASDAQ. They feel that the over-the-counter market offers a trading system that is just as efficient and less costly than the traditional listed markets. As a result, the NYSE is continually updating its computer services, and this has led the Big Board to begin trading distinctly nontraditional securities, such as stock options and other security derivatives. The NYSE has in recent years become much more willing to consider offering a variety of unconventional types of securities.

Streamlining the computer network on the NYSE has resulted in a huge volume increase in the number of shares traded daily on the exchange. Probably the largest percentage of this increased volume is the result of *program trading*. Several institutional members of the NYSE have developed computer programs that generate buy and sell orders. Usually, this type of trading depends on taking advantage of *arbitrage* situations resulting from price discrepancies between index options or index futures and the computer-calculated security prices that make up that index. This type of activity on the NYSE would have been unheard of only two decades ago, but the exchange has certainly seen the profitability of offering these types of transactions. Actually, the NYSE treats any order of 300,000 shares or more as a program trade. Any order of this size is subject to the trading restrictions associated with those generated by a computer in volatile market conditions. You should remember from Chapter 10 that these orders cannot be executed when the market is down over 2 percent unless there is an up-tick. You will probably see more innovative computer programs in the future.

Also, in the future, trading hours are likely to be extended even longer. Eventually, other exchanges around the world will list more and more U.S. companies, and ultimately these exchanges will be networked into an interconnected computer system. This will ultimately evolve into a unified network market, offering the ability to trade securities 24 hours a day—whether in New York, Tokyo, Hong Kong, Frankfurt, Paris, or London. The world is headed toward a completely *inter*dependent global economy. Already business reports throughout the night in the United States update investors on the news and events developing in the Far East markets. How the overseas markets perform each day, either in the Far East or in Europe, is a major factor in forecasting how the U.S. markets might open. More foreign investors participate in the U.S. stock markets or in the outright purchase of U.S. companies. On the other hand, U.S. businesses are expanding as rapidly as possible into foreign countries that had previously been closed to them.

Computers are probably going to cause the traditional stock brokerage giants to lose their dominance over the industry. More and more brokers are likely to gravitate to small *boutique* firms or to organize their own self-employed businesses. The capabilities of computers for stockbrokers will allow them to operate more efficiently as independent advisors, rather than as employees of large corporations. A large number of investors will still seek advice from professional investment advisors. However, with the wealth of information on securities available to everyone from online computer services, future stockbrokers are truly going to have to earn their business. Most of the information that has traditionally been available through securities dealers only will be available to everyone with a computer. More brokers are likely to work out of their homes or in their own offices as self-employed independent financial advisors within the next few years. The computer is going to change the securities industry in as dramatic a fashion as the automobile changed the transportation industry.

How Will Computers Change the Way You Invest?

Computer-savvy investors have a huge advantage over investors who are not. If you currently have money invested in the stock market and you are not online, you should be. If you do not already own a computer, get one. Your computer should have one of the latest CPUs, as much memory as you can afford, a high-capacity hard drive or alternative drive, and a very fast modem or other hardware for providing Internet access. Any new computer that you buy will be sufficient to provide you with all the services you need to be an informed investor. Consider the cost of a new computer as a small investment. Although the computer itself will depreciate, the information you gain from its use will greatly enhance your investment returns. Computer technology has had a dramatic influence on the securities industry; most of it greatly benefits the investor.

There is more information available on the Internet today than was available to professional analysts a few years ago. There are literally thousands of sites on the World Wide Web that are dedicated to providing information on investing. It can be intimidating and overwhelming to someone just starting out; however, if you are unfamiliar with how to navigate the web, start out by just typing in the name of one of the popular search engines or web crawlers such as Excite, Google, Yahoo!, and so on. One very popular way for many investors to find links to other web sites on different investment topics is *www.yahoo.com*. This is the Yahoo! homepage. Once you are on the Yahoo! homepage, you will find many point-and-click menu items, also known as hyperlinks, to take you where you want to go.

If you use a word search engine to find information on a specific topic, you are probably going to find yourself completely overwhelmed. The number of web sites has mushroomed to unmanageable proportions over the last few years. For example, if you want to access some information on bonds, you could type in the word "bonds" in a word search engine and your response might be something like: "Here are the first ten of 1,576,934 matches." Many of these "matches" will have nothing to do with the type of bonds you were looking for. That type of search will likely find many sites with information on bail bonds, James Bond, bonding materials for construction, or any number of unrelated businesses where the word "bond" is used—client bonds, technology bonds, and so on. You might try to narrow down your word search with "municipal+bond." Even that will probably net you out an unmanageable number of matches; you may only reduce the number down to 297,216, or so.

Perhaps a better method of navigating the web is to simply find a site that contains the type of information that you are looking for. Start out with one of sites on Yahoo! or one of the other search engines. Use that site's link from the menu page to begin your search; then, many of the other sites you come to will have hyperlinks to additional sites on the same topic. You can be assured that at least you are looking at sites that relate to the type of information you want. Some of the search engines, such as Yahoo!, will break down a search parameter that is too large into different categories related to that word; thus, you can select the correct category to begin your search.

It would be impossible to present an exhaustive list of all the valuable web sites on the Internet that provide information on investing. Here are a few sites, separated by general topics, that you might find very helpful. Some of these sites may charge you an access fee for their information or services; others are free.

Search Engines or General Information Sites:

www.excite.com	Excite
www.financenter.com	Finance Center
www.google.com	web crawler
www.hotbot.com	Hot Bot
www.infoseek.com	Infoseek
www.lycos.com	Lycos
www.yahoo.com	Yahoo!

Private Organizations and Agency Sites:

www.aaii.com	American Association of Individual Investors
www.afajof.org	American Finance Organization
www.amex.com	American Stock Exchange
www.cbt.com	Chicago Board of Trade
www.cboe.com	Chicago Board Options Exchange
www.cme.com	Chicago Mercantile Exchange
www.ifc.org	International Finance Corp.
www.nasdaq.com	NASDAQ-Amex
www.nasd.com	National Association of Securities Dealers
www.ncfe.org	National Center for Financial Education
www.nyse.com	New York Stock Exchange

News Services and Research Firms:

www.bloomberg.com	Bloomberg News Service
www.cnnfn.com	Cable News Network, Financial News
www.dnb.com	Dun & Bradstreet
www.moodys.com	Moody's Investor Service
www.morningstar.com	Morningstar
www.reuters.com	Reuters Group PLC

Magazines and Other Publications:

www.barrons.com	*Barron's*
www.businessweek.com	*Business Week*
www.forbes.com	*Forbes* Magazine
www.fortune.com	*Fortune* Magazine
www.investors.com	*Investors Business Daily*

www.kiplinger.com   Kiplinger's Personal Finance
www.money.com   *Money* Magazine
www.smartmoney.com   *Smart Money* Magazine
www.wsj.com   *The Wall Street Journal*
www.worth.com   *Worth* Magazine

Government Sources of Information:

www.publicdebt.treas.gov   Bureau of Public Debt
www.ffiec.gov/nic   Federal Financial Institutions
                           Examination Council,
                           National Information Center
www.frbsf.org   Federal Reserve Bank of
                           San Francisco, providing
                           information on Savings
                           Bonds and Treasury bills,
                           notes, and bonds
www.bog.frb.fed.us   Federal Reserve System,
                           Board of Governors
www.sec.gov   Securities and Exchange
                           Commission
www.sipc.com   Securities Investor Protection
                           Corporation

The nature of the securities brokerage industry has radically changed in the last few years. Today you have a choice of setting up an account through a traditional brokerage firm, a discount firm, or an online broker. In some cases, one brokerage firm may offer you all three options. Undoubtedly, the fastest growing method of investing is online. There are several different online brokers with which you can establish an account. Many of the Internet access providers have point-and-click icons that will link you to a choice of online brokers. The account application process is very similar to the way that you establish an account through a traditional firm with a personal broker. You will be asked to fill out a new account form and provide confidential information. Usually, you will be asked to provide your name, address, phone number, date of birth, Social Security number, and email address. A new account application can usually be completed either online or by regular mail. If you choose to register online, you will be able to do so after you create a password to ensure confidentiality. Once your account is established, you can use your password to begin trading—executing your own orders to buy or sell securities. The online service that you selected will provide you with information about entering your buy and sell orders. The commissions charged for the execution of trades by online brokers are usually much lower than those charged by paper-intensive traditional firms.

There are certain drawbacks to cyber-investing. The nature of this process changes the types of securities that most investors select. If investors are aware of some of the potential problems that can result from the means that they use for trading, they can improve their investing success. Online traders are often vulnerable to chat room recommendations and rumors. Such unregulated and unsolicited market analysis is often nothing more than a manipulative strategy by an unethical individual. The NASD has a task force that actively pursues prosecution of this type of illegal market manipulation; however, abuse of investment information on the Internet is still rampant.

Investors' attitudes toward their investments are profoundly affected by cyber-investing. One of the key themes of this book has been that your attitude toward investing should be long-term. As a simple reminder of what you learned at the beginning of this book, when you invest in a company, you are an owner of that company. That equity status of a shareholder is much too easily forgotten by cyber-investors.

Investors today are often unaware of their relationship to their company. Not only do they *not* think of themselves as owners, they do not even think of themselves as investors. They are just speculators looking to make a quick buck.

The ease with which orders can be executed is certainly an advantage of cyber-investing; however, the drawback is that most people are much too nervous and emotional about their money. This, too, is understandable, for you know how hard you had to work to make that money. Consequently, the ease of buying and selling on the Internet can work against you. The commissions for buying and selling are low and entering your orders on the computer is a relatively easy process; therefore, investors may be tempted to pull the trigger too quickly. In other words, many online traders turn into speculators rather than investors simply because of the means in which they execute orders. This type of trading activity certainly characterizes much of the online investing being done today.

Investing requires a great deal of self-discipline. If what you are looking for on the Internet is the stock that seems to be skyrocketing the fastest and the highest, you will be more likely to take that ride. Additionally, you are very likely to be wrong about the timing of both your purchase and your sale. You will be tempted to buy a stock when it is too high and equally tempted to sell it at a loss when it drops. Professional stock market investors refer to this type of trading activity as the **"greater fool theory." It is when you are aware that you are buying a stock that is priced too high, but your hope is that you will be able to sell it at a higher price to someone who is a greater fool than you are.** How do you know if you are the fool, the greater fool, or the greatest fool? You don't; but what does it matter if you are any one of those three choices? Sometimes it is better to have a buffer, such as a physical broker, between you and your investment. The principle of the Greed-Hope-Fear Cycle presented in Chapter 1 was that your emotions usually put you on the wrong side of the market, tempting you to buy when you should sell and to sell when you should buy. You are likely to be tempted to fit into this classic emotional pattern if you invest online rather than through a professional broker. Hopefully, a knowledgeable broker will be able to stop you from making ill-timed decisions.

What Recent Events Will Affect the Economy in the Future?

Over the next few years, you are going to see a trend toward a unified worldwide economy. NAFTA, the North American Free Trade Agreement, was only one of many economic alliances that were forged by other countries throughout the world. Other alliances include the European Union (EU) and the Asia-Pacific Economic Cooperation Forum (APEC) of 18 nations, including the United States, Canada, and Mexico. APEC is really a merger of the members of NAFTA and the Asian-Pacific community. Other smaller trading blocs include the Andean Group and the Southern Common Market, which are two different alliances of South American countries, the Southern African Development Community (SADC), the Central American Common Market, the Australia–New Zealand Closer Economic Relations Pact (CER), and so on.

Once the territorial boundaries between individual nations have been dissolved into economic alliances, renegotiating these alliances into a worldwide free trade organization could be accomplished relatively easily. Citizens of individual nations are much more loyal to their country than they are to alliances of which their nation is only a part. So, the first step toward a worldwide economy has already been completed. The next step will be for the various regional alliances to begin negotiating a global alliance. Thus, the sovereignty of each nation can be compromised with a minimum of opposition.

The rules for world trade are currently being set up by an organization of over 150 member nations in Zurich, Switzerland, called the World Trade Organization, WTO. In 1995 it replaced GATT, the General Agreement on Tariffs and Trade, as the organization responsible for overseeing global trade. The WTO will eventually have far-reaching powers to implement trade agreements, to control tariffs set by individual members, and to formulate world economic policies. It will be the most powerful organization in the world. You can check out the WTO web site at *www.wto.org*.

The unification of the economies in the European Union (EU) with a single currency has demonstrated the effectiveness of economic fusion. The merging of several different countries, cultures, languages, and currencies was once considered completely impossible. Now that it has been accomplished, you are likely to see more mergers in other parts of the world, with the ultimate goal of complete global standardization. This is really much more than an economic process. There are other organizations with similar goals for synthesizing the world's cultures, religions, languages, and so on. I believe this represents an impending threat because of the centralization of too much power and control. If the fairness and ethics of all worldwide economic trade rests in the hands of a privileged few, who wield ultimate power, we are in grave danger.

The concept of an interdependent global economy is one that on the surface makes sense. A nation, or for that matter a community of nations such as the former Soviet Union, that isolates itself from the rest of the world is doomed to failure. The economic system of the Soviet Union perfectly illustrates the ultimate effect of isolationism and restrictions on free enterprise. If individuals are not allowed to profit from their labor, but are required to work for the "common good," they have little incentive to work hard. To take away the rewards for hard work is to take away the incentive.

When the Soviet Union became a communist state in 1917, it not only closed its physical borders, it closed its economic borders as well. It banned free enterprise, labeling it "imperialistic capitalism." It took away most incentives for individuals to raise their own economic status. As a result, after about 70 years, a relatively short period of time economically, the nations of the former Soviet Union reached a point where they could barely produce enough food to feed their own people or to manufacture a product that could be sold at a competitive price to the rest of the world. It became inefficient. At the time of this writing, the exchange rate for the Russian *ruble* was still fluctuating in such a wide range that it was an unacceptable currency for most international trade. It is referred to as a *soft* currency because it has no stable exchange rate. The nations of the former Soviet Union are trying desperately to hoard *hard* currency, primarily U.S. dollars, so that they can regain some international economic power. A free enterprise economy has proven itself the best system for fostering the development of new, innovative products. A free enterprise economy, at its best, allows the individuals who come up with new ideas to benefit financially from them.

So, on the surface a global economy that is based on the free enterprise system makes good sense. The major concern, however, as we approach such "globalization," is who will be in control of all this power? As Lord Acton said, "Power corrupts, and absolute power corrupts absolutely." Even though the concept of a global economy would seem to be a very pragmatic solution to the major problems of world trade, the implementation of this system will inevitably create an even greater problem.

You may not realize it, but right now we are in the midst of World War III. It just doesn't look like the previous two. You may be thinking, there are "hot spots" all around the world where conflicts erupt or are likely to erupt, but that's not a *world* war. No, those conflicts are not what I'm referring to. The casualties of this war are not victims of bullets and bombs, or mines and missiles. The weapons are not tanks, planes, and ships. World War III will not be fought between armies on battlefield fronts. The battle plans for World War III are being formulated by aging men in business suits around conference tables in prestigious locations. This is the frontline of the economic battlefield.

Today the typical U.S. government response to threats against peace and stability anywhere in the world is to "play the economics card." The weapons of this type of war are import-export quotas, boycotts, tariffs, and frozen bank accounts. At no other time has there ever been the possibility of waging war in this manner. It can only happen today because the world is so close to a unified economic system. The rise of global and regional economic alliances and the status of such entities as the World Bank has made economic warfare a reality.

In spite of the fact that we live in an era that has not seen world war in over half a century, we do not live in an age of peace and safety. John F. Kennedy said, "Mankind must put an end to war, or war will put an end to mankind." That comment was a wake-up call that there were already enough nuclear arms in the world at that time to turn it into a global wasteland, if not enough bits of space debris to form another asteroid belt. The potential for complete annihilation has haunted us for so long that it has become an integral part of our psyche. Our only sense of security lies in the assumption that nobody would be so insane as to destroy everything, including themselves. However, some nagging doubts remain. There, indeed, appear to be some in this world who stretch those bounds of sanity.

The response of the free world to this global threat of conventional war was the concept of an economic one. Such a concept is not as bloodless as it sounds. Whether people die of instantaneous nuclear vaporization or prolonged malnutrition due to economic sanctions is of no consequence to their ultimate state. Victims of either type of war are just as dead. War is still hell.

The logistics of waging an economic war make it far less costly than conventional (or unconventional) warfare. Whereas the expense of a buildup of military might contribute to the economic problems of the U.S. government, an economic war enhances the hardship of foreign governments. So, from an American point of view, economic war is better.

However, we are now looking down the barrel of worldwide recession. In Japan, the second largest economy in the world, a collapse of the banking industry appears inevitable. In Europe, the EU has created the situation where economically stronger members support weaker ones. This taxes resources of what should have been a solid economic situation and has made it a troubled one. In Latin America, currency crises, which are often precipitated by Marxist dictators, make real economic growth impossible. Religious restrictions get in the way of sound fiscal policy in many Middle Eastern and Asian countries. The Russian economy is being held hostage by organized crime, the Russian mafia. African countries seem caught in a third world mentality that is not going to change for decades, if ever.

The world looks to the United States for economic support and guidance. After all, if the United States can't provide the necessary support to solve this myriad of global problems, who will? All eyes are on the domestic economy, and it is not exactly a pillar of strength. To stimulate economic growth for U.S. exporting companies, the most likely course of action would be to weaken the exchange value of the dollar against foreign currencies. Weakening the dollar would make goods and services originating from the United States less costly to sell abroad. It would require fewer yen or euros to purchase the same U.S. dollar amount of goods and services. However, from a global point of view, if the dollar is weakened, foreign currencies would need to come down for goods and services produced outside the United States to remain price competitive to consumers here.

This environment appears to be in a catch-22. Weakening the U.S. dollar will help our economy while hurting foreign economies. However, strengthening the dollar would help foreign economies, but hurt our own—upon which the foreign economies depend. The heads of the World Bank and the Federal Reserve Board are constantly confronted by such ambiguous decisions. There is seldom any such thing as a win-win scenario when it comes to global economics.

Additionally, certain socioeconomic groups are today's version of the Luddites, a group of early nineteenth-century protesters in England who attempted to stop the advancement of the Industrial Age by destroying machines. Today's Luddites are bent on stopping the progress of technology in order to force their religious and social beliefs on others. Such fundamentalist groups find technology a deterrent to the advancement of their socioeconomic agenda. They can only hold on to power by destroying the freedom to discuss, let alone to debate, ideas. They must hold on to their tenuous reign by terrorist tactics and control of the educational system. They would burn books and sabotage technology in order to isolate themselves completely. They would throw the world back into the Dark Ages, because the advancement of their cause is predicated upon maintaining a state of ignorance. Achievement of such a goal is becoming increasingly more difficult in a technologically integrated world.

Probably hundreds of books have been written on the impending collapse of the economy, both of the United States and of the world. You are likely to find a book on the current best-seller lists about the impending economic disasters we are now facing. Publishers have always known that negative news sells. Whether the medium is newspapers, magazines, or books, emphasizing, if not sensationalizing, the negative aspects of current economic or political situations is assumed to be a guaranteed money-making formula for a publisher. So, read everything with an attitude of analyzing the potential bias of the source, and always be aware of the possibility of negative slants or sensationalism.

So much has been written forecasting the collapse of the U.S. economy that most people expect anything written about the future of the securities market must surely predict more "doom and gloom." Quite honestly, however, I do not believe that the economy is headed toward catastrophe. It certainly will not collapse in the sense that most of these prophets are forecasting. Admittedly, as I have pointed out several times throughout this book, tremendous economic problems exist. The U.S. government's debt, compounded by continued budget deficit spending, is an extremely serious problem. It is a Damoclean sword hanging over our heads. But, if you remember the story of Damocles, the sword didn't fall. It just made all who occupied the seat under it very uncomfortable. Just as that sword never fell, I do not expect the economy to fall. No economic problems are unsolvable.

The economic problems we are currently facing can and will cause great hardships, but the problems will not cause total collapse. Granted, the solution to the federal debt has no politically easy answers. If it is not dealt with, it will grow to the point where we will experience a good deal of hardship and suffering. If that is what it takes to motivate politicians to act responsibly, then that is what will happen. I do believe, however, that some pressure from the electorate could force those who have the power to cut deficit spending into a less myopic view of their policies. More vocal involvement of individual voters can effect a change of policies before the hardship becomes too intense. No matter what it takes to accomplish, this problem has only two simple solutions: cut spending and/or raise taxes. This will happen. The government cannot demand that we all act fiscally responsible while they do not.

Most people would agree that the best solution to this problem is to cut spending. I agree—cutting spending is the best solution. However, every one of us can always find a just and moral cause that we cannot *afford* to cut. To effectively reduce government spending may mean having to cut spending that would affect *your* own lifestyle. A military base closing near your neighborhood will affect your property values. If you have cancer, or someone close to you does, you will not likely to be in favor of cutting spending for medical research on that disease. Certainly, no one receiving Social Security benefits wants that touched. It is much easier to talk about cutting spending in broad terms than it is to talk about the particulars of what should be cut.

An approach to this problem that appeals to me is a national sales tax. This is a completely different concept of taxation than the current IRS structure. Such a tax would be administered on spending rather than on income. A national sales tax would produce tax revenues in line with that of consumption. Individuals who earn more money usually spend more money, and thus would pay more taxes. The economic problems in many states created by the large population of illegal aliens would be addressed. At least part of the costs of government services would be shared by illegal aliens, and for that matter by foreign tourists as well.

A national sales tax would also have the effect of encouraging savings. Obviously, if you don't spend your money, you won't be taxed on it. Also, the interest you earn on your savings would *not* be taxed. Conceptually, this seems like a good common-sense solution to the current deficit problem. The problem with tax reform, whether a national sales tax, a flat tax, or any other tax proposal, is what to do with tax-free municipal bonds. Any revision of the tax structure that rescinds or nullifies the benefits of tax-free bonds will have a negative effect on state and local government agencies. If municipalities are forced to compete for financing with other taxable bond issuers, such as corporations, many of them would have to make serious spending cutbacks or face bankruptcy. Most municipalities depend on their ability to borrow money at relatively low interest rates, which result from their tax-exempt status. Probably many public services would be privatized.

As I said before, the economy will always exist. It will always have problems. It will always have solutions. *Economic solutions will always create other problems*, and the problems will always be followed by more solutions. I do find, however, other disturbing economic trends, besides the federal debt. One is the question of morality and ethics in the workplace. Many corporate managers today report that it is becoming increasingly difficult to find honest employees. Many employees today feel little or no sense of moral obligation to their employers. In a sense, they are working for themselves, not for the company. I believe this attitude has been fostered by employers who feel no sense of moral obligation to those under them. If the leadership of a company does not set a high standard of ethics for themselves, their employees will surely follow their example.

A good illustration of this symptom of declining morality of corporate leadership in the United States is the issue of executive compensation. I perceive a disturbing trend of excessive financial perks being awarded to many in upper-management today for substandard performance. Not only are upper-management executives compensated with astronomical salaries, but also with hefty bonuses and stock option perks. In recent years, we have seen *most* of the nation's top chief executive officers' annual compensation, including salary and bonuses, top $15 million. The average CEO makes well over 500 times its average hourly worker's pay. This, in my opinion, is a *crime*. I cannot comprehend how any individual's talents or leadership ability can *add* that much value to a company's bottom line.

Our nation's top corporations are being increasingly run by power managers, who focus their management talents on intimidating or manipulating the board of directors and the shareholders of their company into accepting their dictates. In many cases, the board of directors exists only to *rubber stamp* the agendas of the CEO. There needs to be a better system of checks and balances on the power assumed by upper management. The officers of a company should be more accountable—not only to their board of directors, but to their company's shareholders as well.

Several companies today have addressed this problem by tying executives' compensation to performance criteria. A few innovative companies have opted to pay the board of directors primarily in shares of stock, rather than in cash. Thus, the value of their compensation package is tied to the performance of the company. This is an excellent incentive to proactive management. An executive should not be granted a pay raise just because other peers have been. An executive who runs a company into the ground should not be granted a *golden parachute*.

Upper management sets the tone of morality and ethics at their company. A self-serving managerial style sets that example for the rest of the employees. After all, if the CEO, from the laborer's point of view, has a license to *steal*, why can't the employees? Anyone in a position of leadership must maintain the highest standards of morality and ethics. This problem must be addressed by individual shareholders. Individual shareholders need to take more of an initiative to exercise their rights as *owners* of their companies.

As the volume of securities trading has increased in recent years, investors' attitudes have also changed. Perhaps because most new investors choose mutual funds (usually no-load funds) rather than individual stocks, there is very little emotional attachment to the companies in which one is investing. Many equity owners today do not care about the businesses of the companies they own. They just want to make money. This is especially true of no-load funds. Since the typical investor perceives that it costs nothing to "wager a bet" on the success of the fund, most investors take on a very short-term and passive attitude toward stock ownership.

This is the complete opposite of the original intent of the equities markets. The "old-fashioned" attitude that investors were owners usually fostered a sense of loyalty to the products or services of the company owned. Today, however, most investors don't care about their company's business and often don't even know what that business is. Investors today frequently just want to "make a quick buck." Mutual funds, for example, are recommended on the basis of which one had the best quarter. Stocks are selected on the sole expectation of a "quick pop" because of a profitable quarterly earnings report.

Also, executive management of corporations is influenced by this attitude of their shareholders. They feel that constant pressure to perform every quarter, looking at short-term methods of revenue enhancement rather than at long-term business growth strategies. Both shareholders and managers should be reminded that sacrificing the future for the present is a mistake. Investors should make management more accountable for where they are leading the company over the next few *years*, rather than over the next few *months*. If you pay for the present with the future, you will soon find your future has been spent. In spite of the fact that we live in an impersonal computer age, we must return to some of the fundamental values and attitudes on which a free enterprise economy depends.

Remember that the nature of the economy is such that there will never be an ultimate solution to all problems. There are very good reasons for economists or other prognosticators to always be negative, but there are also very good reasons to always be positive. Every solution creates a problem, but every problem has a solution. Do not be drawn into a "doom and gloom" philosophy. Every generation has had its prophets proclaiming, "The end is near!" But it was only "their end," not "the end" that was near.

Wall Street Week with Louis Rukeyser is a very popular weekly television program, and I would encourage you to watch it. Usually, the most watched installments of this program each year are the ones where the panel of experts, who are known as "the elves," make their official forecasts for the upcoming year. "The elves" are mostly technical analysts who look at basically the same, or very similar, indicators and statistics. Each will have a different opinion about which statistics are the most important. Each will emphasize some indicators more than others. However, they all look at pretty much the same information. The conclusions that they draw from this information, however, will vary radically. Some will predict the market will soar dramatically higher, some will predict the market will drop precipitously. Who will be right? No one knows until the year is over.

Obviously, everyone wants to know what will happen. That is why the ratings on these programs are usually the highest of the year. But which "elf" actually comes the closest to being right is more a matter of chance than of skill. No single "elf" will always be the most accurate. Or, you could say they have all been accurate, just not for the right year. You will always find that any market forecaster who attempts to give exact numbers about where the Dow will be on such and such a date will never be consistently correct. Whoever was closest to being correct last year will live off his or her laurels for a year, and more people may follow their advice. But advisors who live by the numbers they predict will inevitably die by their own numbers also.

I am not saying that you should not analyze the market and draw conclusions. Every knowledgeable investor most definitely should. What I am saying is that you should not buy into the line that any one person has much keener insight into the future than everyone else. That is simply not true. Proper analysis is the foundation on which fortunes are made, but no amount of analysis will give you or anyone else the ability to know where the market will be at any given point in the future. So, when you set your goals and lay down your financial strategy to achieve them, keep your plans flexible enough to allow for the uncertainty of the future. Do not follow one guru's advice because he was hot last year.

Regardless of all the hype about who knows the most about the future, whatever is going to happen, will happen. Though everyone is looking for someone who can tell them what happens next, no one really can. The seer who forecasts the Dow is going to 20,000 next year knows no more about the future than the prognosticator who looks at similar statistics and predicts it is going to 2000. The writer who predicts the United States will collapse in less than two years may likely be trying to capitalize on a successfully proven formula for selling books. He or she, like myself, is only giving an opinion and has no more foreknowledge of future events than you do.

The point is not that technical analysts don't know what they're talking about. It is that no one can predict what the market will do on the basis of technical analysis alone. Fundamental analysis, that is, studying and forecasting a company's earnings potential, must be the foundation for good stock selection. If you select top-quality companies that are leaders in their industries, have good management, and good growth potential, you have the secret to successful investing. I am a firm believer that slow and steady wins the race. By the way, this is also the philosophy of most major successful investment advisors. The fact that no one really knows the future makes life exciting. You have to live it to see how it comes out.

In recent years, many traditional principles of stock market investing have come under increased criticism. Following the extended downturn of the market at the beginning of the new millennium, many investment advisors began attacking one of the most sacred principles: "buy and hold"—that is, take a long-term approach. They pointed out that many large, established companies had failed. Thus, they concluded that holding such companies all the way down was a mistake and recommended buying and selling more frequently.

The basis of that criticism was valid. In just a few years some of the largest, oldest, and most well established companies had filed for bankruptcy—Bethlehem Steel, Enron, Kmart, Worldcom-MCI, Pacific Gas & Electric, UAL Corp., and so on. Many others were teetering on the edge of financial crisis—AOL, Charter Communications, Dynegy, Gateway, Lucent, Sun Microsystems, and many, many more. Therefore, several market strategists were advising investors to abandon "old school" rules and to become a bit quicker on the trigger. Shoot first, ask questions later.

Looking back over those years, this advice would appear to be sound, but I remain unconvinced. Hindsight makes everyone look like a genius. Anyone who can read can predict (or should I say *post*dict?) what you should have done in the recent past. Sure it would have been excellent advice if someone had told you to take all your money out of the market at the beginning of the year 2000.

Not coincidentally, some traditional market strategists were advising that. One prominent prognosticator who recommended that investors avoid stocks in 1999 was Warren Buffet. He frequently commented that this was a "bubble market," especially the so-called "dot-coms" and high tech companies. In spite of the fact that he had become the second richest man in the U.S. through prudent stock market strategies, he reiterated many times that he simply couldn't find any bargains to buy. He endured much criticism as the last stage of the bull market ran itself out.

However, the bubble popped. Not only did the market crash, but the U.S. economy slumped into its worst recession since the 1930s. My point in bringing this up is that Mr. Buffet wasn't telling investors to buy and sell frequently in order to survive the bear market. He adamantly criticized the day-trading mentality that had been gaining popularity over the last few years. Mr. Buffet is perhaps the most famous "buy and hold" strategist of all time.

I'd say that nearly every student who takes my class on stock market investing hopes to learn how to get rich. Most, how to get rich quick. I am frequently asked if I am going to teach how to do day trading. My standard answer is that the only thing I'll teach about day trading is why you shouldn't do it.

Frequently, the students who ask that question are the brightest and most gifted—they believe they are smart enough to beat the system. They are motivated, goal-oriented people with brains and talent. Thus, they believe that they have an edge on everyone else and that they can capitalize on that in the securities industry. Everyone wants to be rich, or at least financially secure. However, a problem crops up when achieving wealth becomes the sole motivation in a person's life. Always keep your investment activities in perspective. Treat investing as a means to an end, not an end in itself. Don't waste your life on the pursuit of finding the secret to beating the system—it's a trap.

By nature, corporations are inhuman entities. Don't give up your humanity to them. Materialistic rewards will not result in a satisfying life. Life is more than stuff; it is spiritual. Do something with your life that will benefit the lives of others, not just yourself. Use investments to gain financial security so that you can focus on more meaningful endeavors.

I have always been a voice of praise for the merits of competition in a free enterprise economy. However, the U.S. has just come through a period best described as a lesson in what can happen when free enterprise runs amok. Too often healthy competition has been replaced with cutthroat strategies and dirty tricks politics. Managers are rewarded for unsportsmanlike conduct rather than competitive prowess. Corporate greed has corrupted the hearts of many good people. The only things that swim with the sharks are other sharks. Aspire to be something more than a shark; aspire to be human.

If you have read this book through, you are one of the talented students I was referring to earlier. You are one of the brightest and best. Congratulations, you will be a successful investor. You have demonstrated you have the wherewithal to do what you need to do to be successful. There is just one more bit of advice you need to know.

Don't become a victim of your own success. The financial rewards of investing were never meant to be ends in themselves. Use your brains and talent to accomplish something worthwhile with your life. Do not compromise principles or ethics and morality to achieve your goals. As soon as you do, you lose—if not financially, then spiritually. Don't sell out for a quick buck. Be part of the solution, not the problem.

There, now you really know *what you need to know before you invest*.

Do You Know What You Need to Know?

To check up on what you learned from this chapter, answer the following questions in your own words, then compare your answers with the answer key.

1. What information is available to online investors? What are the advantages and disadvantages of using most Internet search engines to access information?

2. How has the increased use of computers for investing changed the way that individuals make investment decisions? What are the advantages and disadvantages of online trading?

3. How has the nature of computer trading affected investors' attitudes toward the companies they own? Why should investors be aware of how their attitudes are being affected?

4. How might the rivalry between the NYSE and the NAS-DAQ market affect future securities trading?

5. How might the trend toward a global economy affect investments? What potential problems might result from economic globalization?

6. How might privatizing part or all of the Social Security system affect securities markets? What are the pros and cons of such an action?

7. Why is a "doom and gloom" attitude toward the economy justifiable, and why is it also erroneous? How does the nature of the economy itself affect investments?

8. Do you know what you need to know before you invest?

Answer Key

1. More information is available to the general public today than was available to the most sophisticated professional investment advisors several years ago. Keyword searches on most search engines will often result in more responses that the person will be able to check out. Many of the matches found might be on completely unrelated topics. As a result, many web users have found that navigating with hyperlinks from known addresses provides easier access to the information they want.

2. Ready access to so much information is obviously a great benefit to investors; however, one of the drawbacks is that it may sometimes result in hasty, ill-timed decisions. Investors might panic too quickly, selling stocks on negative news without fully analyzing the implications or buying stocks on unsubstantiated rumors.

3. The nature of online investing is changing traditional attitudes toward equity ownership. In the past, stock investors were more aware of their position as shareholder-owners of a corporation. Investors who are looking to trade securities online do not usually have the same personal attachments to their investments; thus, they tend to lose a long-term perspective on their holdings, buying and selling too frequently.

4. The rivalry will likely result in the NYSE offering more nontraditional investment products and in the NASDAQ providing more complete levels of reporting bid and ask prices.

5. The trend toward economic globalization will likely create greater growth opportunities in emerging markets and will probably have a negative effect on well-developed markets. The most likely potential risk that would result from economic globalization is that it would place too much power in too few hands.

6. Allowing Social Security funds to be invested in private markets will undoubtedly benefit those participating in the system. It will result in a huge influx of funds going into equities; however, since the Social Security Administration is one of the largest purchasers of U.S. Treasury securities, the effect of such a move on U.S. debt markets would be very negative—in fact, potentially ruinous.

7. The dynamic nature of the economy is such that there will always be a problem to point to. Also, every solution to that problem will create a new problem. For example, lowering interest rates will stimulate the economy, but will eventually cause inflation. Raising interest rates will slow growth, but may cause a recession. Investors need to be aware of interest rate cycles.

8. I hope you know what you need to know. At the very least, you should be able to avoid common mistakes and

to make well-informed decisions. Good luck. The proof of whether or not you know what you need to know will be in your pocketbook, not just in your head.

The medium may be high tech, but will the message be high tech?

— Appendix —

How Do You Calculate Interest Rates?

Many people have *math anxiety*. As soon as someone starts quoting numbers and mathematical functions, their minds go blank. Math anxiety is usually a result of uninspiring and/or intimidating math teachers. Most people are fully capable of performing all of the mathematical functions they need to know for securities investing. However, those with *high* math anxiety may not realize that they can. If you are one of those individuals who gets sweaty palms if you think that someone is going to ask you to add or to multiply, you don't have to read this appendix. That is why it is in an appendix—it's optional. However, even if you have math anxiety, you may want to read it anyway. This explanation on how interest is calculated is designed for you. After all, even if you don't understand it, you're no worse off than you were before.

The main difference between compound interest and simple interest is that with compound interest, you earn interest on your interest and with simple interest, you do not. If you want to compute the amount of *simple interest* you would earn on a certain amount of principal, you would simply multiply the interest rate (expressed as a decimal) by the principal. Since interest rates are quoted on an annualized basis, that computation would express the dollar amount of interest you would earn in one year. To compute how much interest you would receive in more than one year, you would multiply the principal times the interest rate times the number of years. Since this would only compute the amount of interest you would earn, you would also want to add your original principal amount to this computation to get a total return, or Future Value.

The mathematical formula for computing the Future Value of an investment at the **simple interest** rate is

$$F = P + P \cdot i \cdot n$$

Simplified, this would be:

$$\boldsymbol{F = P(1 + i\,n)}$$

where:

> F = Future Value
> P = Present Value (or Principal)
> i = interest rate (expressed in decimal form)
> n = number of years (that the investment will be held)

If, for example, you wanted to compute the future value of an investment of $1,000 at a 10 percent simple rate of interest for 10 years, you could plug in those numbers into that formula as follows:

$$F - \$1,000[1 + (.10)\,(10)]$$

and you would solve this problem:

> $F = \$1,000(1 + 1)$
> $F = \$1,000(2)$
> $F = \$2,000$

As you may have already been able to deduce before you put these numbers into the formula, $1,000 will grow to $2,000 if it earns 10 percent interest for 10 years at the simple rate of interest. Now let's see how the formula changes if you earn interest at the 10 percent rate on the interest you earn each year. Obviously, at the end of the first year, you would have earned $100 in interest. So, during the second year, you are not just earning 10 percent on $1,000, but you will be earning 10 percent interest on $1,100.

To convert the simple interest formula to one for compound interest, you will simply multiply the interest received by the same interest rate. In other words, in this example the $100 simple interest received at the end of the first year would be multiplied by 10 percent the next year to adjust for compounding. At the end of the first year the totals for both the simple rate and the compound rate will be the same. The interest will not begin earning more interest until it has been paid. If, however, you were to compute how much interest you would earn on your $1,000 of principal, you would use to following mathematical formula:

$$F = \$1,000(1 + .10)(1 + .10)$$

or simplified:

$$F = \$1,000(1.1)(1.1)$$

At the end of the third year, this formula would be:

$$F = \$1,000(1.1)(1.1)(1.1).$$

The simpler mathematical way of expressing this process is to use an exponent, showing that you are multiplying a number by itself that many times. In this case, you would write:

$$F = \$1,000(1.1)^3$$

Obviously, over a 10-year time frame, this would be expressed:

$$F = \$1,000(1.1)^{10}$$

which would be equal to $2,593.74. In other words, if your money is invested at a 10 percent compound rate rather than at a 10 percent simple rate of interest, you will earn an additional $593.74 in 10 years. If you remember Illustration 4.1 in Chapter 4, showing the graphic relationship between a simple yield line and a compound yield curve, that illustration should make more sense now. So, the formula for **Future Value** of an investment at a compound rate of interest is:

$$F = P(1 + i)^n$$

It may also be helpful to understand how you can use this formula to compute Present Value (P). If you want to know how much money you will need to invest now in order to have a specified Future Value (F), you need to know how to solve this equation for P.

You should remember the mathematical principle that if $A = B \cdot C$, then to solve the equation for B, you would divide both sides by C, that is, $A/C = B \cdot C/C$. The Cs on the righthand side will cancel out (that is, are equal to 1), and if you reversed the two sides, you would have $B = A/C$. Now consider:

$$A = F$$
$$B = P$$
$$C = (1 + i)^n$$

By the same token, if you wanted to solve the equation $F = P(1 + i)^n$ for P, you would divide both sides of the equation by $(1 + i)^n$. Then you would have the formula for computing **Present Value** at a compounded rate of interest:

$$P = F/(1 + i)^n$$

So, if you wanted to find out how much money you would have to invest now at a 10 percent compound rate of interest in order to have $100,000 in 10 years, you would have:

$$P = \$100,000/(1 + .10)^{10}$$

or:

$$P = \$100,000/(1.1)^{10}$$

With a calculator you could solve this equation, $P = \$38,554.33$. In other words, an investment today of $38,554.33 at a 10 percent compound annual rate of interest would grow to $100,000 in 10 years. Obviously, if you did not invest that amount of money at a compound rate but rather at a simple rate, you would have to invest $50,000 to achieve the same result. So, another way of looking at the effects of compounding is that you could invest $11,445.67 less at a compound rate than at a simple rate and achieve the same results. That's the beauty of compound interest.

Glossary

American Depositary Receipt (ADR): a designation for shares of foreign companies that trade on U.S. markets. The foreign company will deposit shares of its stock with a U.S. financial institution, which will then issue ADR shares with certificates printed in English and dividends or distributions paid in U.S. currency.

Annuitant: the individual who is designated to receive the distributions made from an annuity contract and upon whose life the insurance benefits will apply. This individual may be different than the contract owner. For example, the owner of an annuity may be a trust and the annuitant the individual who is a trustee of the trust.

Annuity: a contract issued by an insurance company that allows investments to accumulate tax deferred. These contracts are generally used to supplement retirement income, as there is a 10 percent IRS penalty on withdrawals from earnings or capital gains made before the annuitant turns 59½. Also, in the event of the annuitant's death, the value of the contract passes to the beneficiary without going through probate. Annuity contracts may offer either a fixed rate of interest for a certain period of time or variable investments usually run by investment company managers.

Arbitrage: an investment strategy of buying and selling the same or similar securities (usually on different markets) in order to take advantage of price disparities. Riskless arbitrage might involve buying a convertible bond that is selling below the conversion value of the underlying stock and simultaneously selling the stock so the bond could be converted. Risk arbitrage can involve trading large blocks of stock and taking the opposite position on a stock index option. See **Program trading.** Those who participate in arbitrage trading are called *arbitrageurs*.

Ask price: the lowest price at which someone is offering to sell an investment on an auction market; also called *offering price*. See **Bid price**.

Balance Sheet: a financial statement that expresses a company's net worth, or equity, by determining the value of a company's assets at a given point in time and subtracting the company's liabilities.

Bear market: a time period of generally *falling* stock prices, usually several months or years. See **Bull market.**

Beta: a method of measuring the market risk of equity investments, usually stocks or mutual funds. It compares the volatility of the investment with the volatility of the S&P 500 Index over the same period of time. If the percentage change in the price of the investment is the same as the percentage change in the S&P, the investment would have a beta of 1.00. If it changed 50 percent more than the S&P, it would have a beta of 1.50. If it changed 50 percent less than the S&P, it would have a beta of 0.50. The higher the beta, the greater the perceived risk of owning that investment, for the greater the downside potential in a declining market. For instance, if a stock has a beta of 2.00 and the market drops 15 percent, one would expect that stock to drop 30 percent.

Bid price: the highest price at which someone is willing to buy a security on an auction market. See **Ask price.**

Blue Chip: a term used to describe a large company recognized as a leader in its industry. Usually, Blue Chip stocks pay dividends and are considered to be less volatile than stocks of smaller companies. The term refers to the color of the gaming chip with the highest value.

Bond: the formal certificate representing a loan, the terms of which are set by the borrower, the bond issuer. The issuer of the bond will pay a fixed rate of interest to the investor, usually in semi-annual payments, and guarantee the return of the investor's principal at maturity, the due date. An investor in a bond is a lender and has a senior position over equity investors regarding legal claims to the issuer's assets in the event of bankruptcy.

Book value: a calculation from the balance sheet—the shareholders' equity minus preferred equity divided by the number of shares outstanding. Many analysts adjust this calculation by subtracting the value of intangible assets, which are not salable, from the shareholders' equity. Book value is meant to be an indicator of what a shareholder might receive per share if the company's assets were liquidated at the values carried on the financial statements.

Bull market: a time period of generally rising stock prices, usually several months or years. See **Bear market.**

Call option: a type of equity derivative contract, giving the purchaser the right to *buy* a certain number of shares of a company (usually 100) at a set price and expiring within a predetermined period of time. See **Put option.**

Capital asset: a long-term asset, one with a useful life of over one year.

Capital gain or loss: the difference between the purchase price, or some other adjusted-cost basis, and the sale price, or redemption price, of an investment. Capital gains generally qualify for favorable tax treatment.

Capitalization: the term used to describe the total of a company's liabilities and equity from the balance sheet. The debt-to-equity ratio, computed by dividing the liabilities by the equity, is an indicator of the company's financial risk from the way it has structured its capitalization. Generally, the greater the debt, the greater the financial risk.

Cash settlement (of a trade): a special request from the seller of a security to have the settlement date be the same as the trade date; in other words, to have the trade settle on the day of the execution. This allows for an early release of the proceeds of the sale. However, a cash purchaser must be found for the seller, and often the charge for a cash trade is ⅛th or ¼th of a point. Another common settlement option is next day, ND.

Churning: the illegal practice in which a stockbroker generates multiple trades for a client, creating a large number of commissions for the stockbroker, but little or no benefits for the client.

Closed-end fund: an investment company with a fixed (closed) number of authorized shares. This is the opposite of an open-end fund, a mutual fund, that has an unlimited number of authorized shares. Shares of closed-end funds usually trade on organized stock exchanges.

Collectibles: for investment purposes, these can be almost anything that enough people desire to own that the value might appreciate. Many people turn their hobbies into investments. Collectibles can include such items as baseball cards, comic books, rare coins, or stamps. Some financial publications print quotes on popular collectibles, but the investment value of most is very unpredictable.

Commercial paper: short-term corporate unsecured loans, having maturities of 270 days or less. Commercial paper is usually the most common investment in money market mutual funds.

Common stock: the most common method of representing public ownership of corporations. Each share of stock represents a share of ownership in that corporation.

Compound interest: the principle that interest paid also earns interest. If the interest rate paid on the interest is the same as the rate paid on the principal, the formula for compound interest is $F = P(1 + i)^n$, where F = Future Value, P = Present Value, i = interest rate, and n = number of years to maturity.

Consumer price index (CPI): the measure of the changing prices of a market basket of goods and services, representing the inflation rate on the retail level. It is compiled by the Bureau of Labor Statistics and is referred to as the cost-of-living index.

Convertible securities: usually either bonds or preferred stock that have a special feature allowing them to be exchanged for another security, usually common stock, at a predetermined price.

Corporation: the most common type of structure for most large businesses. It is a government-created entity with most of the legal rights and obligations of an individual. A corporation may own property, pay taxes, file lawsuits or be the defendant of lawsuits, and enter into other legal contracts. A corporation is owned by its shareholders. *Public* companies are owned by a large number of shareholders, whereas *private* companies are owned by only a few individuals.

Correlation: used to describe the effects of changing economic factors on investments. Strategists will typically analyze the relationship between securities and variables such as interest rates. The relationship is assigned a number between 1 and +1 called the *correlation coefficient,* showing either a negative or a positive relationship for that security or group of securities. This type of analysis is frequently performed by fund managers, whose goal is to balance out the total portfolio so that some securities will probably appreciate while others may depreciate as a result of certain hypothetical events. For example, foreign securities will probably have a near zero correlation to U.S. interest rates. So, some managers will include them in their portfolio in order to reduce the risk due to rising domestic rates. Thus, though foreign securities may be risky by themselves, their inclusion can lower the overall risk level of a diversified portfolio.

Coupon rate: the interest rate quoted in a bond's description. This rate would be the yield that a bond would pay if it were purchased at par value ($1,000). It is a fixed dollar amount. An 8 percent coupon bond, for example, would pay $80 per year per bond.

Current ratio: a computation from the balance sheet—current assets divided by current liabilities. It shows whether the company has enough readily liquid assets to meet its fixed expenses due within a year.

Current yield: the amount of annual income an investor in a fixed-return security will receive divided by the cost of that investment. If the price of a bond is below par value, the current yield will be higher than the coupon rate. If the price is higher, the current yield will be lower. See **Coupon rate** and **Yield-to-maturity**.

Debenture: a bond for which no specific asset, or collateral, has been pledged as a guarantee for the repayment of the bond. In the event of the bankruptcy of a bond issuer, all collateralized bonds, such as mortgage bonds, first trust deeds, and so on, will be repaid before debentures. Most corporate and municipal bonds are debentures.

Derivatives: in the broad sense, any investment whose underlying value is derived from another investment. Perhaps the most actively traded type of derivative security is a stock option (see **Calls, Options, Puts**). *Mortgage derivatives*, however, are what most people are referring to when they use this term. Mortgage derivatives are securities created from FNMA or FHLMC issues (see GNMA). Speculative mortgage derivatives were responsible for enormous losses in many fixed-income mutual funds in the early 1990s and contributed to the Orange County, California, bankruptcy in 1994.

Discount rate: the interest rate set by the Federal Reserve Board at which the banking regulator will lend money to member banks overnight. Virtually all other interest rates are set at premiums to the discount rate, making this one of the most powerful tools the Fed can use to regulate the economy.

Dividend: a payment usually made quarterly to shareholders of a company. These payments represent a portion of the company's earnings for that quarter. The amount of the dividend is expressed on a per share basis and is annualized. A $1.00 dividend, for example, to a shareholder who owned 500 shares of stock would mean that the shareholder would receive $500 per year (500 × $1.00), or $125 per quarter (500 × $0.25). The board of directors of a company must meet each quarter and declare the dividend payment. See **Trade date–settlement date**.

Dividend yield: the annualized dividend rate divided by the price per share of the security. The dividend yield is analogous to the annualized interest rate on fixed-return investments; however, the dividend rate is not fixed.

Dow Jones Industrial Average: a stock market indicator published by Dow Jones. It is the adjusted average of 30 Blue

Chip stocks. The adjustment is done by changing the divisor. A true arithmetic average of 30 items would be the total divided by 30; however, because of stock splits and company changes, the divisor has been reduced to about 0.2. You can determine how much any one company affects the total Dow by dividing that company's price by the divisor.

Earnings per share (EPS): the bottom entry on an income (or earnings) statement, representing the net income divided by the number of shares outstanding.

Ex-dividend date: the date on which an investor who purchases a stock will *not* (*ex-* means without) receive the next dividend payment. The settlement date for that purchase will be the day after the record date for the dividend payment. See **Trade date–settlement date.**

Fed Funds rate: the rate that banks charge other banks for overnight loans. Though this rate is not set by the Federal Reserve Board per se, the Fed sets targets for this rate that it wants banks to maintain so that bank loan policies will be in line with its economic objectives.

Federal Open Market Committee (FOMC): a group composed of five of the twelve Federal Reserve regional bank presidents and seven members of the board of governors that meets monthly to determine whether to make bank credit more easily available or more difficult to obtain, that is, whether to tighten or to loosen money supply. It does so by requiring banks to either buy U.S. government securities from the Fed to tighten money supply or to sell U.S. government securities to the Fed to loosen money supply.

Federal Reserve Board (the Fed): a government agency created by an act of Congress that regulates the U.S. banking industry and sets domestic economic policy. The Fed has come under recent criticism because its financial position has never been independently audited and its policymaking powers have extended far beyond U.S. boundaries.

Fiduciary: someone who makes financial decisions on behalf of another. Pension fund managers, for example, act as fiduciaries when they make investment decisions for employees' interests in qualified plans.

Fixed-return investments: a general term for bonds, government agency mortgage issues, preferred stock, CDs, or any other investment that makes periodic payments at a set dollar amount to investors.

Forbes 400: a list compiled by *Forbes* magazine of the 400 richest people in America.

Fortune 500: a list of the 500 largest companies in America compiled by *Fortune* magazine.

Future value: the amount of money an investor will have after a given period of time, assuming the investment pays a fixed rate of interest over that period of time. It is computed by the formula $F=P(1+i)^n$. See **Present value.**

Futures contracts: highly leveraged tradable agreements by which the purchaser of a contract may profit from a rise in the price of the underlying commodity and the seller from a decline in the price. Because of the leverage, many speculators are attracted to the futures markets. Futures contracts have considerable upside potential, but also considerable downside risk. The speculator's potential loss is *not* limited to the initial amount of the investment.

G.O. bond: a *general obligation* bond, a type of municipal bond backed by the full taxing authority of the issuer. Such bonds are generally considered more secure than revenue bonds, that are backed by revenues generated from the project for which the bonds were issued.

Glass-Steagall Act: the banking act of 1933 that established the legal separation of the securities industry and the banking industry. The provisions of this act were greatly weakened by legislation in the early 1990s, allowing bank holding companies to participate in most securities businesses, with the notable exception of the primary market.

GNMA, FNMA, FHLMC: GNMA, pronounced "Ginnie Mae," is the acronym for Government National Mortgage Association, a government agency established to create a market for investors in pools, or portfolios, of FHA or VA approved home mortgages. FNMA, "Fannie Mae," the Federal National Mortgage Association, and FHLMC, "Freddie Mac," Federal Home Loan Mortgage Corporation, are other *quasi*-government agencies responsible for creating other mortgage-backed investments. Although FNMA and FHLMC have an implied government backing for their issues, they are legally public companies owned by their shareholders.

Good till-canceled order (GTC): an order to buy or to sell a security that will remain in effect until it is canceled, also called an *open order*. GTC orders are usually entered as limit orders.

Greed-Hope-Fear Cycle: a classic illustration of the psychological effects of market price movements on investors. It demonstrates that one's emotional responses to market movements will typically cause one to buy near the top of market cycles and to sell near the bottom.

Greenmail: the strategy of a hostile suitor's acquiring enough voting shares of a company to threaten to mount a takeover attempt, a change of management, or the election of a new board of directors. The suitor then agrees to sell those shares back to the company, usually at an escalated market price, allowing the management or the board of directors to keep their positions. In other words, it is *legal* blackmail, thus *greenmail*.

Gross domestic product (GDP): the total output of all goods and services produced within the geographical boundaries of a country. It is measured by the amount of spending and investing by all entities in the nation. The GDP Deflator adjusts the actual amount of spending to a constant dollar value. In other words, the deflator takes out the effects of rising prices due to the declining purchasing power of a dollar and expresses the real growth, or decline, of the GDP at a constant dollar level.

Hedging: strategies for limiting the risks associated with some investments. Stock investors may use options to hedge their positions. Bankers may use financial futures or interest rate options to hedge the risk on their loans. Buyers or sellers of large quantities of commodities may use futures contracts to hedge their profit margins.

Income (or earnings) statement: a financial statement showing a company's revenues (or sales) and expenses over a period of time, such as quarterly or annually. It is organized from top to bottom in the order of priority that the company meets its financial obligations.

Indenture: the formal agreement on the face of a bond certificate. It states the legal rights and obligations of the bond issuer and the investor.

Inflation: the measure of the loss of the purchasing power of money due to rising prices and an expanding economy.

Initial margin requirement: the amount of equity required to be deposited when an investor buys a stock by borrowing some of the cost of the purchase from a brokerage firm. This has been set at 50 percent for the last several decades. It is controlled by the Federal Reserve Board and is the only rule-making authority the Fed has in the securities industry. For individual investors this is called Reg. T; for financial institutions, Reg. U.

Insider: according to the SEC, anyone who has access to nonpublic information about a company is considered an insider. It is illegal for *anyone* to profit from an investment made on the basis of insider information about a company. The SEC has vigorously prosecuted many cases of insider trading in recent years.

Institutional investors: organizations or individuals who invest in very large quantities of securities. Influential institutional investors include investment company managers, pension fund managers, corporate or government account managers, and so on.

Interest-rate risk: type of risk associated with fixed-return investments. When interest rates rise, the market value of bonds or other fixed-return investments will decline. This decline is approximately the same percentage amount as the percentage increase in interest rates. If interest rates go up 10 percent, say from 5 percent to 5.5 percent, then the market value of the principal will decline about 10 percent, say from 99 to 90. Note that the percentage change of the price decline is calculated by dividing the ending value into the difference between the beginning value and the ending value, that is,

$$\frac{99 - 90}{90} = 9/90.$$

Investment: the use of money to make more money.

Investment banker: the title of the broker responsible for bringing new issue securities to public markets, the primary market. An investment banker may also be referred to as an underwriter. Usually, investment bankers are divisions of brokerage firms or financial institutions.

Junk bonds: the term used to describe all bonds rated below BBB by Standard & Poors or Baa by Moody's. A popular euphemism for the term "junk" is "high yield." Bonds rated above those levels are considered to be investment grade, and are suitable for fiduciary accounts, such as pension funds or insurance company investments.

Keogh plans: retirement plans for *self-employed* individuals, also called H.R. 10 plans. These plans can allow for larger contributions than SEP-IRAs, but also have more complicated government filing requirements and higher fees. See **SEP-IRA**.

Large-cap: generally refers to companies whose market capitalization is over $3 billion.

Leading economic indicators (LEI): a statistical measure of ten segments of the economy designed to forecast the level of economic activity for the upcoming year. There are also indexes of lagging indicators and coincident indicators, that are released at the same time as the LEI.

Leverage: the use of a smaller amount of capital than the total cost of the underlying investment to control the total investment. Leverage allows the investor to receive a greater percentage capital gain or loss. Examples of the use of leverage would be margin accounts, call and put options, and commodities futures contracts.

Limit order: an order to buy or to sell a security at a minimum price. A limit order to buy will usually be at or below the current ask price of the security, and a limit order to sell will usually be at or above the current bid price. See **Good-till-canceled order.**

Liquidity: the ease with which an investment may be turned into cash with little loss in market value.

Listed securities: security investments that trade on an established exchange, as opposed to the over-the-counter market. The exchanges themselves set the minimum requirements that a company must meet to be listed. If a company fails to maintain these requirements, it may be *delisted*.

Load: the fee charged to invest in a mutual fund. In addition to a load, mutual funds may charge annual fees for administration and operating expenses and 12b-1 fees for promotional costs.

Long-term capital gain: the difference between the purchase price and the sale price of an investment held for over one year, if the sale price is higher than the purchase price. If the sale price is lower, the investor will have a long-term capital loss.

M2: the most watched measure of money supply. It is the total of M1, that includes all cash and currency in circulation and deposits in checking and saving accounts, and investments in money market mutual funds and CDs. The Fed may attempt to limit the growth of the money supply, and thus control inflation, by raising interest rates.

The market: in daily use this term usually refers to the Dow Jones Industrial Average. The changes in the DJIA are a market barometer, computed by the mathematical average, of the changing prices of 30 companies. These companies are selected on the basis of being leaders in their industry groups.

Market capitalization (Market cap): the total number of shares outstanding times the current market price of the stock. This is different than the *capitalization* of a company, that represents the total of the company's debt and equity. See **Capitalization.**

Margin: the percentage of equity that an investor has in an account where some money has been borrowed from the brokerage firm. An account that is at 30 percent margin has a 30 percent equity position.

Market order: an order that will be executed at the best available price at the time it is received by the specialist for a listed stock or the market maker for an OTC stock.

Mark to the market: the process of journaling (or transferring) money between an equity margin account and a short account in order to maintain a credit balance equal to the full market value of the short position in the short account. An investor who sells short must have an equity balance or deposit money in a margin account equal to 30 percent of the proceeds of the short sale. If the price of the short security goes up, money from the margin account must be added to the short account (marked to the market) to equal the full market value of the short.

Mid-cap: generally refers to companies whose market capitalization is between $1 billion and $3 billion.

Minimum maintenance requirement: the minimum equity balance all margin investors must maintain in their accounts. The NYSE sets this minimum at 25 percent of the total market value, but most *brokers set it at 30 percent* in order to stay in compliance with the NYSE requirements. This is different from the *initial* margin requirement, Reg. T, of 50 percent. The maintenance requirement becomes significant if the market value of the investment drops.

Money market funds: open-end mutual funds that invest only in very short-term debt securities. Since the market value of these securities does not change, the share price of a money market fund should remain stable. Usually, this share price is set at $1.00. The most frequently used investment in money market funds is *commercial paper*, corporate loans with "short maturities." Most money market fund investments mature within about 30 days. So, part of the portfolio will usually turn over every day. Thus, the interest rates money market funds pay will change daily.

Money supply: the total amount of cash and liquid investments in circulation. It is reported every Thursday by the Fed. M1 is the total amount of coins and currency in circulation plus checking accounts, savings accounts, and travelers checks. M2 is M1 plus money market mutual fund and CDs. M3 is M2 plus institutional money funds and jumbo CDs. The most watched measure of money supply is M2. It is important because the growth of the money supply could be inflationary. If it exceeds the Fed's target, the Fed may move to slow its growth by raising interest rates.

Municipal bonds: fixed-return investments issued by state or local governments or government agencies. The interest paid on municipal bonds is exempt from federal income tax and from state income tax to residents of the state in which the bond was issued.

Mutual funds: professionally managed portfolios of investments in which each share of the fund represents ownership of many individual securities; also referred to as open-end funds. See **Load** and **Open-end fund.**

NASDAQ: the sophisticated automated quotation system for over-the-counter trading. In the newspaper, stocks that are eligible for NASDAQ trading are often listed as the national market or national over-the-counter.

National Association of Securities Dealers (NASD): the self-governing agency of the securities industry responsible for setting academic and ethical standards for brokers. It is also very active in arbitrating disputes between brokers and their clients. The NASD is to brokers what the American Bar Association is to lawyers.

Net asset value (NAV): the calculation of the per share value of the total of the investments in a mutual fund or a closed-end fund. With mutual funds, the NAV is usually determined daily by dividing the closing market value of all the investments in the fund by the total number of shares outstanding. Mutual funds may be liquidated at NAV, minus any fees if applicable.

Net profit margin: a financial ratio from the income statement— net income (or earnings) divided by net sales (or revenues). This calculation tells the analyst what percentage of the total sales the company is able to keep after all expenses.

Odd lot: any number of shares less than 100, a round lot. A quantity of shares such as 563 would be referred to as a *mixed lot*, composed of five round lots and an odd lot.

Open-end fund: the designation for an ordinary mutual fund. It has no fixed capitalization and can issue any number of shares.

Options: a type of security derivative. See **Call option** and **Put option**.

Over-the-counter market (OTC) a method of securities trading conducted via an interconnected computer network, rather than in one central location as with an exchange. See **NASDAQ.**

Par value (pv) of bond: the principal or face amount of the bond. The amount the bond investor will receive at maturity.

Par value (PV) of stock: the arbitrary per share value that is assigned for the purpose of balance sheet accounting. If the par value is $1, and a company has ten million shares outstanding, the balance sheet will carry the equity value of the common stock at 10 million dollars. Most additional equity value on the balance sheet will result from retained earnings. The par value of stock has nothing to do with the market value.

Penny stock: a low-priced and highly speculative equity. Although the term implies that it would refer to securities priced under $1, it is frequently used to describe any low-priced security. Most brokerage firms do not allow purchases of penny stocks on margin.

Poison pill: a corporate strategy to discourage hostile takeover attempts. In the event a hostile suitor acquires a certain percentage of a company's stock, a poison pill allows the company to issue more shares or to convert preferred stock. These new shares would be issued only to current shareholders, those who purchased their stock before the hostile suitor. Thus, it is almost impossible for the suitor to amass a voting majority. It is a poison pill because the dilution of stock, the issuance of additional shares, will cause the stock's price to drop. Additionally, some poison pills permit dividend payments, allowing management to deplete shareholders' equity.

Portfolio: usually used to describe the list of all the financial investments owned by one individual or institution.

Preferred stock: a fixed-income *equity* investment. Shares of preferred stock are rated like bonds, pay fixed-income-like bonds, and are vulnerable to interest-rate risk like bonds. However, preferred stock shares trade on equity markets like common stock.

Precious metals: gold, silver, and platinum. Some financial advisors recommend keeping a certain amount of investors' portfolios in precious metals, usually 10 percent to 15 percent. The rationale for this is that so-called *hard assets* are inflation hedges, and they will retain their value better than financial assets in the event of a recession or a depression. However, over the last two decades there has been no correlation between the price of gold and the rate of inflation whatsoever. The trading pattern of precious metals reveals that they are speculative commodities.

Present value: the inverse of the Future Value formula, $P = F/(1 + i)^n$. This formula calculates how much money must be invested at the present time to receive a predetermined value in the future at a fixed rate of interest. See **Future value.**

Price earnings ratio (PE): an important financial ratio computed by dividing the current market price of a stock by the most recent annual earnings per share, that is, the total of the last four quarterly earnings reports. This is also referred to as the *earnings multiple*, for it is the number that, if multiplied by the most recent annual earnings per share (the total of the last four quarters), would result in the current market price.

Producer price index (PPI): the Department of Labor's measure of inflation at the wholesale level. It is reported monthly, a day or two before the Consumer Price Index.

Program trading: the use of computers to generate buy and sell orders for large blocks of securities. Program orders are frequently entered in risk arbitrage trading, involving the securities of major indexes and the options or futures contracts of the underlying indexes. Program trading has been linked to high market volatility. The NYSE has imposed restrictions program trading when the market goes through periods of high volatility.

Prospectus: a document issued for all companies on the primary market, representing full disclosure of the company's business. No other information may be disseminated regarding a new issue except the prospectus, and all potential investors in a new issue must receive a prospectus.

Proxy: someone who votes on behalf of another. Each year companies send out proxy solicitation cards to shareholders to vote on matters coming up at the annual shareholders' meeting.

Put option: a type of equity derivative contract that gives the purchaser the right to sell a set amount of stock at a set price within a predetermined period of time. See **Call option.**

Random walk theory: the belief that market movements are completely unpredictable, that there is no predictable cause-and-effect relationship between economic developments and security prices.

Real estate investment trust (REIT): a type of closed-end investment company that invests in a portfolio of real estate properties or mortgages. As an investment company it must *pass through* at least 90 percent of its net income to its shareholders.

Red herring: the preliminary prospectus that must be issued to all prospective investors before a company goes public. It is so named because of the red lettered disclaimer on the cover.

Return on assets (ROA): a calculation from financial statements—net income divided by total assets.

Return on equity (ROE): a calculation from financial statements—net income divided by total shareholders' equity, net
worth. This is an important financial ratio, showing whether
the return that the company has received on its equity is sufficiently higher than that of the riskless rate of return to com-
pensate shareholders for risk.

Revenue bond: a type of municipal bond where the interest payments and the repayment of principal are secured by the revenues generated from the bond project. Common revenue
issues would include solid waste disposal bonds, toll road or
toll bridge bonds, water revenue bonds, hospital bonds, and
so on.

Risk: the uncertainty about the predictability of the future.
Macroeconomic risk would describe those factors that affect
all securities, such as inflation, interest rates, or other economic cycles. It also includes such uncertainties as changing
political policies or federal regulations. *Microeconomic risk*
would describe the factors that only affect a specific company.
Micro risk factors would include competition from other businesses, an overly leveraged balance sheet, or industry business
cycles.

Riskless rate of return: the interest rate available on U.S.
Treasury securities. Because of credit risk, all other bond
issuers must pay a higher rate of interest than the riskless
rate. So, when the Treasury raises interest rates, all other
bond issuers—corporations, municipalities, government
agencies, and even foreign bond issuers—must raise their
rates to a higher premium over the riskless rate.

Round lot: one hundred shares of stock, the most frequently used
multiple for securities trading. The volume section of the
stock quote information in the newspaper will list the number of round lot trades for that day. To determine the actual
number of shares traded, you would add two zeros to the
number of round lots reported.

S&P 500 Index: a "value weighted" index, as opposed to a *price
weighted* average such as the Dow Jones Industrials. It is

computed by multiplying the current market price of each of the 500 companies in the index by the number of shares outstanding for each company. In other words, it is the average of the total *market value* of the companies in that index. An index, as opposed to an average, uses an arbitrarily arranged base number as a beginning so that changes in the index will represent percentage changes from that base. This index is almost universally used by mutual fund managers and institutional investors as a statistical representation of the overall market. Speculators can invest in index options or futures on this index or on other S&P indexes such as the 100 and thus *bet* on the market.

Secondary markets: all security exchanges and the over-the-counter market. The primary market is the process of bringing an initial public offering (IPO). Once the IPO has been priced, the securities begin trading on the secondary markets, the NYSE, the AMEX, OTC, and so on.

Secular: used in the securities industry to imply a long-term trend. You may have a *secular* bull market, for example; however, it may go through several bear cycles.

Securities: a broad term for the types of investments issued by businesses, usually corporations, and available through broker/dealers.

Securities and Exchange Commission (SEC): the U.S. government agency that is the chief regulatory body for the securities industry. It was created by the Securities Exchange Act of 1934.

Securities Investors Protection Corporation (SIPC): a corporation that acts as a government agency providing insurance protection to investors' accounts in the event of the bankruptcy of member brokerage firms. Currently this insurance coverage is limited to $100,000 for cash and $500,000 for investments. The SIPC is to the securities industry what the FDIC (Federal Deposit Insurance Corporation) is to the banking industry.

SEP-IRA: acronym for simplified employee pension–individual retirement account, a retirement plan for *self-employed* individuals. A participant can contribute up to 15 percent of after-tax earned income from the business to a SEP-IRA, and all profits from investments in the SEP-IRA are tax deferred until withdrawn. See **Keogh plans.**

Short sale: the act of selling shares of a security that are borrowed from a lender, usually a brokerage firm. This strategy is used to profit from the price decline of the security. The shares are hopefully sold at a higher price than what the short seller will pay to buy them back in the future. See **Mark to the market.**

Small-cap: generally refers to companies whose market capitalization is less than $1 billion.

Specialists: the members of a stock exchange whose primary function is to match buy and sell orders. Specialists may also buy and sell shares for their own accounts—within limits—in order to maintain a fair and orderly market. In other words, if there is an imbalance of sellers, specialists must be ready to buy shares for their own accounts to help control market volatility. If there is an imbalance of buyers, the specialists must be sellers.

Speculation: an investment strategy that employs a higher level of risk than investing. Speculators expect a higher rate of return or quicker results than would generally be possible with a conservative investment strategy.

Stock rights: contracts that give current shareholders the opportunity to purchase additional shares. Stock rights are issued prior to a company's plan to increase the number of shares outstanding. Since these additional shares will *dilute* current shareholders' percentage ownership of the company, the rights offering will allow them to increase the number of shares that they own to maintain the same percentage ownership. Also, since the dilution will cause the stock's price to drop, the exercise price of the rights will usually be at a price below the current market price of the stock. Rights offerings will usually precede stock offerings by a month or two.

Stock split: a method by which companies can issue more shares of stock to current shareholders. This practice, however, will cause the price of the stock to be reduced by the same percentage as the amount of increased shares. Shareholders should realize that a stock split does not materially benefit them. If a stock splits 2-for-1, the number of shares owned will double, but the price of each share will be cut in half. Stock splits are usually the result of management's decision to keep the share price at a low enough level to make a round lot affordable to most investors. Note that a stock split does not cause dilution, as a stock offering does. See **Stock rights.**

Stop order: an order to sell a security at a price lower than the current market price of that security, or an order to buy a security at a price higher than the current market price. A stop order will become a *market order* when the stop price is reached. Traders often use stop orders to limit the potential loss on an investment or to preserve a predetermined profit margin, if the security has appreciated. These orders may also be referred to as Stop Loss orders. Another variation of the stop order is the *stop-limit order*. It is a stop order that becomes a limit order when the stop price is reached. See **Limit order.**

Tick: the term used to describe the smallest unit of incremental change in securities prices, usually $\frac{1}{8}$th of a point or $0.125 per share. Also, an up-tick would indicate that the last price at which the security traded was higher than the previous price. A down-tick would indicate that the last price was lower than the previous price.

Trade date–settlement date: When you invest in a security, the day of the purchase is the trade date; and the day by which you must pay for the purchase is the settlement date. For all regular way transactions, the settlement date is three *business days* after the trade date. A business day is any day that banks are normally open, that excludes weekends and holidays. When a security is sold, the settlement date is the day that the proceeds can be paid out. Trade dates and settlement dates are important considerations for investors who are concerned about dividend payments. The settlement date for a stock purchase must be on or before the *dividend record date* in order for the investor to receive the next dividend payment. If a security is purchased just two business days before the record date, that is, the ex-dividend date, the trade will settle the day after the record date, too late for the investor to receive the next dividend. See **Dividend.**

Transfer agent: the institution, usually a commercial bank, that is responsible for registering security certificates and recording changes of ownership.

Treasury bills: the shortest term fixed-return securities issued by the U.S. Treasury Department. T-bills are sold at a discount to face value ($10,000 minimum) and are available in three-month, six-month, or one-year maturities. The interest rate on T-bills defines the riskless rate of return.

Treasury bonds and notes: fixed-return securities issued by the U.S. Treasury Department. New issue *T-notes* mature in two to ten years, and *T-bonds* in ten to thirty years.

Triple witching days: the third Friday in the months of March, June, September, and December. On these days three derivative securities contracts expire: stock options, index options, and commodity index futures. The market can trade with unusual volatility on or around these days because of large blocks of stock being bought or sold due to program trading tied to options or futures contracts.

Variable-return securities: another common designation for stocks, or other securities like warrants, that do not provide a fixed rate of return.

Warrant: a contract that, like a call option, gives an investor the right to buy shares of an underlying security at a set price and that expires within a certain period of time. Usually, warrants have much longer terms (several years) than stock options. One warrant usually gives the holder the right to buy one share. Also, warrants trade on securities exchanges.

Wash sale: the term used to describe the repurchase of a security, or an equivalent security, within 31 days of the date of the sale, if the security was sold at a capital loss. Current IRS rules do not allow an investor who sells an investment *for a capital loss* to claim that loss as a tax deduction if the investor executes a wash sale.

Yield-to-maturity: the formula derived from compound interest tables that computes the total return of a fixed-return investment, including the coupon interest and the change in the value of the principal from the time of purchase to the time of maturity.

Zero coupon bond: a fixed return investment that *does not pay* interest at regular periodic intervals. A zero coupon bond is purchased at a discount to par value, and the interest is represented by the appreciating value of the bond until maturity. Series EE U.S. savings bonds and Treasury bills are examples of the structure of zero coupon bonds. Investors should be aware that they will have to pay income taxes each year on *taxable* zero coupon bonds, corporate zeros for example, even though no actual income was received. These bonds may also be identified as OIDs, original issue discounts.

Recommended Reading

Bernstein, William J. *The Four Pillars of Investing*. New York: McGraw-Hill Trade, 2002.

Graham, Benjamin, and David L. Dodd. *Security Analysis*. New York: McGraw-Hill Trade, 1996.

Kasriel, Paul L., and Keith Schap. *Seven Indicators That Move Markets: Forecasting Future Market Movements for Profitable Investments*. New York: McGraw-Hill, 2002.

Levitt, Arthur, and Paula Dwyer. *Take on the Street: What Wall Street and Corporate America Don't Want You to Know*. New York: Pantheon Books, 2002.

Lynch, Peter, and John Rothchild. *One Up on Wall Street: How to Use What You Already Know to Make Money in the Market*. New York: Fireside, 2000.

Richelson, Hildy, and Stan Richelson. *The Money-Making Guide to Bonds*. Philadelphia: Bloomberg Press, 2002.

Sowell, Thomas. *Basic Economics: A Citizen's Guide to the Economy*. New York: Basic Books, 2000.

Stein, Robert. *Inside Greenspan's Briefcase: Investment Strategies for Profiting from Key Reports and Data*. New York: McGraw-Hill, 2002.

Index